NEW CENTURY BIBLE
COMMENTARY

General Editors

RONALD E. CLEMENTS
(Old Testament)

MATTHEW BLACK
(New Testament)

ACTS

THE NEW CENTURY BIBLE COMMENTARIES

EXODUS (J. P. Hyatt)
LEVITICUS AND NUMBERS (N. H. Snaith)*
DEUTERONOMY (A. D. H. Mayes)
JOSHUA, JUDGES, AND RUTH (John Gray)*
EZRA, NEHEMIAH, AND ESTHER (L. H. Brockington)*
JOB (H. H. Rowley)
PSALMS Volumes 1 and 2 (A. A. Anderson)
ISAIAH 1-39 (R. E. Clements)
ISAIAH 40-66 (R. N. Whybray)
EZEKIEL (John W. Wevers)*
THE GOSPEL OF MATTHEW (David Hill)
THE GOSPEL OF MARK (Hugh Anderson)
THE GOSPEL OF LUKE (E. Earle Ellis)
THE GOSPEL OF JOHN (Barnabas Lindars)
THE ACTS OF THE APOSTLES (William Neil)
ROMANS (Matthew Black)
1 and 2 CORINTHIANS (F. F. Bruce)
GALATIANS (Donald Guthrie)
EPHESIANS (C. Leslie Mitton)
PHILIPPIANS (Ralph P. Martin)
COLOSSIANS AND PHILEMON (Ralph P. Martin)
1 PETER (Ernest Best)*
THE BOOK OF REVELATION (G. R. Beasley-Murray)

*Not yet available in paperback
Other titles are in preparation

NEW CENTURY BIBLE COMMENTARY

Based on the Revised Standard Version

ACTS

WILLIAM NEIL

WM. B. EERDMANS PUBL. CO., GRAND RAPIDS

MARSHALL, MORGAN & SCOTT PUBL. LTD., LONDON

Library of Congress Cataloging in Publication Data
Neil, William, 1909-
The Acts of the Apostles.

(New century Bible commentary)
Reprint. Originally published: London: Oliphants,
c1973. (New century Bible)
Bibliography: p. 11
Includes indexes.
1. Bible. N.T. Acts — Commentaries. I. Title.
II. Series. III. Series: New century Bible.
BS2625.3.N44   1981   226'.607   81-5577
ISBN 0-8028-1904-4 (pbk.)   AACR2

CONTENTS

PREFACE

It is vital for the life of the Church and of the ordinary Christian to be able to turn to the book of Acts as substantially the true story of our origins, of how the faith we profess was first proclaimed, of how the first Christians viewed the role of the Church in the world, how they lived and worshipped, how they organized their community life, how they preserved their sense of belonging to the same body.

After more than twenty years study, teaching and discussion of the book of Acts I believe that we have very strong grounds for treating it with the utmost respect as a basically accurate account of what happened, recorded by a man whose evidence we have good cause to trust. Despite the recent weight of scholarly opinion which would question this judgment there is every reason to hope that a more widespread recognition of the general historical reliability of Acts may re-emerge in the not too distant future.

W. N.

University of Nottingham.

ABBREVIATIONS

BIBLICAL

OLD TESTAMENT (*OT*)

Gen.	Jg.	1 Chr.	Ps.	Lam.	Ob.	Hag.
Exod.	Ru.	2 Chr.	Prov.	Ezek.	Jon.	Zech.
Lev.	1 Sam.	Ezr.	Ec.	Dan.	Mic.	Mal.
Num.	2 Sam.	Neh.	Ca.	Hos.	Nah.	
Dt.	1 Kg.	Est.	Isa.	Jl	Hab.	
Jos.	2 Kg.	Job	Jer.	Am.	Zeph.	

APOCRYPHA (*Apoc.*)

1 Esd.	Tob.	Ad. Est.	Sir.	S. 3 Ch.	Bel.	1 Mac.
2 Esd.	Jdt.	Wis.	Bar.	Sus.	Man.	2 Mac.
			Ep. Jer.			

NEW TESTAMENT (*NT*)

Mt.	Ac.	Gal.	1 Th.	Tit.	1 Pet.	3 Jn
Mk	Rom.	Eph.	2 Th.	Phm.	2 Pet.	Jude
Lk.	1 C.	Phil.	1 Tim.	Heb.	1 Jn	Rev.
Jn	2 C.	Col.	2 Tim.	Jas	2 Jn	

OTHERS

AV   *Authorised Version*
RSV   *Revised Standard Version*
NEB   *New English Bible*
E.T.   English Translation
LXX   Septuagint (the ancient Greek translation of the Old Testament)

BIBLIOGRAPHY

The literature on Acts is of vast dimensions. The following selection includes some of the most important recent works on the subject.

W. F. Albright, *New Horizons in Biblical Research*, Oxford, 1966.
C. K. Barrett, *Luke the Historian in Recent Study*, London, 1961.
M. Black, (ed.), *The Scrolls and Christianity*, London, 1969.
— *The Scrolls and Christian Origins*, London, 1961.
F. F. Bruce, *The Acts of the Apostles*, London, 1951.
H. J. Cadbury, *The Book of Acts in History*, London, 1955.
— *The Making of Luke–Acts*, New York, 1927.
G. B. Caird, *The Apostolic Age*, London, 1955.
H. Conzelmann, *Die Apostelgeschichte*, Tübingen, 1963.
— 'The First Christian Century', in *The Bible in Modern Scholarship*, ed. J. P. Hyatt, London, 1966.
— *The Theology of St. Luke* (E.T.), London, 1960.
O. Cullmann, *Peter* (E.T.), London, 1953.
W. D. Davies, *Paul and Rabbinic Judaism*, London, 1948.
M. Dibelius, *Studies in the Acts of the Apostles* (E.T.), London, 1956.
G. Dix, *Jew and Greek*, London, 1953.
C. H. Dodd, *According to the Scriptures*, London, 1952.
— *The Apostolic Preaching and its Developments*, London, 1936.
G. R. Driver, *The Judaean Scrolls*, Oxford, 1965.
J. Dupont, *The Sources of Acts* (E.T.), London, 1964.
B. S. Easton, *Early Christianity* (ed. F. C. Grant), Greenwich (Conn.), 1954.
E. E. Ellis, *The Gospel of Luke* (New Century Bible), London, 1966.
C. F. Evans, 'The Central Section of St. Luke's Gospel', in *Studies in the Gospels*, ed. D. E. Nineham, Oxford, 1957.
H. Flender, *St. Luke, Theologian of Redemptive History* (E.T.), London, 1967.
F. J. Foakes-Jackson, *The Acts of the Apostles*, London, 1931,
F. J. Foakes-Jackson and K. Lake (eds.), *The Beginnings of Christianity*, London, 1920–33, 5v.
R. H. Fuller, *The New Testament in Current Study*, London, 1963.
B. Gärtner, *The Areopagus Speech and Natural Revelation* (E.T.), Uppsala, 1955.
W. W. Gasque, and R. P. Martin (eds.) *Apostolic History and the Gospel*, Exeter, 1970.
M. G. Goulder, *Type and History in Acts*, London, 1964.
R. M. Grant, *A Historical Introduction to the New Testament*, London, 1963.
G. Graystone, *The Dead Sea Scrolls and the Originality of Christ*, London, 1956.
M. Green, *Evangelism in the Early Church*, London, 1970.

E. Haenchen, *The Acts of the Apostles* (E.T.), Oxford, 1971.

R. P. C. Hanson, *The Acts*, Oxford, 1967.

J. H. E. Hull, *The Holy Spirit in the Acts of the Apostles*, London, 1967.

A. M. Hunter, *Interpreting the New Testament 1900–1950*, London, 1951.

— *Paul and his Predecessors*, London, 1940.

E. Käsemann, *New Testament Questions of Today*, London, 1969.

L. E. Keck and J. L. Martyn, *Studies in Luke–Acts*, London, 1968.

W. L. Knox, *The Acts of the Apostles*, Cambridge, 1948.

G. W. H. Lampe, 'Acts', in *Peake's Commentary on the Bible*, London, 1962.

— *St. Luke and the Church of Jerusalem*, London, 1969.

G. H. C. Macgregor, *The Acts of the Apostles*, in the Interpreter's Bible, IX, New York, 1954.

I. H. Marshall, *Luke: Historian and Theologian*, London, 1970.

W. Neil, *The Truth about the Early Church*, London, 1970.

S. Neill, *The Interpretation of the New Testament, 1861–1961*, Oxford, 1966.

J. C. O'Neill, *The Theology of Acts*, London, 1961.

R. B. Rackham, *The Acts of the Apostles*, London, 1901.

Sir W. M. Ramsay, *The Bearing of Recent Discovery on the Trustworthiness of the New Testament*, London, 1914.

M. H. Scharlemann, *Stephen: A Singular Saint*, Rome, 1968.

C. H. Scobie, *John the Baptist*, London, 1964.

A. N. Sherwin-White, *Roman Society and Roman Law in the New Testament*, Oxford, 1963.

James Smith of Jordanhill, *The Voyage and Shipwreck of St. Paul*, London, 1848.

K. Stendahl, *The Scrolls and the New Testament*, London, 1958.

E. Sutcliffe, *The Monks of Qumran*, London, 1960.

J. P. M. Sweet, 'A Sign for Unbelievers', in *New Testament Studies* XIII. iii, 1967.

W. C. van Unnik, *Tarsus or Jerusalem?* (E.T.), London, 1962.

H. Wansbrough, 'Acts of the Apostles', in *A New Catholic Commentary on Holy Scripture*, London, 1969.

M. Wilcox, *The Semitisms of Acts*, Oxford, 1965.

C. S. C. Williams, *The Acts of the Apostles*, London, 1957.

R. R. Williams, 'Church History in Acts', in *Historicity and Chronology in the New Testament*, ed. D. E. Nineham, London, 1965.

INTRODUCTION

to

The Acts of the Apostles

INTRODUCTION*

1. LUKE—HISTORIAN OR THEOLOGIAN?

When Vernon Bartlet wrote his commentary on Acts for the
original *Century Bible* in 1901, the authorities he referred to most
frequently were Adolf Deissmann and W. M. Ramsay. The points
on which their opinions were quoted were mainly archaeological,
serving to confirm and illuminate further what was obviously
regarded then as a reliable record of the first thirty years of the
history of the Church, written by Luke the physician and companion of Paul on his missionary journeys (Col. 4:14; Phm. 24; 2 Tim.
4:11). It was generally accepted that as a careful historian, and
indeed as an eye-witness of much of what he describes, Luke had
written Acts soon after writing his Gospel and as a sequel to it, to
show how the faith that had its origins in Galilee and Jerusalem
was carried by the followers of Jesus, principally by Paul, from the
Levant through the Mediterranean lands until it reached the
capital of the civilized world—Rome itself.

This had been the traditional view of Acts and its author from
the time of the Christian Fathers, and it went unchallenged until
towards the middle of last century, when the Tübingen school
questioned both the historical value of Acts and the identity of its
author. They had come to the conclusion that in the early Church
the feud between the Jewish Christians, led by Peter, and the
Gentile Christians, led by Paul, was intense and bitter. But this is
not at all the situation which Acts describes. Certainly there is
tension between the two sides, but the willingness of the parties to
compromise for the sake of the unity and well-being of the Church
is heavily underlined. Thus the Tübingen scholars maintained
that, since Acts so grossly misinterprets the true situation as they
saw it, its historical value is negligible and its author could not
have been a contemporary, far less a companion, of Paul. Acts is,
they insisted, an eirenical document, written about a century after
the events it records; and it is designed to smooth over the early

* With the permission of the publishers, Hodder and Stoughton Ltd, I have
drawn in this Introduction on my Croall Lectures, delivered at the University
of Edinburgh in 1967, and published with the title *The Truth about the Early
Church* (1970).

dissensions between the Pauline and Petrine factions in the early
Church by making Peter and Paul speak with one voice and work
together in harmony.

This presumption that Acts must be wrong because Tübingen
must be right was of course strongly challenged, not least in this
country by J. B. Lightfoot. But at the end of the nineteenth century
the massive contribution of Sir William Ramsay bade fair to
negative the sceptical conclusions of the Tübingen school. Ramsay
had begun by treating Acts as an untrustworthy second-century
document, but, on the basis of his own archaeological investi-
gations in Asia Minor, he had radically changed his views. He
now maintained with a wealth of supporting evidence, not only
that Acts was written by Luke the physician and companion of
Paul, but that Luke's accurate and detailed knowledge of the
geography, customs and provincial government of the Roman
Empire showed him to be a wholly reliable historian of the life
and times of the early Church.

This swing back to the traditional view was furthered in the
first half of the present century by the weighty support of two
outstanding New Testament scholars, Adolf von Harnack and
B. H. Streeter. Both of them agreed with Ramsay on the Lucan
authorship of Acts and on its general trustworthiness as a historical
record. Contrary opinions were of course not lacking in this period.
Johannes Weiss in Germany and A. C. Clark in England argued
that Luke could not have written Acts, and in their monumental
five-volume work, *The Beginnings of Christianity*, Foakes-Jackson
and Kirsopp Lake took a generally sceptical view of the value of
Acts as history. On the other hand, just before the midpoint of the
century, the influential pen of W. L. Knox, in a small but erudite
volume on *The Acts of the Apostles*, powerfully defended the traditional view against its critics. On the whole, it seemed that by 1950
the main body of scholarly opinion was by and large in agreement
that Acts was the work of Luke, the companion of Paul, and that,
within the limits imposed on any first-century historian, he could
be relied on to have left us a generally trustworthy record of the
first three decades of the Church's history.

The last twenty years, however, have been marked by what is
no less than a revolution in this estimate of the book of Acts and
its author. A good account of its beginnings is given by C. K.
Barrett in *Luke the Historian in Recent Study* (1961). As a result of this
revolution, 'Luke the historian' has given place to 'Luke the

theologian'. Sir William Ramsay's picture of Luke, whose meticulous attention to historical and geographical details could vouch for the general reliability of his record, has been succeeded by a picture of our author as a man who is primarily an evangelist and a creative theologian, more concerned with the proclamation of the Gospel than with historical reporting, and ready to sacrifice the factual accuracy of his narrative to didactic considerations.

This new approach to Luke had been pioneered in England by C. F. Evans in 1955, with an essay in *Studies in the Gospels* (ed. D. E. Nineham) on 'The Central Section of St Luke's Gospel'. Evans maintained that in his record of Jesus' last journey to Jerusalem Luke had been less concerned with the actual historical order of events than with presenting Jesus as the new Moses in a 'Christian Deuteronomy'. Setting out the events and topics of Deuteronomy in parallel columns with Luke's version of the last journey of Jesus, Evans claimed that Luke had deliberately selected and arranged his material to demonstrate his thesis.

Two years earlier Hans Conzelmann had published his important study of Luke–Acts in Germany, although it did not appear in English until 1960 under the title of *The Theology of St Luke*. In Conzelmann's view this two-volume work Luke–Acts is a rewriting of the story of Jesus and its sequel from Luke's own distinctive point of view. Luke sees the history of salvation in three stages: the period of Israel; the period of Jesus; and the period of the Church. He may thus, in the words of Eduard Lohse, be called a 'theologian of redemptive history', and he wrote Acts to record the highly significant beginning of the mission of the Church to evangelize the world in the power of the Spirit.

Conzelmann has subsequently (1963) written a short commentary on the book of Acts in which he develops this view of Luke as one of the creative theologians of the New Testament, and his approach is shared by Ernst Haenchen in his massive commentary on Acts, first published in 1956. For Haenchen, the book of Acts is not a straightforward account of the apostolic age written by a contemporary, but a work of art written for the edification of the Church in his own day towards the end of the first century by a theologically-minded author who manipulates the facts of history to serve his own purposes.

The metamorphosis of 'Luke the historian' into 'Luke the theologian' was carried a stage further by J. C. O'Neill in his study of *The Theology of Acts* (1961). For O'Neill, Luke was not the

companion of Paul, but an apologist of the second century, writing
somewhere between A.D. 115 and 130. He was one of the fore-
runners of the 'catholic' period in the history of Christian thought
(see below, pp. 48ff.), and he wrote to persuade the educated and
politically powerful in the Graeco–Roman world to commit their
lives to the service of the kingdom of God.

M. G. Goulder, a pupil of Austin Farrer, in his *Type and History
in Acts* (1964), finds in Luke the same kind of theological ingenuity
as Farrer had found in Mark. Seen through the eyes of a thorough-
going typologist, Acts reveals itself, not as straightforward history,
but as a story that is told in cycles, a spiral construction which
repeats the basic pattern of the death and Resurrection of Jesus
in the lives of the Apostles. It is in effect a re-enactment of the
story of the Gospel and, indeed, of much of the Old Testament as
well. Where no types can be found, as in sections of Paul's journeys,
we may regard Luke's narrative as more or less factual. Where
typology can be clearly detected, as in events such as the Ascension
and Pentecost, we are bound to treat them as unhistorical. Luke
excelled as a writer of the myths which now dominate the Christian
calendar.

Thus the trend of recent scholarship has been to move away
from the traditional picture of 'Luke the historian' to 'Luke the
theologian' or even to 'Luke the mythographer'. To the names of
those scholars already mentioned who have in the past twenty
years invited us to take a new look at Luke could be added many
more, not least Philipp Vielhauer, Ernst Käsemann and Ulrich
Wilckens. However much they disagree among themselves they
would not ascribe to Luke the title of 'historian' in any normally
accepted sense of the word, and certainly not as it was used by
Ramsay, Harnack, Streeter and Knox.

There is indeed much in the new emphasis on Luke the theologian which is open to criticism, and particular arguments of
individual scholars are still being debated. But we may be grateful
to recent studies of Luke–Acts for many new and valuable insights,
and it would seem that a case has been made out for revising the
traditional picture of Luke the historian, and for seeing our
author as much more of a theologian than was previously thought
to be the case. What really concerns the reader of Acts, however,
is whether in the light of this Luke can still be regarded as in any
sense a reliable recorder of the history of the apostolic age.

2. LUKE—THEOLOGIAN *AND* HISTORIAN

In the traditional view of the authorship of Acts, stress was laid on the point that anyone who had been in Paul's company on his missionary journeys, and had subsequently compiled a narrative which was to a large extent based on his own personal knowledge, must be regarded as a thoroughly trustworthy witness. Sir William Ramsay went so far as to say that if Luke, the companion of Paul, did not write Acts, it could not possibly be accepted as reliable history.

This is an overstatement. The historicity of Acts does not depend on whether its author was 'Luke, the beloved physician' of Col. 4:14 or not. Few upholders of the traditional view of the author have claimed that he had first-hand knowledge of the events he describes in his book earlier than half-way through Paul's second missionary journey, when the appearance of the first personal pronoun in the narrative at 16:10 is claimed to indicate the point at which the author joined Paul's party at Troas. For the earlier part of his book—i.e., for more than half of its contents—he is dependent on such information as he has been able to glean from other sources apart from himself.

As far as those parts of Acts are concerned where the author may himself have been involved, we have seen reason to believe, as a result of recent study, that we are dealing with a man who has a distinctive theological point of view, and this would undoubtedly affect his presentation and interpretation even of events in which he himself took part. For the rest of his narrative, of events where he was not present, its historicity will depend on the accuracy of such information as came his way, whether written or oral, and his method of dealing with it. Moreover, we could not expect a first-century writer, whoever he was, to step outside his times and address his task with the objectivity of a modern historian. Thus it would be no guarantee of the absolute historical accuracy of Acts if it could be proved beyond a shadow of doubt that its author had been a companion of Paul and had been an eye-witness of much of what he records.

Nevertheless, if the evidence of Acts indicates that the author had an accurate knowledge of the political situation in the period he is describing; if his account of legal procedure in the course of his narrative turns out to be in accordance with the judicial practices of the time; if his geographical references are detailed and factual in those parts of his story where it appears that he himself was involved, and if what he tells us about Paul's missionary campaigns can be seen to tally generally with what the Apostle himself tells us in his letters, there would seem to be a reasonable probability that the traditional view of the author as the companion of Paul is the correct one, and that by and large we have in Acts an invaluable and trustworthy guide to these all-important first thirty years of Church history.

The cautionary words 'by and large' are necessary, in view of the limitations of any ancient historical writing. As can be seen from the preface to his Gospel (Lk. 1:1–4), we are not dealing with an author who claims to be infallible. It would be natural to expect that such events as those in which the author himself took part would convey a greater sense of first-hand and accurate reporting than others which came to his knowledge at second- or third-hand. We shall not lose faith in our author's general trustworthiness if it transpires that occasionally he gets his facts mixed up, or if his attitude to some features of his story is that of a first-century, and not a twentieth-century, chronicler.

If there is one major criticism that may be levelled against the recent exponents of the thesis that Luke was a theologian rather than a historian, it is that they pay too little attention to the established findings of a past generation of scholars which point in the opposite direction. It is generally recognized that Sir William Ramsay latterly pressed his advocacy of Luke's reliability as a historian almost to the point of claiming his infallibility, and came dangerously close to insisting that archaeology proves the New Testament to be true; but, in his heyday, on the basis of his own study of inscriptions in Asia Minor, he did reach certain conclusions about the book of Acts which are still relevant.

Ramsay was convinced that the writer of Acts knew the world of Paul in the intimate way that could only have come from first-hand knowledge; particularly is this evident in his use of official titles, which, in the days of the Roman Empire as in our own day, were a peculiarly tricky problem. Yet, as he pointed out in pp. 96–7 of *The Bearing of Recent Discovery on the Trustworthiness of the New Testament* (1914), the officials whom Paul and his party encountered were exactly those who should have been there at that time: proconsuls in senatorial provinces, Asiarchs in Ephesus, *stratēgoi* in Philippi, politarchs in Thessalonica. This type of argument does not of course prove that Luke was there, but it does suggest a writer who took the trouble to get his facts right, and who might well have been on the spot himself.

Another contribution from an older generation which is still worthy of respect is the monograph of James Smith of Jordanhill on *The Voyage and Shipwreck of St Paul* (1848). Smith had made a study of ancient ships and methods of navigation, and argued that Ac. 27 must have been written by an eye-witness who was not himself a sailor. The view seems more likely that the eye-witness was the author of Acts himself rather than that canvassed by Conzelmann and others, that Luke found somewhere a good story of a voyage to Rome including a shipwreck and inserted into it a few references to Paul.

It is surely also not without significance, as H. J. Cadbury pointed out in pp. 241-52 of *The Making of Luke–Acts* (1927), that the writer of Acts is interested in the geographical details of Paul's journeys. He refers to Perga as being in Pamphylia, Antioch as Pisidian, Lystra and Derbe as cities of Lycaonia. Philippi is the leading city of part of Macedonia and a colony, Tarsus is in Cilicia, Myra in Lycia. He speaks of a place called Fair Havens in Crete near the town of Lasea, and of Phoenix, a Cretan harbour, looking north-east and south-east. He notes the addresses of the people in his story and the places where the missionaries find lodgings: at Philippi Paul stays with Lydia, in Thessalonica with Jason, in Corinth with Aquila and Priscilla. Paul leaves their home and goes to lodge with Justus, whose house was next door to the synagogue. In Joppa, Peter stays with a tanner by name Simon, whose house was by the sea.

Now, of course the author of Acts may have found all these details and many more like them in some written documents which came into his hands long after the events he is recording. It is surely equally possible at least that he mentions these things because he had a good memory for what he had himself seen or heard. In either case it is difficult to understand why an author whose sole concern was theological instruction should have bothered to include such trifling matters.

In his recent Sarum lectures, *Roman Society and Roman Law in the New Testament* (1963), A. N. Sherwin-White has shed new and interesting light on our problem from the angle of classical studies. He shows that the author of Acts was well versed in the intricacies of Roman law as it was practised in the provinces of the Empire in the middle of the first century; in the case of Paul's trials before

Felix, Festus and Gallio, the legal procedure is accurately described. On the question of the status and privileges of Roman citizens such as Paul, Sherwin-White maintains; 'Acts gets things right both at the general level, in its overall attitude, and in specific aspects.' He concludes that in Acts 'the confirmation of historicity is overwhelming . . . (and) . . . any attempt to reject its basic historicity even in matters of detail must now appear absurd. Roman historians have long taken it for granted' (pp. 173, 189).

We shall have to consider later (pp. 31–4, and *ad loc.*) how far the picture of Paul that emerges from the pages of the book of Acts squares in general and in detail with the evidence of Paul's own letters. It can be shown that there is no real discrepancy. But even without this additional consideration there does seem to be good reason to hesitate before substituting the new image of 'Luke the theologian' for the older image of 'Luke the historian'. That he was much more of a creative theologian than was at one time thought to be the case would seem to be established; but it would appear to be equally clear that, whoever he was, the author of Acts was extremely well informed about the political and legal institutions of the first century A.D., that he had a wide-ranging knowledge of the Mediterranean world, and that his meticulous recording of detail in matters which we can verify would lead us to believe that, in other matters on which we have only his evidence, we are dealing with a reporter on whom we can rely.

If this is so, the dichotomy between 'Luke the historian' and 'Luke the theologian' is a false one, for the author of Acts emerges rather as a theologically-minded historian or a historically-minded theologian. In either case, his narrative reveals him as being concerned with both theology and history, a writer who clearly sets the events he records in a distinctive theological framework, but at the same time makes it plain that it is historical events which he is relating. Was this man the Luke of ancient tradition, the Gentile doctor who accompanied Paul on his journeys, or was he an unknown writer at the end of the first century—or even in the first half of the second century—who had no direct knowledge of the events he was describing?

Despite the various caveats we have already noticed, which forbid us to assume that someone who lived closer to the period he is recording will necessarily be a more reliable reporter than someone writing at a later date, most readers of Acts would

probably have more confidence in the accuracy of the narrative
if they could be reasonably certain that the author was in one way
or another in close contact with the people and places that feature
in his story.

3. THE SOURCES OF ACTS

Before the end of the second century, and certainly from the time
of Irenaeus (c. A.D. 180), the author of Acts was generally identified
as Luke, a Syrian from Antioch, a doctor by profession who had
been a disciple of the Apostles and who had been the companion
of Paul until Paul's martyrdom. He was said to have written the
third Gospel and later *The Acts of the Apostles*, and to have died
unmarried in Boeotia in Greece at the age of eighty-four.

Most of the statements in this traditional view of the author of
Acts have been challenged in modern times by one scholar or
another. It has been argued that our author could not have been a
native of Antioch or even a Gentile, that his alleged medical
vocabulary as likely indicates that he was a horse-doctor as a
physician, that he could not have been Paul's companion because
he never regards Paul as an Apostle on the same level as the
Twelve, and that if he was the writer of Acts he was a different
man from the writer of the third Gospel.

Many of the scholarly arguments in this as in all other fields of
New Testament criticism cancel each other out, and here as elsewhere we cannot expect cast-iron certainties, but must be content
with reasonable probabilities. The traditional view has not been
conclusively proved to be wrong, and many of us would prefer to
give more weight to the tradition of the Church than to the hypo-
theses of individual scholars. The reliability of Acts does not in the
last resort depend on whether its author came from Antioch or
Macedonia, or whether he was a Gentile or a Hellenistic Jew, or
whether he was the 'beloved physician' of Paul's letter to the
Colossians. Nor, for that matter, if his information was sound, does
he necessarily need to have accompanied Paul on his journeys.

But if we read the book of Acts as dispassionately as we are able,
it is difficult to resist the conclusion that this fascinating account
of the first three decades of the Church's history is not only a
masterly study by a theologically-minded historian, but also a
vivid piece of first-hand reporting by someone who had been

himself deeply involved in the events he describes. When in the course of his narrative the author, whom we may as well call 'Luke' as anything else, changes from using the word 'they' to using the word 'we', and when at these points in his story the record acquires additional realism and shows greater attention to detail, it would seem to be misdirected speculation to fail to draw the obvious conclusion. To say that this is simply an attempt on the part of the author to hoodwink his readers into the belief that he had himself been on the spot, or that it is a literary device for which parallels can be found in pagan literature, or that the 'we' passages have been inserted into the narrative from a different source, is surely to put a premium on critical ingenuity at the expense of common sense.

Taken at its face value, the book of Acts squares admirably with the traditional picture of its author as a member of Paul's missionary team. The evidence of the 'we' passages suggests that he joined the Apostle half-way through his second journey at Troas, was left behind at Philippi presumably to follow up the work of the initial campaign there, and rejoined the Apostle a few years later as one of the delegates of the younger churches entrusted with conveying funds for the relief of the mother church in Jerusalem; and that from that point Luke was with Paul through his arrest in Jerusalem, his imprisonment in Caesarea, and his last voyage to Rome.

Luke enters the stage about half-way through the book of Acts. From then on he was either himself present during the events that the narrative describes, or close enough to them through his association with Paul and other missionaries to have a fair knowledge of what was going on in the Church at large. For the first half of his book, which tells the story of the birth of the Church in Jerusalem and of how it spread through Palestine to Antioch in Syria, which became the great new centre of Gentile Christianity, and where Paul established his headquarters, Luke could gather information from his many missionary contacts: Paul himself, Philip the Evangelist, Barnabas, doubtless some of the twelve Apostles, and perhaps John Mark. Being the kind of man his book shows him to have been, Luke would make good use of his time in Caesarea where he had two years at liberty while Paul was in prison.

Under the influence of Harnack, scholars in the first decades of this century exercised their ingenuity in identifying written sources which Luke was alleged to have used in composing the early part of his book, which covers the story of the Church before he himself came on the scene. Largely as a result of the work of Martin Dibelius, whose highly important essays on Acts began to appear in Germany in 1923, and were collected posthumously under the title, in the English translation, of *Studies in the Acts of the Apostles* (1956), this quest for written sources has been largely abandoned. It was Dibelius who first established a case for Luke as a creative author who himself shaped the first part of his story from the information that was available to him, rather than as a literary editor compiling documents which had been used before. As for the second part of the book, we may leave the question open whether Luke made notes as he went along in some sort of travel-diary, or whether he amplified some kind of itinerary of Paul's journeys which covered episodes in the missionary enterprise when Luke himself was not present.

After a searching examination of the whole subject, the most recent writer on the subject, the Roman Catholic scholar Jacques Dupont in *The Sources of Acts* (1964), recognizes that it is impossible 'to define any of the sources used by the author of Acts in a way which will meet with widespread agreement among the critics'. He comes to the conclusion, which he shares with Père Benoit, that the book of Acts was written in stages, and that it is 'based, not on sources coming from another author, but on Luke's own notes' (pp. 166–7). Scholars of Harnack's generation set out on the quest for the sources that lie behind Acts on the assumption that Luke must have used the same methods in composing Acts as he had used in composing his Gospel, where he combined Mark, Q, and his own special material. This newer view that in the case of Acts it was only his own material that he was using, and that it went through several stages of editing and re-editing by the author himself, would account for some of the features of the book that seem to suggest pre-existing sources.

We seem, then, to see a more complete picture of Luke emerging from all this—a theologically-minded historian who is also an author in his own right, the creator of a book which has a unique place in the New Testament and which deals with a unique period of Church history. There is no certainty about where or when he wrote it. Perhaps it was in Rome, perhaps in Greece, and probably in the seventies or eighties of the first century. Dibelius makes the point that Luke's name must have been attached to both his volumes from the beginning. He suggests that it is most unlikely that two books dedicated to a named patron, in this case Theophilus (see on 1 : 1), could have been sold to educated readers in the bookshops of the day without the author's name being known. He surmises that they may have appeared under the titles of *Luke's Acts of Jesus* and *Luke's Acts of the Apostles*.

4. THE PURPOSE OF ACTS

But why did Acts appear at all? What was Luke's purpose in writing it? First of all, let us remember that we are dealing with Part II of a two-volume work. Few scholars, ancient or modern, have dissented from this view. But for the fact that in the traditional arrangement of the New Testament writings the Fourth Gospel comes between the two parts of Luke's work, this point would hardly need emphasizing. It does help to remind us, however, that this theologically-minded historian is primarily an Evangelist. Whatever other motives our author may have had in mind in writing this literary masterpiece, his fundamental object was to proclaim the Good News. The book of Acts, like the third Gospel, tells the story of what God has done for the world through Jesus, and the main clue to our understanding of what made Luke write them both is that, as Harnack said, he was an 'enthusiast for Christ'.

Little support is now given to Streeter's view that Luke wrote his two volumes to serve as a legal brief for Theophilus, charged with the task of defending Paul on trial for his life in Rome. The only advantage of this theory would seem to be that it solves the problem of why the book of Acts ends where it does, with Paul in prison awaiting trial, without going on to tell us the outcome. We shall have to look at this point more closely later (pp. 29–30). There is so much in both the Gospel and Acts that would be quite irrelevant for any advocate preparing a speech for the Apostle's defence that this particular suggestion appears to be quite inadequate to cover the facts.

Dibelius draws a distinction between the readers for whom the Gospel was designed and those whom Luke had in mind when he wrote Acts. The Gospel, says Dibelius, was written for the Church; but Acts was written for the world—it was meant for the bookmarket, for private reading by educated pagans (p. 148). O'Neill similarly claims that in Acts Luke is preaching the Gospel primarily for unbelievers (p. 173). But it seems unnecessary to limit Luke's purpose in this way. Surely he is writing both for the Church and for the world, and above all for the Church in the world. He is thinking not only of intelligent enquirers outside the Church who want to know what Christianity is all about, but also of intelligent enquirers inside the Church who want to know how it all began.

Luke's work has sometimes been called an apologia for Christianity. But this again is to limit its scope: Luke is not primarily defending the faith, he is proclaiming it. And it is here that the more recent emphasis on Luke as a theologian finds its place. What makes his two-volume work unique in the New Testament is that he does something that no other Evangelist or letter-writer, not even Paul, attempts to do. Mark in his Gospel tells of the redemptive acts of God in the life, death and Resurrection of Jesus. His Gospel ends on a note of expectancy: the Lord will come again in glory, and the time will not be long. For Paul the story of redemption begins where Mark leaves off. He has little to say of the ministry of Jesus, for in his mind it was but the prelude to his death and Resurrection which ushered in the new age, where the risen and glorified Christ is present with his people through his Spirit.

Thus, as C. K. Barrett points out, Mark only hints at the future life of the Church, and Paul only hints at the historical Jesus. Neither of them deals with the relationship between the Jesus of history and the Church. But this is precisely what Luke does; in his two-volume work he builds a bridge between the two. It is thus not without significance that he tells the story of the Ascension twice: once at the end of his Gospel, and again at the beginning of Acts.

In Luke's mind the Ascension of Christ has two aspects: in the Gospel it is the end of the story of Jesus, in Acts it is the beginning of the story of the Church, which will go on until Christ comes again. Thus for Luke, as Barrett says, 'the end of the story of Jesus is the Church, and the story of Jesus is the beginning of the Church'. For Mark and Paul Jesus is the End—God's last word. With this Luke agrees, but for him Jesus is also the beginning of something else. In one way or another the whole of the New Testament sees the time after the Resurrection as the last chapter in history; for Luke, however, the last chapter is a new chapter, and Christ 'is not the close of all history, but the starting point of a new kind of history, Church History'. Luke is thus entitled, Barrett concludes, to be called 'the father of Church History', since no one before his day had realized that there was such a thing, and no one else in the New Testament had the same vision of something that had just begun but whose end was on the far horizon (pp. 53–8).

But Luke's Church history in Acts is no mere recital of what happened in these early decades; it is history written by a theologian and a preacher. Luke is convinced that God's redemption of the world and renewal of its life continues through the work of his servants in the Church. There is nothing casual or accidental in its growth and progress; the hand of God is in everything that happens; the Church advances irresistibly in the power of the Spirit. God's plan for the salvation of the world, which began through Israel and was crystallized in the life, death and Resurrection of Jesus, proceeds on its victorious way to its appointed end despite all obstacles and human perversity.

So M. G. Goulder is right to urge us to see in the pageant of Acts a re-enactment of the Gospel story and of the great themes of Old Testament redemptive history. How could Luke have written otherwise when he saw in his mind's eye the whole majestic sweep of God's dealings with man from the Creation to the Parousia? In this great panorama he concentrates on one tiny period of thirty years—three short decades, but how critical they are for the Church and the world. His version of the Gospel traces the descent of Jesus back to Adam, the type of mankind. The story he tells in Acts leads us from Jerusalem to Rome, the heart of civilization as Luke knew it, the symbol of the world as it is, and of mankind in need of salvation.

Streeter suggested that an alternative title for the book of Acts might be 'The Road to Rome', for this is indeed the significance of Luke's work. Whatever minor motifs Luke had in mind, such as the establishment of Christianity in men's minds as a constructive and not destructive element in the social order, his main concern was to show that, in God's plan for the renewal of the life of mankind, Jerusalem, the heart of old Israel, was the goal of Stage I, while Rome, the centre of the world, was the goal of Stage II. From there the future lay open, and time would not be reckoned in decades but, for all Luke knew, in centuries and millennia. Meanwhile, however, his task was to recall the foundation and first definitive period of the Church. The acts of the twelve

Apostles and, above all, of the thirteenth Apostle, Paul, were basic to the whole enterprise of the evangelization of mankind.

5. LUKE AND PAUL

It has often been said by writers about the book of Acts that Luke made Paul his hero. Certainly the other Apostles, even Peter, are given much more sketchy treatment. More than half of Acts is devoted to the life and work of Paul, although Luke makes it quite clear that in the expansion of the Church through the pagan world countless other Christians, named and unnamed, had a part in spreading the Gospel among the Gentiles. Clearly it is not, as might at one time have been thought, the uncritical hero-worship of a simple medical missionary; not only does Luke paint his picture of Paul with 'warts and all', but, as we have seen, our author is a man of independent judgment with a theological view-point of his own.

In underlining the significance of Paul's contribution so heavily, he must have had a better reason than admiration of Paul as a tireless and intrepid adventurer for Christ. It was certainly not because our author was a devotee of Pauline theology. He does not distinguish Paul's characteristic view of salvation from that of the other Apostles. Justification by faith is mentioned, but no more (13:39), and the significance of the death of Christ plays little part in Luke's summaries of Paul's preaching. Luke does not regard it as a peculiarly Pauline emphasis that circumcision should not be obligatory for Gentiles; on the other hand, he goes out of his way to point out that Paul regarded observance of the Law as incumbent upon Jews.

It has often been pointed out that Paul might not have written any of the letters whatever, for all the notice Luke takes of them, or of the theological ideas expressed in them. Even allowing for the fact that Paul's letters do not seem to have been generally known much before the end of the first century, one would think that, if Luke wrote Acts in Rome at any time after Paul's death, he would have at least known the contents of the letter to the Romans; or, if he wrote it in Greece, one or other of the letters to Corinth or Philippi or Thessalonica must have come his way.

The most likely explanation of this neglect is that Luke was not particularly interested in Paul as an individualistic theologian;

but then, neither was the Church in general in the seventies or eighties of the first century. Probably Luke, like others in the early Church, honoured Paul for more practical reasons. He saw him as one of the great martyrs of the young Church, who had preached the Gospel, and witnessed to his faith, and given his life for his Master in the heart of the Empire; but more than that he honoured him because he had brought the message of salvation from Jerusalem to Rome.

This was why Luke made Paul his hero, if we like to put it that way. In fulfilment of Old Testament prophecy, Jesus had come to bring light into the darkness of the Gentile world. From Pentecost onwards his Spirit had driven his followers, above all Peter, to recognize that their task was to be his witnesses 'in Jerusalem and in all Judaea and Samaria and to the end of the earth' (1:8). This was the succession in which Paul stood, and none of the other Apostles had done more to make this mission to the Gentiles a reality. When Paul reached Rome, God's plan for the salvation of the world was in principle accomplished. However far ahead the last act in the divine drama might lie and whatever unexpected reverses might yet be encountered before God's purpose for the world was effected through his Church, Luke would see to it that no one could be in any doubt as to the mighty role that was played under God's hand by this one-time scourge of the saints, who became the chief architect of the Israel of God.

It is for this reason that the book of Acts ends as it does, with Paul in Rome awaiting trial, under house-arrest, but still in his confinement allowed to preach the Gospel, as Luke says, 'quite openly and unhindered' (28:31). The older view that Luke left the story of Paul in mid-air because he wrote Acts at that very point in time—that is, before Paul's martyrdom, which is generally dated at A.D. 64—is difficult to substantiate nowadays. Among other things, it would mean that Acts was written before Mark's gospel appeared, say, in A.D. 65, and since the third Gospel, the first of Luke's two volumes, clearly depends on Mark for much of its contents, Acts must be later than both of them.

What happened to Paul after Luke's story ends is to some extent conjectural. Did his case go by default, as Ramsay believed; or was he casually released as the result of an imperial act of clemency, as Sherwin-White (pp. 118–19) has suggested? Or was he acquitted, and did he then embark on further missionary journeys;

and, if so, was it to Spain, as Clement of Rome seems to suggest, or did he return to the East, as the Pastoral Epistles imply? The answer involves us in many problems, not least the authenticity of the letters to Timothy and Titus. But, whatever preceded it, Paul's martyrdom in Rome at the same time as Peter's as a result of the Emperor Nero's victimization of the Christians for the burning of the city in A.D. 64 is so firmly embedded in early Church tradition that we may take it as established.

This fact would be so well known to most of the readers of Acts that there was no need for Luke to include it. In any event, his primary aim is not to write a full-length life of the Apostle but to show how God used him to bring the Gospel to the nerve-centre of the pagan world. Luke ends his story of the life of Jesus with the picture of the Disciples after the Ascension spending all their time in the Temple at Jerusalem praising God for what they had seen and heard (Lk. 24:53). He now completes the sequel to this story with the picture of Christ's greatest disciple, after surviving countless hazards and surmounting gargantuan obstacles, installed by God's invincible purpose in the heart of the Roman Empire, proclaiming the Good News of man's salvation 'unhindered'. With this expression, which is literally Luke's last word in Acts, he is saying that, largely through Paul's activities, the Church is now on the march, and nothing can stop it. Paul has built the vital bridge from Jerusalem to Rome. The Cross is in the field.

If, however, Luke has so deep a sense of the significance of Paul in the history of the Church, we may well wonder why he does not more obviously give Paul the status of apostolic authority which he accords to the Twelve, a status which, if we are to judge by Paul's own letters to Galatia and Corinth, he himself regarded as all-important (Gal. 2:8; 1 C. 9:1). On the Damascus road he had received a direct commission from Christ himself, and, whatever views others may have taken of what that implied, Paul certainly regarded his own authority in the Church as no less than that of the Jerusalem Apostles. B. S. Easton insists that Luke is determined to keep Paul in his place. While recognizing him as an Apostle, like Barnabas (14:14), Luke never disguises the fact that he considered his status in the Church as being inferior to that of the Twelve (*Early Christianity*, pp. 60–2), and Haenchen uses the same argument to deny that the author of Acts could possibly have been a companion of Paul. No one who knew Paul well, says

Haenchen, could conceivably have failed to emphasize his claim to be an equal of Peter and the others (*The Acts of the Apostles*, pp. 114–16).

It is difficult, however, to think that Luke regarded Paul, to whose activities he devotes sixteen chapters of his book, as significantly inferior to Matthias, who was chosen to take the place of Judas Iscariot as one of the Twelve, but who, after his election in chapter one, is never even mentioned again in the remaining twenty-seven chapters. Moreover it is likely that, by the time Luke came to write Acts, twenty years or so after Paul's martyrdom, the importance of the Twelve as a body compared with their associates was no longer a burning issue. They had been undoubtedly the Founding Fathers of the Church. They had served their turn as a symbol of the twelve tribes of Israel, translated into a Christian setting, worthy of respect as guarantors of the faith in the earliest days of the Church, but from Luke's point of view they had passed into history. He would not have been adding anything to his eulogy of Paul if he had asserted his right to be ranked equal with a body of men, most of whom were unknown even by name to the Gentile world. What had mattered greatly to Paul thirty years earlier in his running battle with Jewish-Christian extremists seeking to discredit the Apostle, on the grounds that he lacked the status and authority of the original Twelve, was at the time of the writing of Acts largely a matter of academic interest.

In this, as in other respects, Luke's portrait of Paul serves as a catalyst of some of the apparently contradictory impressions we get of the Apostle from his letters. The relationship between Acts and Paul's letters is one of mutual illumination, and, while obviously the evidence of the Epistles is primary, the framework provided by the book of Acts is invaluable. From Luke's narrative we see Paul in perspective against the skilfully delineated background of the Jewish and Gentile world, as part, albeit a major part, of the great forward movement of the Church in the first three decades of its history. Many of the battles which Paul is fighting in his letters have been won; much of the dust stirred up in his many controversies has settled. Luke as a participant in much of Paul's story can now look back in tranquillity and see the whole amazing drama of these early years unfolding.

The Jerusalem that Paul knew is in ruins; the old mother-church is scattered; the Jewish-Gentile controversy that bedevilled Paul's ministry has been largely solved by political developments outside the control of the Church. In all of this Luke cannot but see the hand of God. So the cause of Gentile freedom from Jewish legalism for which Paul fought so valiantly can be viewed dispassionately, and seen to be part of the teething troubles of the infant Church. As we have noted, Luke is a theologian in his own right, but he is more of a churchman in his theology than a Paulinist. Judging from Luke's writings, the profundities in Paul's thinking which evoked a response in minds like those of Augustine, Luther and Barth made little impact on our author's understanding of Christianity. It is perhaps just because he is the kind of man who is not dazzled by Paul's dialectical skill and theological expertise that Luke can give us in Acts a picture of the Apostle which not only adds much to what we learn from Paul himself in his letters, but also enables us to form a truer estimate of Paul as seen through the eyes of a highly intelligent friend and fellow-worker.

A generation ago scholars were still busy refuting the views of Reitzenstein, Bousset, Kirsopp Lake and others that Paul had turned Christianity into a Greek mystery-religion, and had corrupted the simple Palestinian Gospel of Jesus; that sacramentalism, redemption by a dying and rising Saviour, initiation by baptism, mystical union with Jesus as *Kurios* (or 'Lord'), all derived from Paul's hellenization of Christianity. There is very little if anything of this now. The whole trend in recent decades has been to emphasize the Hebrew background of Paul's thinking, as indeed the Apostle himself unmistakably asserts, and as Acts confirms; like a good missionary, he used terminology that meant more to Gentile audiences than Jewish ideas, like that of the Messiah and the Kingdom, but the Gospel that he preached was essentially the same as that which, according to Luke, was preached at Pentecost. Gregory Dix's *Jew and Greek* is an admirable exposition of this view.

Probably the most important book on the subject is W. D. Davies's *Paul and Rabbinic Judaism*. Davies's thesis is that, although his life was dedicated to the conversion of the Gentiles, Paul remained a Hebrew of the Hebrews and baptized his rabbinic heritage into Christ. From another angle, A. M. Hunter in *Paul and his Predecessors* has shown how much the theology of Paul derives from the Jewish Christian tradition which he took over at his conversion, and an interesting suggestion has come from W. C. van Unnik in *Tarsus or Jerusalem? The city of Paul's youth*, that the

Apostle was no more than born in Tarsus, but spent his boyhood
and schooldays in Jerusalem.

The argument turns on what is meant by Ac. 22:3, where Paul
at his arrest in Jerusalem claims that he was born in Tarsus yet
brought up in this city (i.e., Jerusalem) at the feet of Gamaliel.
If this means what van Unnik says it means, it implies that even
what little early Greek influence the Apostle could hardly help
absorbing in the imperial city of his boyhood must now be
questioned, and he emerges as an out-and-out Jerusalem Jew
until his conversion. But even if van Unnik is wrong, it has become
increasingly clear of recent years that there was far less difference
than was thought to be the case between Judaism as it was known
in Palestine in Paul's day, and Judaism as he would have known
it in the Jewish colony of the Greek city of Tarsus. The hellenization of the ancient world had infiltrated even into the tradition
of Israel, and whether Paul was brought up in Tarsus or Jerusalem
there is no need to look for the sources of his ideas anywhere but
in Judaism.

When we add to this the new light which is being shed on aspects
of Paul's thought by the Dead Sea Scrolls, the Palestinian imprint
on his thinking becomes even more pronounced. He tells us himself in his letters that he was a Pharisaic Jew of the strictest type
(Gal. 1:13f.; Phil. 3:5f.), and this is confirmed by Luke in
Acts (23:6). The further evidence of Acts is that, after his conversion to Christianity, his concern for his own kinsfolk as the
legatees of God's promises and the people of the Covenant persisted. It was not merely missionary strategy that took him first
to the synagogues in his missionary campaigns, but a deep sense
that the Gospel must first be preached to the Jews.

There were almost no lengths to which Paul was not prepared
to go to demonstrate his respect for the Law as the divinely ordained way of life for those who bore the Jewish name. Antioch
was his base of operations, but Jerusalem was his spiritual home.
The Temple and its festivals—Passover and Pentecost—as well
as the material needs of his Jewish–Christian brethren, seem
never to have been far from the forefront of his mind. On his
last visit to the Holy City he accedes to the request of the Jerusalem church leaders that he should openly identify himself as a
true son of the Law by associating himself in the Temple with some
Jewish–Christians who had undertaken Nazirite vows (21:17–26),
and in the last scene of all that Luke describes in Acts he is

pressing the claims of Christianity as the fulfilment of the Law and the prophets upon the leaders of the Jewish community in Rome (28:17–28).

For this intensely loyal Jew had through his shattering experience on the Damascus road learned to see the limitations of the Law. His vision of the risen Christ brooked no denial. Jesus of Nazareth who had died a felon's death under the curse of the Law was indeed the Messiah of psalm and prophecy. The salvation of the world lay through the Cross, and not through the Law of Moses. Contrary to everything he had been brought up to believe, Paul was forced to acknowledge that the despised Nazarenes were the true people of God, and from this recognition it followed inevitably that the barrier that separated Jew from Gentile had been broken by what God had done in Christ. Jews and Gentiles, each following their own tradition, were now to be gathered into one household of faith, the Church which is the body of Christ. It is a striking fact that in Luke's three accounts of Paul's conversion (chapters 9, 22, 26) he focuses attention on two aspects: Paul is summoned to come into the Church and, at the same time, is called to go out into the Gentile world.

It is the great merit of Luke's delineation of Paul that he shows him in the story of Acts not to have been an individualistic theologian, patenting his own brand of Christianity and foisting it upon the world. Rather he depicts him as a true Israelite, deeply conscious of what the Old Testament heritage meant for Christians, yet deeply conscious also of the common faith which he shared with all other Christians, and of his membership of a common fellowship into which he had been welcomed at his conversion. Of Paul's genius as an interpreter to the world at large of the 'breadth and length and height and depth' of the love of Christ (Eph. 3:18) Luke has little to say, for his task is rather to show Paul's greatness in action as the master mind of the Christian mission, a Hebrew of the Hebrews who nevertheless made the Gentile world his parish.

6. LUKE AND PETER

We shall have occasion later to look more closely at the role of the twelve Apostles as a body in the structure of the early Church as Luke describes it (pp. 51–2). In the first chapter of his book

(Ac. 1:13) Luke has given us the names of eleven of them: Peter, John, James, Andrew, Philip, Thomas, Bartholomew, Matthew, James the son of Alphaeus, Simon the Zealot, and Judas the son of James. Then, as he tells us, to fill the vacant place of Judas Iscariot a new apostle, Matthias, was added to complete the Twelve. As we have already seen, Matthias is never mentioned again; but, astonishingly enough, neither are most of the others. Apart from Peter and John, and a mention of James by name only to record his death (12:2), as individuals the Twelve fade out of the narrative.

Clearly Luke regarded them as a body as highly important, but his problem when he came to write Acts must have been that he could find out little about them. This is perhaps not surprising. As Haenchen has pointed out (pp. 81–2), the first generation of Christians was deeply interested in what Jesus had said and done, and this was what the Twelve and their successors proclaimed; what the Apostles themselves had said and done only became of interest to a later generation, such as that for which Luke was writing, but there was all too little that he could find to tell them. Men who were living in expectation of the end of the world and the return of Christ, as were the first-generation Christians, would remember the message of the preachers rather than details about the preachers themselves.

Accordingly it is 'the Acts of the Apostles' in the wider sense that Luke describes in his narrative, primarily those of Paul, and his associates—Barnabas, Silvanus, Timothy and the rest—for he had no lack of information about these, or of Stephen and Philip, who are also part of Paul's story. But it would be true to say that, as in the novels of Sir Walter Scott, Luke's thumb-nail sketches of minor characters make them come alive more vividly than the more important personages in the narrative. True, we get a clear picture of Stephen as a brilliant pioneer of the more radical type of Christianity, and of Barnabas as a man of great integrity, wide sympathy and much wisdom; but, compared with Philip and Silvanus, for example, who played major roles in the work of the mission, little people with walking-on parts, like the worthy gaoler at Philippi, Rhoda the flustered maid-of-all-work in Mary's house in Jersualem, and Demetrius the trade union organizer in Ephesus, are much more memorable.

The picture of Paul so dominates the scene that the other Apostles tend to be dwarfed. Yet there is one exception, and we

may leave out of account for the moment James, the brother of the
Lord, the *éminence grise* of the mother church at Jerusalem whose
shadow falls darkly across Paul's mission to the Gentiles (see on
12:17); he was not an Apostle in the sense of being a missionary.
The exception to the generalization that Luke's narrative is
largely about the acts of the thirteenth Apostle is, of course, Peter.
It would not be far from the truth to say that what Luke describes
in his book are the Acts of Peter and Paul.

From the beginning of his story, Luke shows Peter to have been
the undoubted head of the Church, its chief spokesman and
acknowledged leader. He assumes the authority which our Lord
conferred on Peter at Caesarea Philippi (Mt. 16:16–19), and this
authority is accepted by all, although Luke in his Gospel, presumably without knowledge of Matthew's fuller account, follows
Mark in his abbreviated version of how Peter acclaimed Jesus as
the Messiah. It has never been any easier for Protestants to accept
the scriptural evidence about the place of Peter in the early
Church than it has been for them to do justice to the status of
our Lord's Mother. Mariolatry and exaggerated papal claims have
done a grave disservice to both. In the case of Peter, Protestantism
has often sought to counter Catholic claims by overstressing Paul
and underrating the Rock on which Jesus promised that he would
build his Church. The book of Acts gives us a truer perspective.

From the beginning of the Church's story Peter occupies a
unique position. He it is who, even before Pentecost, insists that
the vacant place of Judas Iscariot must be filled and who pre-
sides over the appointment of Matthias to complete the number of
the twelve Apostles. At Pentecost it is Peter who as spokesman
explains to the assembled crowd the meaning of the visitation of
the Holy Spirit. In the healing of the cripple at the Temple it is
Peter's action which first rouses the ire of the authorities against
the Nazarenes, and it is Peter again who successfully justifies
what has been done in the name of Christ. The macabre tale of
the notorious Ananias and Sapphira is marked by the general
acceptance of Peter's disciplinary authority within the Church,
and, although we are told that other Apostles had the gift of
healing, it is only of Peter that it is said that the popular estimate
of his healing power was so great that even his shadow falling
across a sick man was believed to be efficacious. Peter is quite
clearly the head of the Church in its earliest stage (chapters 1–5).

This supremacy of Peter in the Jerusalem church is not only

attested by Acts but also confirmed by Paul. He tells us in his
letter to the Galatians that on his first visit to Jerusalem three
years after his conversion it was Peter he went to see (Gal. 1:18).
It would seem that even then, although James the Lord's brother
was becoming a power to be reckoned with among the Jerusalem Christians, Peter was still pre-eminent. When a more radical
spirit came into the Church, under the influence of Stephen and
the Hellenists, and the first persecution of the Nazarenes resulted
in the beginning of missionary enterprise by the fugitives among
the Samaritans, the conservative Twelve, including Peter,
represented a type of Christianity which was sufficiently in-
distinguishable from Judaism to make it possible for them to
remain unmolested in Jerusalem. Yet Peter, accompanied by
John, was delegated by the Twelve to go down to Samaria and
welcome the converts there into the Church (chapters 6–8).

From then on he seems to have himself embarked on missionary
activities among Jews. We hear of him at Lydda and Joppa, and
it was presumably as a result of wider missionary work of this
kind carried on by the Twelve that James, the Lord's brother,
became head of the local church in Jerusalem. But, according to
Luke, it was the encounter with Cornelius, the Roman centurion
in Caesarea, that transformed Peter, the staunch Jewish Christian,
into the first protagonist of the mission of the Church to the
Gentiles (chapters 9–10). So much is made of this incident in the
book of Acts that it is plain, as Dibelius has pointed out (p. 118),
that for Luke Cornelius is not the main character in the story,
but Peter: is not Cornelius' conversion to Christianity that matters
so much as the fact that Peter is given such unmistakable indication that the Gospel is for Gentiles as well as Jews. By the
undoubted prompting of the Holy Spirit, the head of the Church
is forced to recognize the importance of the Gentile mission. All
that we are told about Peter subsequently suggests that, although
he was tactically the leader of the Jewish Christian mission as Paul
was of the Gentile Christian mission, 'in the entire tragic debate
whose echoes we hear in all the letters of Paul'—the question as
to how far Jewish practices should be incumbent upon Gentile
Christians—'Peter himself', in Oscar Cullmann's words, 'no
doubt stood nearer to Paul than did the other members of the
Jerusalem mission' (*Peter*, p. 45).

According to Acts, Peter left Jerusalem after his escape from
prison during Herod's persecution of the Church, and went off 'to

another place' (12:17). Whether Luke has any definite place in mind or whether he was simply clearing the stage for the appearance of Paul, who from this point onward is the centre of attention, is not clear; certainly he sees the careers of Peter and Paul as following parallel lines, and does not think of them in any sense as rivals for the leadership of the Church. According to early tradition, both of them witnessed for their faith by martyrdom in Rome, so that, as Cadbury says (*The Book of Acts in History*, p. 132), 'even in their death they were not divided'. As an associate and admirer of Paul, and because of his deep sense of the importance of the mission to the Gentiles, Luke has made Paul the hero of his story; but not at the expense of Peter, who from the record quite clearly stands out in Luke's mind as the Rock on whom the whole Church was founded.

7. THE SPEECHES IN ACTS

As we have seen, it was Martin Dibelius who, so to speak, turned the tide of scholarly opinion back from the frustrating quest of sources which the author of Acts was supposed to have used for the earlier part of his book, covering the period before he entered the stage himself as the missionary companion of Paul. Dibelius has persuaded most critics that it is to Luke himself that we must turn, seeing him as author rather than editor—not a compiler who pieced together material that had been used before, but a creative historian who in the first half of his book gives us a picture of the life of the Church before the impact of Paul upon it, based on such information as he had been able to collect.

Now, if by that Dibelius, who, unlike most of the recent German writers on the subject, believed that the author of Acts was actually, as tradition maintained, the doctor from Antioch who accompanied Paul on his journeys, had meant that Luke had used the ample opportunities which the book of Acts suggests to find out from first-hand witnesses what had happened in the Church in Jerusalem and Palestine generally before he came on the scene, we should be happy indeed to follow his lead. For we should then have an invaluable insight into the beliefs and practices of the first Christians, based on actual reminiscences of what had happened on this or that occasion and what had been the substance of the earliest Christian preaching.

But this is not at all what Dibelius meant when he called Luke 'the first Christian historian'. He reckons that, apart from some popular stories, such as those of the healing of the cripple in the Temple and the dramatic tale of Ananias and Sapphira, Luke had little to go on. He linked these few stories together, supplied himself the narrative summaries of the Church's development and, above all, wrote all the speeches or sermons that are credited to Peter, Paul, Stephen and the rest out of his own head. This may indeed enhance our opinion of Luke as a literary craftsman, but it does not encourage us to turn to the book of Acts if we are looking for evidence of what the earliest Christians believed. For in Dibelius' view (pp. 123-85) the sermons that Luke incorporates in his narrative are much more models of what he considered preaching in his own day should be like than, in any sense, reflections of how the earliest Apostles proclaimed the Gospel.

This is, of course, a crucial issue. It is not without value for us today to know how the message of Christianity was presented to the world in the last decades of the first century, but we already have the letters of Paul which tell us how the faith was being expressed by the middle of the first century. If the book of Acts is to add anything to this, it must be because it enables us to go further back still. We may follow Gregory Dix (p. 27) in dividing the history of the apostolic Church roughly into three decades: the first (A.D. 30-40), when Christianity was still a movement within Syrian Judaism; the second decade (A.D. 40-50), when the Jewish Christian mission went out among the Jews of the Dispersion; and the third (A.D. 50-60), when the Church leapt from the Syriac to the Greek world.

Again, speaking generally, the third decade is covered by Paul's letters and, to some extent, by his sermons and speeches in the second half of the book of Acts. But it is to the first half of the book of Acts, and there alone, that we should want to turn—to the preaching of Peter and Stephen—to find the form and substance of the Christian message as it was being proclaimed in the first two decades of the Church's history, beginning with Pentecost and ending with the first appearance of Paul's letters. If, as many of the most recent writers on the book of Acts maintain, Luke, or whoever they think the author of Acts may have been, composed himself the sermons and speeches he includes in his history, putting them into the mouths of Peter and Stephen, we have no grounds for believing that we can by studying Acts hope to penetrate beyond Paul into the thoughts of those who were Christians before him. According to these scholars, we can regard the theology of Acts, not as representing the first stage of Christian belief, but merely what Luke thought the first Christians might have believed, or should have believed, or how Christians in his own day several decades later formulated their own faith, or in the author's view ought to formulate it.

No one would dispute the fact that taken as a whole the theology of the early chapters of Acts is less developed and less profound than the theology of Paul's letters. Scholars before Dibelius generally took this to mean that in these chapters we come very close to what the first Christians believed about God, about Christ, about the Church, about salvation. If we are to say now that the theology of Acts reflects the faith of the Church in the latter decades of the first century, we should have to label as an erratic, not only Paul himself, but also the authors of Hebrews and the Johannine literature, who are manifestly much more complex in their theology than the missionary preachers in the early chapters of Acts. J. C. O'Neill, the most radical of recent critics in his dating of Acts, which he places in the first half of the second century, is hard put to it to account for some of the titles given to Jesus in the book, which are not found, or very rarely found, elsewhere in the New Testament. The older view would have been that this is a clear indication of a stratum of primitive theology which Luke has preserved. O'Neill has to account for this awkward piece of evidence by saying (p. 145): 'chapters three, four and five (of Acts) provide an exuberance of uncommon titles because Luke is striving to give an archaic and scriptural ring to that part of Acts.'

If it is admitted that there is an archaic flavour about the theology of Acts, it is surely at least as likely that this points in the direction of an author who knew that this was the type of belief that was held in the earliest years of the Church's existence as that a literary artist of a later date deliberately set out to embellish his narrative with details which would evoke a picture of a stage of history about which he knew relatively next to nothing. C. H. Dodd in pp. 34ff. of his seminal study, *The Apostolic Preaching and its Developments*, contended that the distinctively Hebraic character of the earlier speeches in Acts indicated that the author had at his disposal Aramaic sources of one kind or another, which would of course take us back very close indeed to the actual preaching of the first missionaries. But more recently this has been disputed by scholars who claim that the semitisms in Acts are either merely imitations of the Septuagint or echoes of liturgical formulae. This basic conflict of opinion on the trustworthiness of the speeches makes it possible for us to find within the same covers of an important recent volume, *Studies in Luke–Acts* (ed. Keck and Martyn), on the one hand Eduard Schweizer maintaining with Dibelius that the speeches in Acts are Luke's own composition, so that Paul speaks exactly like Peter and Peter exactly like Paul (p. 214), and C. F. D. Moule, on the other hand, insisting that this uniformity is not established, and that Peter sometimes speaks like the Peter of the first Epistle of Peter, while Paul on occasion speaks like the Paul whom we know from his own letters (pp. 173ff.). Yet, despite his claim that Luke was responsible for the contents of all the speeches, Schweizer is forced to admit (p. 212) that where Christ is spoken of in the early chapters of Acts Luke is drawing on older traditional material. It would seem then that in what has been called the post-Dibelian era, even within the ranks of those scholars who would not consider that in the speeches of Acts we have access to the thought of the first Apostles but only to that of Luke, there is a recognition that some elements in these speeches and sermons are older than the finished products. (For a full discussion of this question, see M. Wilcox, *The Semitisms of Acts*.)

Vincent Taylor said about the 'kenotic' theory that if we dismiss it at the door it comes back through the window. The same thing might apparently be said about the reliability of Luke's evidence as to the beliefs of the early Church; however much the author of Acts may have contributed to the shaping of sermons and speeches that he puts into the mouths of Peter, Paul and Stephen, he does appear to have preserved in them, not only individual characteristics which differentiate the speakers, but also elements which on any but the most sceptical view would seem to take us back into the earliest stratum of the Church's faith as it was proclaimed in the first decades of its history.

Now, no one doubts the sincerity or honesty of those scholars who would deny that the book of Acts is a trustworthy guide to the beliefs of the first Christians, but there seems to be such a thing as an inherent bias towards conservatism or radicalism which makes it possible for two scholars to examine the same evidence and come to diametrically opposed conclusions. We may take as an example of this within the field that we are considering Paul's speech on Mars' Hill in Ac. 17.

Dibelius had again led the modern trend with his essay on *Paul on the Areopagus* (1939), in which he roundly maintained that the theology of the speech was foreign to Paul and to the whole of the New Testament. It was written by Luke as an example of a sermon to Gentiles in his own day, its ideas are hellenistic, not Jewish, and its motifs are Stoic in origin. Only its conclusion can be described as in any way Christian. This approach has been followed by Conzelmann and Haenchen in their commentaries, and specifically by Philipp Vielhauer in an influential article 'On the "Paulinism" of Acts' (Keck and Martyn, pp. 33–50). Vielhauer compares Paul's speech in Athens with the passage in Rom. 1 in which Paul also deals with man's natural knowledge of God, and comes to the conclusion that the two are incompatible. The speaker on the Areopagus is, he says, as distant from the real Paul as he is close to the second-century apologists.

An entirely opposite view, however, is taken by Bertil Gärtner in a special study, *The Areopagus Speech and Natural Revelation*. Gärtner is critical of the whole Dibelian attitude to the speeches in Acts, and considers that they give reliable evidence of the apostolic message as it was preached by Peter and Paul. He draws attention to the personal characteristics which distinguish the different speakers, and underlines the different types of audience that they are addressing. He examines Paul's speech to the philosophers of Athens in detail, and finds that, while some of the ideas are expressed in a form which has affinities with Stoic thought—doubtless as a point of contact with the audience—the whole substance of the speech is thoroughly in line with Pauline theology as revealed in his letters, and derives wholly from Old Testament and Jewish tradition. He finds closer parallels to the ideas expressed in the speech in the Pentateuch, the Psalms, the Wisdom literature, the Apocrypha and the New Testament itself than in the pagan philosophers.

In a vital matter of this kind, where we are concerned with the trustworthiness of the evidence for the beliefs of the first Christians and where equally competent scholars reach opposite conclusions, many of us would feel that, unless a clear and indisputable case can be made out for dismissing traditional views in biblical scholarship, the benefit of the doubt should always be given to the tradition of the Church.

It has already been suggested here that the new look at the author of Acts as a theologian in his own right is not incompatible with the old look at Luke as a careful historian. In the matter of the sermons and speeches in Acts, from which we should hope to distil the essence of the earliest proclamation of the Gospel and the faith of the first Christians, we can reach conclusions which are reasonable and profitable without subscribing to the view that the words that the author of Acts has put into the mouths of Peter, Paul and Stephen are the product of his own imagination.

Not even the most dyed-in-the-wool traditionalist would contend that the speeches and sermons in Acts are verbatim recordings of what the Apostles said; even in these days of short speeches and short sermons, we cannot conceive of anything quite so brief as the addresses in Acts. It is therefore not a matter for dispute that what Luke gives us in Acts are summaries of sermons and speeches, and that to do this he exercised the function of an editor rather than that of a reporter.

How far this editorial function extended is the crucial question and, as we have seen, one answer that has been frequently given in recent years is that the editor produced the sermons and speeches out of his own head. We may safely go part of the way with Dibelius and his disciples in conceding that there are sufficient similarities in the addresses that Luke incorporates in Acts to indicate that the same hand has been at work in shaping them all. There are indeed characteristic nuances and phrases which mark out one speaker from another, and the particular circumstances in which the sermon or speech was delivered result in noticeable differences in style; but that a single mind is behind them all, the mind of a singularly gifted theologically-slanted historian, appears to be beyond question.

As a by-product of the recent interest in historiography and its importance for New Testament studies, much attention has been given to parallels between the methods of the author of the book of Acts and those of ancient historians in general. The works of Jewish historians such as Josephus and the writers of the books of the Maccabees, as well as those of classical historians such as Suetonius and Tacitus, have been drawn into the discussion of how historians in roughly the same period as Luke dealt with the speeches they included in their narratives.

It has been noted that some ancient historians felt themselves free on occasion to enliven their books with speeches which they regarded as some sort of light relief—to display their own skill in oratory or rhetoric. These flights of fancy were, however, condemned as irresponsible by the more sober writers of their time, and the canons of Thucydides in particular were followed by the most reputable authors. In a famous passage in his *History of the Peloponnesian War*, Thucydides had said: 'As for the speeches which were made by different men either when they were about to begin the war or when they were already engaged therein, it has been difficult to recall the words actually spoken with strict accuracy, both for me about what I myself heard and for those who from various other sources have brought me reports. So the speeches are given in the language in which, as it seemed to me, the several speakers would express, on the subjects under consideration, the sentiments most befitting the occasion, though at the same time I have adhered as closely as possible to the general sense of what was actually said' (*Hist.* i. 22).

This implies that Thucydides formulated the speeches in his narrative in his own words and in his own style on the basis of what he had actually heard if he was present himself, or what had been reported to him from people who had been there. Only when this kind of information failed him did he resort to composing the kind of speech that he believed the particular speaker would have made, in the light of what he knew about his character and point of view. We may take it that Luke was, no less than Thucydides, a reputable historian, who was not only, as a Gentile, guided by the canons of pagan historiography but also, as a Christian, debtor as well to the Old Testament and Jewish background he shared with the missionaries whose sermons and speeches he had to record.

If, as we have earlier maintained, our author was no second century apologist or late first century *littérateur*, but the companion of Paul on his journeys, with first-hand knowledge of some of the events he describes and ready access to information about the earlier days before he joined the missionary enterprise, we may be confident that the sermons and speeches in the first half of the book of Acts, covering roughly the first two decades of Church history, give us, in the Thucydidean 'general sense', a reliable guide to the faith of the Church from its beginning in Jerusalem on the first Whitsunday.

It is difficult to imagine that a theologically-minded historian, writing, say, in the eighties, who was so meticulous about recording the political and legal niceties of the fifties, when he was himself involved in Paul's campaigns, should not have taken the trouble to find out from his many contacts what precisely had happened in the Church's infancy in the thirties and forties and, above all, the precise terms in which the new faith had been proclaimed. It was not Luke's own period. The Church had expanded, and as he knew it first it was making its impact on the Gentile world. But he was writing a history of the Church from its beginnings, and it was his business to find out what had been said and done in that early and, to him, unfamiliar Palestinian setting when the Gospel had been preached by Jews to Jews, before it had to be restated in terms that were meaningful to pagan minds.

8. THE CHURCH IN ACTS

Whatever discrepancies occur in Luke's three accounts of Paul's conversion, the words which the Apostle claimed to have heard never vary: 'Saul, Saul, why do you persecute me?' (9:4; 22:7; 26:14). Paul had had no hand in the trial and death of Jesus, but he had, we are told, 'laid waste the church' (8:3), and on the Damascus road he was confronted with the truth that Christ and his Church are inseparable.

However, it is not only in the mind of St Paul that Christ and his Church are conceived to be inextricably bound together. The terms in which the first Christians expressed this, according to Luke's account in Acts, are no longer current coinage, but the convictions that lay behind them are beyond question. Jesus was the Messiah for whom Israel had long waited. By putting him to death, just as they had done with the prophets who spoke of his coming, said Stephen at his trial before the Sanhedrin (chapter 7), the Jews had finally forfeited their claim to be the people of God. By the same token, in accepting Jesus as both Messiah and Lord, his followers fulfilled the role of the Remnant of which Isaiah had spoken. They were the new Israel.

In this conception of the nature of their community the first Christians were faithful to the intention of Jesus. It is clear both from his choice of twelve disciples, symbolic of the twelve tribes of Israel, and from his institution of a new covenant to replace the covenant of Sinai, that Jesus' purpose was to create a new people of God which would be at once continuous with old Israel yet freed from its restrictive practices, and which would take over Israel's historic assignment to bring the world to the knowledge of God. So in its earliest days the young community, in obedience to the intention of its Founder, filled the twelfth place in the apostolate formerly occupied by Judas, so that the symbolic structure of the new Israel should be preserved.

When Paul in his letters speaks of the Church as the Body of Christ, or when he equates being in the Church with being in Christ, he is not importing into Christianity ideas foreign to its character or novel in its development. By the very nature of their Old Testament background and Hebrew upbringing, the first Christians could not think of the Messiah apart from Israel, or of themselves as the Remnant being in any way separable from either. When Stephen at his trial has a vision of Jesus as Son of Man, he sees him in the role which Jesus claimed for himself in his own trial before Caiaphas (Mk 14:62). Both go back to Dan. 7:13, where the mysterious figure of the Son of Man is at once head of the new community of the kingdom of the saints and representative of it. The witness of Acts to the earliest stratum of Christian belief is thus that Christ and his people are one: Jesus and his Church are inseparably united.

But what was the form of the Church in its earliest stage as we see it in the book of Acts? John Allegro in his various writings on the Dead Sea Scrolls has no doubt that the organization of the early Church was largely dependent on the Essene pattern. He has dismissed the Gospels as the product of Christian myth-makers, who modelled their picture of Jesus on the Teacher of Righteousness of the Qumran sect, and who built the Church on the lines of the Righteous Teacher's community. He has claimed that, not only is the office of the Christian bishop founded on the office of the 'inspector' or 'overseer' (mebaqqer) of the Essene community, but also that the source of the names and offices of the original Apostles is to be sought in the administrative structure of the Qumran sect.

It would be agreed by most scholars today that there are parallels between the practices of the Dead Sea sect and the early Church. Both were protestant movements which sought to reform Jewish religion; both were lay communities dedicated to the pursuit of truth and holiness; both could be called followers of a righteous teacher; and both were awaiting the Messianic Age.

They believed in sharing their possessions; they partook of common meals; and they practised baptism. Both of them called themselves 'the elect' and followers of 'the Way'.

None of this need surprise us when we remember their common period, locality and background; their common Old Testament heritage; and their nonconformist origins. It would be more surprising if the organization of the early Church owed nothing to an older, well-established and to all accounts efficiently administered, neighbouring sectarian movement. But this is something quite different from saying that the Christian Church was the creation of dispossessed Essenes, who imposed on it the pattern of their own community life, and reinterpreted their own beliefs into Christian myths in order to propagate their teaching more successfully in the Gentile world.

It may be, as has been suggested by several scholars, that after the destruction of the monastery at Qumran in A.D. 68, large numbers of the Dead Sea sect joined the young Christian Church and brought with them their more rigid tradition of discipline and order. It is also possible that, among the 'great many of the priests' referred to in Ac. 6:7 who were converted to Christianity, some at any rate were Essenes, and that through them Essene influences penetrated into the life of the Church.

It does not seem, however, as if these influences, such as they were, made any marked impression on the life of the Church in the earliest stage of all with which we are concerned. Father Joseph Fitzmyer's careful study, 'Jewish Christianity in Acts in Light of the Qumran Scrolls' (Keck and Martyn, pp. 233–57), examines the parallels between Essene and early Christian practice in such matters as terminology, sharing of property, the use of the Old Testament, organizational structure, and the common meal. Father Fitzmyer concludes that these features of Essene tenets and practices 'often shed important light on passages of Acts that describe the early Jewish Christian Church'. He considers that 'it is possible at times to think in terms of a direct contact or a direct imitation of Essene usage' (as in the common designation of both Christianity and the Qumran community as 'the Way'), but he rightly insists that we 'cannot prove from such points of contact that the early Jewish Christian Church developed out of an exclusively Essene framework', and that the most that we can say is that the early Church was 'not without some influence from the Essenes'. In his view 'the influence of Qumran

literature on Acts is not as marked as it is in other New Testament
writings, for example John, Paul, Matthew and Hebrews', and
that such parallels as do exist, 'striking though they may be, are
not numerous'.

We have long been familiar with the fanciful claim that Jesus
himself was an Essene, and the less fanciful possibility that John
the Baptist may have had some relationship with the Qumran
community. It would be foolish to deny that both Jesus and John
the Baptist, or for that matter Paul, may have had some contact
with the sect, and that evidence of this may be detected in their
teaching and practice. Similarly with the early Church. It has
never been the claim of Christianity that its authority rests on its
complete originality; apart from anything else, its obvious dependence on the faith and morals of the Old Testament would
preclude any such suggestion. If the Dead Sea Scrolls now indicate that it was indebted also to nonconformist as well as to mainstream Judaism, we may echo G. R. Driver's verdict that, in the
last analysis, it is 'the person and position of Christ which make
the ultimate difference between the Gospel and the Scrolls' (*The
Judean Scrolls*, p. 548) and, by the same token, between the
Church and the Qumran community (see also: M. Black, *The
Scrolls and Christian Origins*; E. Sutcliffe, *The Monks of Qumran*).

Among recent German writers on Luke, it has been maintained,
particularly by Ernst Käsemann, that our author's ecclesiastical
background is 'primitive Catholicism' (*Frühkatholizismus*). Vielhauer, for example, says that Luke 'no longer stands within earliest
Christianity, but in the nascent early catholic Church' (Keck and
Martyn, p. 49), and Käsemann himself asserts that 'the Lucan
work as a whole is totally incomprehensible if it is not seen that
only in the stream of apostolic tradition does one also belong to the
one Holy Church as the earthly realm of salvation' ('Paul and
Early Catholicism', *New Testament Questions of Today*, p. 247).

Catholicism, primitive or present day, is a loaded word for
some Protestants. It is difficult, however, to see why it should be
regarded as a criticism of Luke if he shows that the primitive
Church was catholic in the sense that we mean when we affirm in
the Creed that we believe in 'one holy catholic and apostolic
Church'. C. K. Barrett is alarmed when Käsemann says that in
Acts 'the Word is no longer the single criterion of the Church, but
the Church legitimizes the Word, and the apostolic origin of
ecclesiastical office affords the guarantee for legitimate preaching'.

Barrett thinks that when we use the phrase 'primitive Catholicism' we ought to mean that attitude to the Church reflected in the letters of Clement (*c.* A.D. 95) and Ignatius (*c.* A.D. 115) with their 'ecclesiastical, ministerial, authoritarian and sacramental' emphasis. By contrast Luke, according to Barrett, sees the Apostles, not as administrators, but as preachers of the Word, and the Church not as 'a hierarchical *Heilsanstalt* (or agency of salvation) but as a loosely-knit evangelistic and pastoral organism' (pp. 70ff.).

Commenting on this, R. R. Williams says: 'Dr Barrett, when he reads Acts, sees in it a classical picture of the early Church already well-committed to the Reformed doctrine of the Word of God,' and continues: 'I trust I shall be forgiven if, as an Anglican bishop, I see in it a Church equally governed by, and devoted to, the Word of God, but also a Church in which the institutional arrangements—ministry, sacraments, and calendar—have their part to play in the preservation and propagation of that Word.'

Mainstream Christianity has always relied on Acts, as Williams points out, for justification of many of its practices: the commemoration of Ascension Day and of Whitsunday goes back to Ac. 1 and 2; the celebration of Holy Communion on the first day of the week is taken to be exemplified in the service at Troas in Ac. 20, when Paul preached his record-breaking sermon. We learn from Acts that baptism was the normal rite of admission to the Church, and some would find justification for infant baptism in the administration of this sacrament to the Philippian jailer and 'all his family' (16:33). The laying-on of hands by the Apostles in the case of those recently baptized has been regarded as the original pattern for confirmation, and so on (*Historicity and Chronology in the New Testament*, ed. D. E. Nineham, pp. 145, 160). We must agree with Williams that, on the evidence of Acts, the early Church was more than merely a collection of preaching centres.

It confuses the issue, however, to say that we find exclusive support in Acts for any particular form of the Church as we know it today; the earliest Christians were not Anglican or Reformed, or even primitive Catholic in the Ignatian sense. No branch of the Church can claim to reproduce in its present practice or structure the Church that Luke describes in Acts; all branches—including Pentecostalists, Salvation Army and Quakers—may claim to be in continuity with it, in that they worship the same Lord and live by the same Spirit. But is this enough? Some branches of the Church would say 'No', and would claim proprietary rights to be the only true Church or to have certain features which are essential to the Church.

Before looking at the evidence of Acts itself, let us return to the question of the reliability of Luke's information. If we are dealing with a late first-century or early second-century theologian, who either reflects the concerns of the Church of his own times or creates an artificial picture of a period of Church history about which he knew next to nothing, then it does not really matter very much to us today what he has to say about the form of the Church in its earliest days. Like the faith of the Church in the same period, it would be Luke's own brain-child—of some interest, certainly, but not vital to the current ecumenical discussion.

If, on the other hand, there is every reason to believe that our author was himself involved in part of the story he describes in Acts, and for the earlier part of his book had easy access to accurate information about what went on before he joined Paul's missionary enterprise, then we must take what he says about the earliest form of the Church very seriously indeed. Since his book as a whole reveals him to be a man who took the trouble to record the niceties of the provincial and legal administration of the Empire in his day, and to be a stickler for accuracy in geographical details, it would surely be reasonable to expect that he would be no less concerned to get his facts right on ecclesiastical polity in the first three decades of Church history, which form the subject of his narrative.

Should it be, therefore, that what emerges from Luke's pages is a Church of which the form is in many respects imprecise and often obscure, it would be wrong to conclude that Luke did not know any better. On the contrary, it would be more likely that he knew only too well that in the period he is describing the Church was finding its feet, and that consequently it has no absolute form or order that in some way constitutes its essence and from which it must never depart if it is still to be called the Church. What in fact we find is that some features are present in a primary form which later become more significant, and that other features which seem to have been regarded as even more important are, for one reason or another, gradually dropped. It is very much easier to glean from the book of Acts what is of the essence of the Church in matters of faith—such as the transcendence of God, the Lordship of Christ and the forgiveness of sins—than it is to say what is of its essence in matters of Church order.

Let us begin with the Church itself, the *ekklesia*. We have seen already that the first believers, being Jews, regarded themselves as the new Israel committed to the service of the Messiah whom God had sent, and whom they now acknowledged as their risen Lord. They came to call themselves the Church, using the word *ekklesia*, because it linked them with their Old Testament background as the new people of God (see on 5:11). But, on the evidence of Acts, their earliest description of themselves was 'the brethren', or 'the disciples', or 'all who believed'. The word 'church' in Acts usually means the local congregation, and looked at together the young congregations are spoken of as the 'churches'. Only twice is the word 'church' used to mean the whole company of Christians (9:31; 20:28), and there is no suggestion that Paul's later conception of the Church as the Body of Christ, or John's doctrine of the mystical union of Christ with his Church, had as yet been envisaged; indeed, Luke on occasion uses the word *ekklesia* to denote a pagan assembly (19:32, 39, 41).

There is a similar lack of precision in the sacramental life of the Church. Baptism was insisted on as a rite of admission, but it seems to have been much more akin to John the Baptist's baptism of repentance for the forgiveness of sins than to the Pauline or Johannine conception of baptismal regeneration. Again, Paul and John emphasize the deep significance of the Eucharist; Luke knew all about this too, for he had recorded its institution at the Last Supper in his Gospel. But, although it looks as if regular eucharistic celebrations were an integral part of the life of the earliest Christians (2:42), they seem to have formed part of a communal meal, and are described simply as the 'breaking of bread' (2:46). Similarly, the laying on of hands by the Apostles, which has been thought in the case of the Seven to have been an act of ordination (6:6), was administered to all and sundry in the case of the Samaritan converts (8:17).

When we turn to the government of the Church in its earliest days, the situation is equally fluid and imprecise. To begin with, the twelve Apostles dominate the scene, but more as the embodiment of the new Israel, as former companions of Jesus, and as witnesses to his Resurrection, than as a supreme ecclesiastical court; Peter, who receives most mention, appears primarily in the role of an active Evangelist. The others, generally unspecified, were presumably also travelling missionaries. The teaching of the Apostles, which for Luke means their preaching, was regarded as the authoritative proclamation of the Gospel.

After the Council of Jerusalem they disappear from Luke's record, and no mention is made of the appointment of any successors to preserve continuity of their office. The Twelve occupy a unique place, but there are others, whom Luke also calls 'Apostles' —Paul and Barnabas, for example (14:14)—and even more anonymous Evangelists who established Christian communities in Phoenicia, Cyprus, Damascus and Antioch, when they had been driven out of Jerusalem after Stephen's martyrdom. Stephen had been one of the Seven appointed by the Jerusalem mother church, ostensibly to assist the Twelve, though the Seven are called neither 'deacons' nor 'elders'. More likely they were appointed to placate the more radically minded Greek-speaking section of the Christian community.

We find James, the Lord's brother, emerging as head of the local Jerusalem church, presumably on account of his relationship to Jesus, and associated with him are presbyters or elders. When the Church expands into the Gentile world it seems to have been the practice of Paul to appoint elders to look after the young congregations following the initial missionary campaign (14:23). At one point these elders are called *episkopoi* ('bishops') (20:28), so that at this stage the two offices are the same. On the other hand, the local church at Antioch seems to have been led by men who are described as 'prophets' and 'teachers' (13:1).

Thus the overall picture of the government of the Church as a whole in its earliest stage is one of diversity, which we might even call pragmatic. Apart from the unique position of the twelve Apostles there is no common pattern, and certainly nothing that could be called 'Church order' in the modern sense. Leadership was essential in each congregation, but it seems to have been stereotyped neither in form nor by designation. The authority and continuity of the Church was safeguarded, not by apostolic succession, but by adherence to the apostolic tradition concerning Jesus, by the legacy of the Old Testament and by the presence of the Spirit.

9. THE HOLY SPIRIT IN ACTS

The book of Acts has often been called 'The Gospel of the Holy Spirit'; but Luke, although clearly he has a theological turn of mind, is not a professional theologian of the calibre of Paul, and we should not expect from him a doctrinal exposition of his convictions on the subject of the Spirit in the Pauline manner. What we should expect, and what we get, is a practical demonstration of the Spirit at work. For Luke, everything that happens in the life of the Church from the beginning to the end of his story is in one way or another controlled, inspired and furthered by the Holy Spirit. He sees the Church as the people of God advancing towards the fulfilment of God's purpose for the world, not in their own strength, but in the power of the Spirit. It is a Spirit-filled Church, and its members are ordinary men and women who have been endowed with this unique gift from God.

As in the case of their attitude to Christ, where they were more concerned with his past and present activity than with formulating any doctrine about his relationship to God, so, in the case of the Holy Spirit, the first Christians did not attempt to systematize their views. Because they were Jews, they could on occasion speak of the Holy Spirit almost as a personification of God (e.g. 15:28), like Wisdom in the minds of the Wisdom Scribes; but mostly, and certainly in the beginning, the Spirit was more simply regarded as the power of God at work in human affairs. As W. L. Knox has put it (p. 92): 'It would seem that Acts reflects the gradual and quite unrationalized development by which the relation of the Spirit to God in himself and to Jesus as the exalted Christ is passing from its purely Jewish form of belief in a spiritual action of God or the Lord on the mind and soul of the disciple into the later Christian conception of a "person" within the divine Trinity. His relation to God and to Christ seems to be completely vague and undetermined.'

Similarly, there is no clear-cut theological or ecclesiastical pattern of how and when the Spirit can be expected to be given; normally it is thought of as accompanying baptism on admission into the new community. Peter said to the crowd at Pentecost: 'Repent, and be baptized . . .; and you will receive the gift of the Holy Spirit' (2:38). But the Samaritan converts to Christianity were baptized, we are told, without receiving the Spirit, which only happened to them later through the laying on of hands by the Apostles (8:12–17); yet obviously it was not invariably channelled through the Apostles, or through the laying-on of hands by anyone at all: Cornelius and his family circle, we are told, received the gift of the Spirit before they were baptized (10:44–8), and the Apostles themselves received the Spirit at Pentecost while, as far as we know, most of them may never have been baptized at all (cf. Jn 1:35ff.).

Yet, however imprecise the first Christians may have been in this as in other respects—so imprecise as to refer to the Holy Spirit in Peter's words as 'this (thing)' (2:33)—they were never in any doubt as to its reality as a new power which had come into their experience at Pentecost. Schooled as they were on Old Testament prophecy, they had been taught by Isaiah, Ezekiel, Joel and Zechariah to associate a great outpouring of the Spirit of God with the coming of the Messiah and the birth of a new age. Jesus himself had pointed to his own ministry as proof that the Spirit was mightily at work (Lk. 11:20), and his Resurrection had convinced his followers that they were now living in the time of which the prophets had spoken.

In Luke's interpretation of the situation, their minds were thus prepared by the absence of the Spirit after Christ's Ascension to expect its return, as happened at Pentecost. The Holy Spirit of God, which had been seen at work uniquely in the words and works of Jesus, was now being given by Christ to his Church to continue his work in the world. It is not surprising, in view of the remarkable events which the Apostles had themselves seen in the ministry and Resurrection of Jesus, that it was the more dramatic evidence of the presence of the Spirit—such as speaking with tongues, miracles and prophecy—that at first attracted most attention. It would be a complete travesty of the situation, however, to think that these were ever regarded as mere marvels or portents, or to overlook the fact that, side by side with them from the beginning, went the recognition of the presence of the Spirit in less spectacular ways as the power that could change men's lives and build a Christian community.

Whether the tradition of the absence of the Spirit between the Ascension and Pentecost came to Luke, as Knox suggests (pp. 85f.), as a symbolic parallel with the rabbinical story that Moses was summoned to heaven to receive the Torah, which he then brought down to men—in which case Christ was regarded as sending down the new Law at Pentecost to be written on men's hearts—or whether, as Conzelmann maintains (*The Theology of St. Luke*, p. 184), the idea comes from Luke himself, to make a clear distinction between the period of Christ and the period of the Church and the Spirit in the divine economy, the day of Pentecost marks the beginning of the Church's mission.

Like the story of the Ascension, the story of Pentecost is to be read as a pictorial expression of a theological fact, rather than as a literal description of a particular event; what hand Luke himself had in the shaping of it is impossible to say. The symbols of wind and fire, suggesting the divine presence, express the profound spiritual experience which the Apostles shared on the first Whitsunday. We may hazard the guess that the overpowering religious ecstasy, which issued in 'speaking with tongues' (glossolalia), was communicated to the more sympathetic in the crowd, giving rise to the tradition of a 'miracle of languages', while the less sympathetic regarded the Apostles as being merely under the influence of drink.

The Old Testament prophets had to some extent been similarly caught up in such ecstatic experiences, and Peter had no doubt that this was the great outpouring of the Spirit of which Joel had spoken. It was the first, but by no means the last, occasion in the story of the early Church, as recorded in Acts and in Paul's letters, where this undoubtedly genuine religious experience came upon individuals and groups. Paul's concern in his letter to the church at Corinth, where he seeks to keep this particular manifestation of the presence of the Spirit within the bounds of decorum during divine service, is no criticism of the reality of the experience; it has recurred at many points in the history of the Church, and it is a feature of early Christianity which is preserved among Pentecostalists today. With regard to its present practice, if we are to be guided by Paul, we may echo J. P. M. Sweet's judicious conclusion, that 'we must reject any claim that tongues are the exclusive or even the normal sign that a Christian has received the Spirit', and that 'his (Paul's) authority cannot be claimed for regarding glossolalia as a necessary part of Christian life'. The most we can say—but with the authority and emphasis of Jesus himself—is: 'Do not forbid it' (1 C. 14:37–9); and, on Paul's own authority: 'Do not quench the Spirit' (1 Th. 5:19) (*New Testament Studies*, XIII, iii, pp. 256–7).

In these days of psychosomatic medicine, the miraculous element in Acts should present less of a problem than it did to an earlier generation, for most of the miracles recorded are cases of exorcism or physical healing. No doubt some of the stories that came to Luke, like some of the miracle stories in his Gospel, had lost nothing in the telling, and pious regard for the Apostles had added its quota of imaginative embellishments. But we cannot

eliminate the miracle stories from Acts any more than we can
eliminate them from the Gospels, and there is no good reason why
we should try.

For the restoration of wholeness to mind and body in the case of
the diseased and the mentally disturbed was done in the name of
Jesus by men who had been endowed with his Spirit to continue
his work. Some of the acts of healing which Luke records were
performed by the same men who had earlier been given authority
by Christ himself in Galilee to preach the Gospel and to heal the
sick. What they and other missionaries were now doing in a wider
field was part of the same ministry; they were channels of the
healing power of Christ: Peter said to the paralysed, bed-ridden
Aeneas: 'Jesus Christ heals you; rise' (9:34). It is no diminution
of our gratitude to God for modern medical science, and the
devoted care of all concerned in the work of healing, to say that
there is still evidence of the direct and miraculous power of the
Spirit to heal, most spectacularly at Lourdes, but also through
undenominational faith-healers and through the intercessory
activity of divine healing groups in various branches of the Church
today. When Luke describes glossolalia and healing miracles as
signs of the Holy Spirit at work in the life of the early Church,
he is not a credulous simpleton, far less an inventor of pious
marvels, but a sober recorder of a particularly rich outcrop of
manifestations of the Spirit which have never since been completely absent from the Church, but which, in the unique period of
its beginning, appeared with unusual intensity.

Prophecy was the third obvious mark of the presence of the
Spirit that occurs frequently in Luke's narrative. Akin to speaking
with tongues, it had in Paul's view a greater value for the edification of the Church in that, although prophets were also
ecstatics, they were at least intelligible. Prediction of coming
events formed part of the prophet's function, as it did in the Old
Testament; but by far his greatest contribution in the early
Church, again as in the Old Testament, was inspired preaching
—preaching that conveyed the unmistakable sense that this was the
Word of God, and that the preacher was moved by the Spirit.

In less startling and unfamiliar ways than those just described,
the Spirit is shown by Luke to have been the main driving-force
in the day to day life of the earliest Christians. It was the Spirit
who gave the Apostles, these 'uneducated common men' as Luke
calls them (Ac. 4:13), that extraordinary 'boldness' which enabled

them to face the threats of the Sanhedrin with equanimity; who strengthened them to meet persecution, not with resignation, but with exultation; who gave the young community so close a sense of fellowship that it instituted a common fund for the relief of the poorer members; who led it to make its criterion of 'a good man'—like Barnabas, for example—that he was 'full of the Holy Spirit and of faith' (11:24).

On occasion, there is mention of the 'comfort' of the Holy Spirit (9:31), and no doubt this was a real element in early Christian experience as it is today. But the Holy Spirit administers different kinds of comfort, and as often as not in the life of the early Church it was uncomfortable comfort that the Spirit provided.

Throughout the whole of Acts we are given the impression that it was not far-sighted statesmanship that brought the first Jewish Christians to the realization that the whole world was their parish; rather, we get a picture of men as prone to religious conservatism as the main body of the Church has always been, as tied to their own past history and tradition, as reluctant to venture out into the unknown future with its problems and uncertainties, but driven almost against their will by the unmistakable urge of the Spirit to venture forward into uncharted and intimidating waters with only their faith to sustain them. Luke shows us that, if they had been left to themselves, the members of the first Christian community might well have begun and ended as a little coterie of orthodox Jews, content to meet and celebrate the coming of the Messiah within the confines of the Holy City. But the Spirit moved Stephen to public utterance about the role of Christ in the wider world, as it had been revealed to him; in consequence, he became the first Christian martyr, and through his protest his supporters were forced, this time certainly against their will, to leave their homes and to take refuge wherever they could. Yet, no matter where they went, they were moved to plant the seed of the Gospel, and new Christian communities began to appear up and down the eastern Mediterranean lands.

It was the Spirit, we are told, who prompted Philip the Evangelist to accost the God-fearing African official riding south along the Gaza road, and to baptize him after instruction as the first member of the Church from outside the tradition of Israel. It was the Spirit who forced the reluctant Peter to recognize that the Church must embrace Gentiles as well as Jews, beginning with so unlikely a convert in Jewish eyes as an officer of the imperial army. When the more cautious Apostles at Jerusalem heard with some dismay of this and of the conversion of large numbers of Samaritans, those ancient enemies of all good Jews, their doubts were silenced by indisputable evidence that the Holy Spirit was pressing them to acknowledge as brothers in Christ people who by every natural inclination they would have preferred to regard as beyond the pale.

So in the rest of his story, which covers the great expansion of the Church from its Palestinian setting through Asia Minor, Greece and finally to Rome, Luke shows that it was nothing but the prodding of this uncomfortable Comforter, the Spirit, that urged on Paul and his associates, despite hazard and opposition, illness, mob-violence and rough justice, to spread the Gospel, not always where they wanted, but where they were meant to go. It is a moving and exhilarating account, which leaves us in humble wonderment that men of ordinary flesh and blood could endure and survive and still press on with what they believed to be their God-given assignment, a story that is only explicable in the light of the supernatural power with which they were endowed.

This is the mood in which we begin to wonder whether Luke's whole story of the first three momentous decades of the Church's history is not too good to be true. This inspiring procession of men and women wholly dedicated to the service of Christ and the furthering of his Kingdom—this impressive evidence of the fellow-ship of all believers, their compassion and care for one another, their joy in tribulation, their unwavering confidence in the good outcome of their enterprise despite all setbacks, their firm con-viction of the divine origin of their faith—can we be persuaded that there ever was such a beginning to our present theological uncertainties, our interdenominational embroilments, our hesitant moral witness? In such a mood we might well conclude either that Luke's picture is a flight of fancy, an ideal that never existed, or that he is describing a state of affairs so far removed from twentieth-century realities that his book has virtually nothing to say to us.

This is no new problem. The contrast between first beginnings and later developments was felt very early in Christian history, but the right conclusions were not necessarily drawn. For example, Eusebius, writing in the fourth century A.D., looks back wistfully and says that in the first epoch of its history, the Church was 'a pure and incorrupt virgin. If there were any who tried to corrupt the sound doctrine of the preaching of salvation, they still hid in a dark hiding place. But when the sacred chorus of the Apostles in various ways departed from life, as well as the generation of those who were deemed worthy to hear their inspired wisdom, then also the faction of godless error arose by the deceit of teachers of another doctrine.'

Conzelmann makes the wry comment: 'This is a picture, an idea, not historical reality. In history there was error in the Church from its beginning. There never was such a sacred chorus. There was faith and weakness, there was God's message and men's error, there was—Church in history' (*The Bible in Modern Scholarship*, ed. J. P. Hyatt, pp. 225–6). One might suspect indeed that Eusebius had never read the book of Acts, for Luke certainly gives no countenance to such an idyllic conception of the first chapter of the Church's story. Luke had himself known some members of the 'sacred chorus', and he belonged to the generation of those who, according to Eusebius, 'were deemed worthy to hear their inspired wisdom'. He certainly testifies that the Gospel of salvation was soundly proclaimed, and that this was well reflected in the quality of the day to day life of the Church.

But he does not shrink from showing us the seamy side as well. He does not draw a veil over the wrangling in the Jerusalem congregation concerning the distribution of poor relief, or the plain dishonesty of Ananias and Sapphira. He faithfully records the suspicion with which Paul had to contend within the Church after his conversion, on account of his past black record; the official criticism of Peter for stepping out of line in admitting an officer of the Roman army into the jealously guarded circle of the faithful, and for mixing generally with these impossible Gentiles. Nor does Luke disguise the fact that Mark left Paul's missionary team just as they were getting under way in their first great evangelistic enterprise, and that his defection led later to a violent quarrel between Paul and Mark's kinsman Barnabas. Our author does not pretend that there was not hot, and no doubt bitter, debate at the Council of Jerusalem on the question of whether Gentiles should be allowed to become full members of the Church without submitting to circumcision and accepting other traditional Jewish tenets.

Luke is thus not describing a Church that never was, a paradise on earth peopled by haloed saints, but a Church where there was as there has always been, in Conzelmann's words, 'faith and weakness', 'God's message and men's error'. This is surely the crowning evidence of the general reliability of the story that the book of Acts has to tell. If Luke had been, as many recent writers have suggested, a late first-century or early second-century theologian, looking back at the foundation of the Church which he loved but of whose early beginnings he had no direct knowledge, he would surely have painted a more glamorous picture of the first generation. Instead of that, he shows us 'a band of men whose hearts God had touched' (1 Sam. 10:26), but who were still sinners in need of daily repentance and daily forgiveness.

Similarly, if Luke had been, as has been suggested, a convinced exponent of primitive catholicism, reflecting back into the life of the first Christian decades the more developed ecclesiastical system of the end of the first century or the beginning of the second, surely he would have left us a tidier canvas. We might have been shown the twelve Apostles directing the expansion of the Church from Jerusalem, ordaining a proper ministry, formulating a body of doctrine, exercising strict discipline, and handing on their authority to duly appointed successors. Instead of that, Luke gives us both doctrinally and ecclesiastically a thoroughly untidy picture, and the most obvious explanation of that is that this is how it was, and that Luke knew it at first hand to have been so. Perhaps a man who wrote a book which can be called the 'Gospel of the Holy Spirit' understood better than most of us what our Lord meant when he said: 'The wind blows where it wills' (Jn 3:8).

THE ACTS
OF THE APOSTLES

THE PROGRESS OF THE GOSPEL FROM JERUSALEM
TO ANTIOCH 1:1–12:25

Title. The oldest manuscripts call the book simply 'Acts of Apostles'. This is a more accurate description, since the narrative is not an exhaustive account of the activities of *the* (Twelve) Apostles, but a selective record of the history of the first three decades of the life of the Church in which other Apostles feature more largely than most of the Twelve. It has been suggested that the book may have been put on the book market, under the title of 'Luke's Acts of the Apostles', as a companion volume to his Gospel, 'Luke's Acts of Jesus'.

1. first book: i.e., the Gospel to which this is a sequel, and with no suggestion that there is a third book to follow later.

Theophilus: meaning 'lover of God', which some have thought suggests that it was a pseudonym. More likely he was Luke's patron, who helped to launch the book on the market; but nothing is known of him. The fact that he is not addressed as 'most excellent' as in the preface to Luke's Gospel does not indicate that relations between the two men have become either cooler or more friendly.

began: this implies that the works and words of Jesus, recounted in the Gospel, were the real beginning of the story of the Church, and that Jesus is still acting through his Spirit in the missionary campaigns of the Apostles.

2. taken up: referring back to the Ascension described in Lk. 24:51. There the original text probably read simply: 'he parted from them', the words: 'and was carried up into heaven' appearing only in some manuscripts. There is no doubt, however, that Luke meant to round off his account of Jesus in the Gospel with the Ascension to mark the end of the most significant chapter in the story of God's plan for the salvation of the world, as he will shortly (verse 9) describe it again as the prelude to the birth of the Church, which derives its life from the gift of the Spirit given by its ascended Lord.

commandment: still harking back to the last chapter of Luke's

Gospel (24:45–9), where Jesus before his Ascension outlined the programme of world mission to his eleven remaining disciples.

Holy Spirit: the first mention of the Spirit who so dominates the narrative of Acts that this book has often been called: 'The Gospel of the Holy Spirit.' Luke implies here that the power of the Holy Spirit with which Jesus had been endowed from his baptism onwards was the same power that was now to be given to the Church, founded on the Apostles whom he had chosen, to continue his work on earth.

3. proofs: Luke is emphasizing that it was not visions of Christ that the disciples saw after the Crucifixion, but unmistakable appearances of the living Lord himself.

forty days: it has been suggested that between the writing of the Gospel and the writing of Acts Luke came to hear that there was a longer period between the Resurrection and the Ascension than he had known about when he wrote the last chapter of his Gospel. Superficially, it seems that there he speaks of the Ascension as having taken place on Easter Day; closer examination, however, indicates that a longer period is involved, and that there is no inconsistency between the two accounts. Here Luke says that on various occasions during approximately six weeks after the Resurrection the disciples received further teaching from Jesus. The number 'forty' would recall the 'forty days' during which Moses was said to have received divine instruction on Mount Sinai. There he was given the programme of action for old Israel, as the Apostles are now given the message that is to be preached by the new Israel.

kingdom of God: the rule of God on earth, beginning with Jesus' own ministry, had been the main theme of the Gospel. This had been the Good News which the disciples were now to proclaim to the wider world. We may take it that, in harmony with what he has already said in the last chapter of his Gospel, Luke implies here that the disciples had to be taught the full meaning of the coming of the 'kingdom of God' through Jesus in the light of his death and Resurrection. The period between the Resurrection and the Ascension is thus the point at which, under divine guidance, the first missionaries of the Church received clarification of many things that still puzzled them, and were taught to see how the life, death and Resurrection of Jesus were in accordance with the Scriptures, and together constituted God's mightiest act for the salvation of the world.

4. staying: The unusual Greek word may mean 'eating with
them' (*RSV mg.*). If so, it would connect up with Lk. 24:43.
Jerusalem: for Luke, Jerusalem is supremely important as the
centre of Israel's faith and the place of the Lord's Passion. Now it
is also to be the place where the Holy Spirit is given to the
disciples, in the power of which the Good News will be carried
from the Holy City to Rome, the heart of the pagan world. Thus
the Apostles must not leave Jerusalem before Pentecost, 'for out
of Zion shall go forth the law, and the word of the LORD from
Jerusalem' (Isa. 2:3).
promise: God's promise through the prophet Joel (2:28-9)
that in the messianic age there would be a great invasion of his
Spirit into the lives of men. Jesus declares that this is now about to
happen.
5. water . . . Spirit: John the Baptist's mission had included
baptism by immersion in the Jordan as an outward sign of the
inward cleansing power of God's forgiveness for the penitent
sinner. Some, at any rate, of the Apostles had been baptized by
John (Jn 1:35), but full rebirth in the Christian sense involves
baptism both by water and by the Spirit (Jn 3:5). This complementary gift of the Spirit could not be given to the Apostles until
after Christ's Ascension. The Lord would send from heaven the
power they needed to renew their own lives and to launch the
Church on its mission.
6. restore the kingdom: since these early verses of Acts so
clearly recapitulate the last section of Luke's Gospel, we may think
of the disciples involved in the events described here as a wider
circle than the eleven Apostles. Luke obviously attaches primary
importance to the latter here, as throughout his narrative of the
early days of the Church. But there has already been reference in
Lk. 24 to Cleopas and his companion on the road to Emmaus,
where they are described as Apostles (Lk. 24:10-13), as well as
to 'those who were with' the Eleven when Jesus appeared to them
on Easter Day (Lk. 24:33). Thus, if we think in terms of this
larger inner circle of believers, we can understand the apparent
discrepancy between the appearances of Jesus to some of the
disciples in Galilee (Mk 14:28; 16:7; Jn 21) and our Lord's
injunction to the disciples in verse 4 not to depart from Jerusalem.
Some had gone to Galilee after the Resurrection, but had now
returned; others had probably never left Jerusalem.
    This would also account for the surprising question now as to

whether the Lord intended to **restore the kingdom to Israel,**
in view of the fact that during the 'forty days' he had apparently
been instructing his followers as to the true nature of the Kingdom
of God. The question, implying the common expectation of a
national triumph for the Jews over the Romans by the agency of
the Messiah, could hardly have been asked by those who had so
recently been enlightened. It could, however, have been asked by
others who had not heard the Lord's words on the subject, and
who had now gathered together for this final scene before his
Ascension.

7. times or seasons: Jesus' reply, in keeping with his words
in Mk 13:32, turns their thoughts away both from any nationalist
conception of the Kingdom and from any expectation of an
immediate realization of God's total purpose. It is for God himself
to set the time for its fulfilment. Meantime the task of Christ's
disciples is to work for the final triumph of God's rule on earth,
not merely in Israel, by the mission of the Church.

8. to the end of the earth: not by their own strength, but only
by the supernatural power of the Spirit which was shortly to be
given to them, could this mission of preaching the Gospel and
healing the sick be accomplished. The disciples were to witness to
Christ—that is, to tell what they themselves had seen and heard—
beginning in Jerusalem, whose inhabitants knew Jesus as the
prophet from Nazareth but not Jesus as the Christ of God. From
there the message was to be carried through Judaea and Samaria
as far as civilization extended (cf. Isa. 49:6). For practical purposes this meant Rome, and this verse summarizes the progress
of the Gospel as Luke recounts it in the chapters that follow.

THE ASCENSION 1:9–11

It would be a grave misunderstanding of Luke's mind and purpose
to regard his account of the Ascension of Christ as other than
symbolic and poetic. He is not describing an act of levitation, or
bracketing the last event in the story of the historical Jesus with
the legendary end of Elijah or Hercules. He is aware that theological truth can often be best conveyed by imaginative word-
pictures. In this case, the truth to be conveyed to the reader is that
the end of the story of Jesus and the prelude to the story of the
Church was the apostolic conviction that the risen Christ was now
raised to the right hand of God, exalted as Lord and King. When
the purpose of the post-Resurrection appearances of Jesus had

been achieved, they came to an end, and the Son who had become man in the mystery of the Incarnation returned to the Father in the mystery of the Ascension. It was the faith of the early Church as reflected throughout the *NT* that the crucified Christ, raised to life by the Easter miracle, reigns in glory and mercy, sharing men's concerns, until God's final victory over evil is accomplished by the power of his Spirit working through the Church. Luke emphasizes the Ascension as the necessary prelude to Christ's gift of the Spirit to the Church at Pentecost.

9. he was lifted up: this conveys pictorially the conviction that Christ is now exalted and transcendent. So long as we know, like Luke, that God is not only 'up there', but 'down here', we can still, *pace* the astronauts, speak like Luke of God and heaven as being 'above' us.

cloud: the characteristically biblical symbol for the mystery and glory of God's presence, the Shekinah, into which Christ is now received.

10. two men . . . in white robes: these are obviously intended to be angelic beings bringing a message from God, as on Easter morning the women outside the empty tomb received similar clarification in their perplexity (Lk. 24:1–7).

11. why do you stand looking into heaven? As the women at the sepulchre were brought to their senses and shown the significance of the empty tomb, so here God's word to the Apostles recalls them to reality. They are not to waste time in idle speculation. Their mission is on earth and their task awaits them. **in the same way:** the Apostles are assured that Christ will come again. We are not meant to think in terms of a physical descent, any more than of a physical ascent. The divine message confirms the universal *NT* conviction of the ultimate triumph of Christ who, as Lord and Judge of all, will be the same Jesus as they have known in the flesh.

BETWEEN THE ASCENSION AND PENTECOST **1:12–14**

12. they returned to Jerusalem: the note of exhilaration reflected in Lk. 24:52 is not referred to; but it is no doubt implied, as the Apostles await the baptism of the Spirit.
Olivet: the Mount of Olives, E. of Jerusalem across the Kidron valley on the way to Bethany (cf. Lk. 24:50).
a sabbath day's journey: the distance pious Jews were allowed to travel on the Sabbath, about three quarters of a mile.

13. the upper room: the first meeting place of the Church, probably to be identified with the scene of the Last Supper (Lk. 22 : 12), traditionally the *coenaculum* in the house of Mary, mother of John Mark (12 : 12).

staying: i.e. accustomed to meet.

Peter . . . James: the same list, with slight variation in order, as in Lk. 6 : 14–16, with the omission of Judas Iscariot.

14. prayer: probably, as in Lk. 24 : 53, in the Temple.

women: their wives, or the women of Lk. 8 : 2–3; 24 : 10, or both. The mother of Jesus is singled out for special mention, and it is implied that his brothers (Mk 6 : 3) at one time sceptical (Jn 7 : 5) had by this time become believers. Paul refers to the appearance of the risen Christ which probably caused the conversion of James, the Lord's brother (1 C. 15 : 7), and perhaps of the other brothers as well.

REPLACEMENT OF JUDAS ISCARIOT **I : 15–26**

It is significant that the first official action of the small Christian community was to restore the apostolate to the original number that Jesus had appointed (Lk. 6 : 13). From the outset, the Church regarded itself as the new Israel, inheriting the mission of the traditional twelve tribes to bring the nations of the world to the knowledge of God. There must therefore be twelve Apostles, in compliance with the intention of Jesus, and the authority of the apostolate which had been damaged by the treachery of Judas must be restored.

Peter emerges right from the beginning as the undisputed head of the Christian community. It was upon him that Jesus had promised to build his Church (Mt. 16 : 18), and Peter's gift for leadership, his courage and his wisdom from the Ascension onwards more than compensated for his momentary denial of his master during Jesus' trial (Lk. 22 : 54–62). Like the other speeches and sermons in Acts, the address that follows is obviously not a verbatim record of Peter's actual words but Luke's own summary of what he had been informed was the substance of Peter's statement.

15. in those days: i.e. between the Ascension and Pentecost.

the brethren: the earliest name for the Christian community.

a hundred and twenty: it has been suggested that, since in Jewish constitutional law a town congregation had to have one hundred and twenty members before it could elect members to

the Sanhedrin, Luke is anxious to show that the election of
Matthias was legally correct. But perhaps the number is not
necessarily significant, except as an approximate estimate of the
number of Christians in Jerusalem at this time. There were at
least five hundred to whom the risen Christ had appeared
(1 C. 15:6), but presumably most of these were still in Galilee.

16. the scripture had to be fulfilled: under the guidance of
Christ himself (Lk. 24:27), the first Christians found answers to
many puzzling aspects of the ministry of Jesus by searching the
Scriptures. Why, for example, had Jesus chosen as one of his
closest followers a man who betrayed him? Such a psalm as 41:9
indicated that treachery on the part of a friend was one of the
afflictions to be expected by the righteous. Inevitably such a
Righteous Sufferer became the prototype of Christ. More precisely Peter found in Ps. 109:8 and 69:25, which he quotes in
verse 20, words which appeared to point to the fate of Judas and
the need to fill his place in the apostolate.

David: it was the belief of the first Christians that David was
the author of all the Psalms and that, like the prophets, he was the
mouthpiece of the Holy Spirit. This led them to take on occasion,
as here, a mechanical view of the relationship between *OT* words
and *NT* events which we should now question. *NT* writers on the
whole, however, see the relationship as more organic than
mechanical, in that they see Gospel events as a general fulfilment
of God's promises to Israel. As might be expected, since both
Christianity and Essenism had a common origin in the faith and
practice of Israel, each group found in the *OT* justification for its
beliefs and confirmation of events in its own history. It is evident
from the Dead Sea Scrolls that the method of interpreting the
OT used by the Qumran sectaries was in many respects similar to
that of the early Jewish Christians.

19. Field of Blood: however Judas met his death, he had
apparently had a violent end. Luke's version of the story, a
parenthetical comment inserted into Peter's speech in verses
18–19, differs from that of Mt. 27:5–8, and is presumably a local
explanation of an odd place name.

22. a witness to his resurrection: it is a mark of the importance that the early Church attached to the historical evidence
for their faith that the qualification insisted upon for the candidate
who should fill the vacancy in the apostolate was that he should
have been an actual eye-witness of the events in the ministry of

Jesus from the beginning; only such a man, it was felt, could testify with authority to the truth of his encounter with the risen Christ. It was presumably for this reason that James, the Lord's brother, who later became head of the Jerusalem church, was passed over on this occasion, and it was no doubt partly because he had not been a companion of Jesus in his Galilean ministry that Paul was later to be looked at askance by the more rigid Jewish Christians.

23. they put forward two: there were perhaps not many who fulfilled the requirements of verse 22. The two named here may have been among the seventy of Lk. 10:1.

Joseph . . . and Matthias: nothing more is definitely known of either of these, and they are not mentioned again in Luke's narrative.

24. they prayed: the whole congregation having put forward two names (although the 'Western' text suggests that Peter himself nominated the candidates), they prayed to Christ to indicate which of the two he had chosen to replace Judas.

26. they cast lots: as in 1 Sam. 14:41, when it was by the use of the sacred Urim and Thummim. Here it means presumably shaking two stones, with the names of the candidates on them, in a container until one or other fell out. In this way it was thought that the human element or chance was ruled out, and that the Lord had made the selection. It is perhaps more likely that this was the procedure adopted, rather than that, after prayer, they 'gave their votes'. Since the apostolate was a unique office this was not treated as ordination (see on 6:6), and appointment by lot was not practised again by the Apostles. Nor, when a vacancy in the Twelve occurred later by the death of James, the son of Zebedee (12:1–2), was his place filled. The Twelve provided an original and collective witness to the historical Jesus and his Resurrection, and were thus the supreme authority in the earliest stage of the Church.

Note on the Western Text

In a commentary on the English text of Acts it is unnecessary to dwell at length on the problems of the Greek text. It is reckoned that the 'witnesses' (i.e. MSS., versions or translations of the Greek into other languages, quotations of the *NT* in the writings of the early Christian Fathers, and papyri) which preserve most probably the text that Luke wrote are those which are considered to be the most valuable for the text of the rest of the *NT*. In the case of Acts, however, the text of a group of MSS. and versions originating mostly in the West (hence called the 'Western' text) provides a number of interesting variant readings which are noted in the course of the commentary. Each should be considered on its own merits, since on occasion the Western text may represent more correctly what Luke originally wrote. (The text of Acts is dealt with fully by J. H. Ropes in Jackson and Lake's *The Beginnings of Christianity*, III and, more recently, by A. F. J. Klijn in *A Survey of the Researches into the Western Text of the Gospels and Acts* (1949).)

THE CHURCH IN JERUSALEM 2:1–7:60

THE GIFT OF THE SPIRIT 2:1–13

For Luke this is the real beginning of his story in Acts. The coming of the Spirit at Pentecost brings the Church to birth, and endows it with the divine power without which it could not have fulfilled its appointed mission as set forth in 1:8. Nothing less than this heaven-sent gift in Luke's view could have changed simple fishermen into fearless Evangelists and made them the spearhead of an irresistible missionary campaign which swept through the Roman Empire or could have transformed in the short space of thirty years an obscure Jewish sect into a world-wide religious movement. As in his treatment of the Ascension, Luke conveys the significance of Pentecost in symbol and word-picture. The basic event was a communal religious experience, as a result of which the Apostles embarked on the first stage of the Church's mission. Luke, however, dramatizes this in terms of the 'wind' of the Spirit of God and the 'fire' of the Power of God together with the breaking down of the barrier of language, symbolizing the beginning of the reconciling power of the Gospel.

If we accept that Luke is an original theologian as well as an historian, we shall not be disturbed by the apparent discrepancy between the account of the giving of the Spirit in the Fourth Gospel and what Luke has to say here. Nor shall we be too concerned at the difference between the nature of 'speaking with tongues', or glossolalia, elsewhere in Acts (10:46; 19:6) and in Paul's Epistles (1 C. 12, 14), where it is represented as the same kind of inarticulate ecstatic babbling as was common among the 'sons of the prophets' in the *OT* as well as in Christian revivalism past and present, and Luke's transformation of this common occurrence into a 'miracle of languages' at Pentecost. In John's Gospel the Holy Spirit was given to the disciples by the risen Christ on the day of the Resurrection (Jn 20:22), and clearly the Holy Spirit must have been at work on the hearts and minds of the disciples throughout the whole period between the Crucifixion and Pentecost. Luke, however, pinpoints the gift of the Spirit as having taken place precisely at Pentecost, since there were so many theological overtones associated with that particular day, and since in fact it was at this juncture that the Church went into action with a new-found consciousness of the power of the presence of Christ. Similarly the ecstatic experience of 'speaking with tongues' suggested irresistibly to him the reversal of the mythical curse of Babel, when men's impious pride had been punished by their being separated from one another by the diversity of language (Gen. 11:1-9), where now men from all nations could be brought into one fellowship by the power of the Spirit.

1. Pentecost: the Christian Whitsunday. This was the second of the three great Jewish annual festivals, falling between Passover and the Feast of Tabernacles or Feast of Booths. Its name means 'fiftieth', since it was celebrated fifty days after Passover, and, as it was held seven weeks after Passover, it was also called the 'Feast of Weeks' (Exod. 34:22). It was a harvest festival, when offering was made of the first-fruits of the wheat crop (Lev. 23:15ff.). As such it would be seen by Luke as an appropriate occasion for the appearance of the first-fruits of the Spirit in the launching of the Church's mission. Pentecost had also come to signify for Jews the commemoration of the giving of the Law at Sinai fifty days after the Exodus Passover. For Luke this, too, would be seen as having a Christian fulfilment in the giving of the Spirit fifty days after the Christian Exodus Passover, the Crucifixion and Resurrection. **all together in one place:** this would seem to refer to the whole company of 'the brethren' of 1:15 and, in view of 2:6, the 'place' was more likely to have been somewhere within the Temple precincts, perhaps Solomon's Portico (3:11; 5:12), rather than in the seclusion of the upper room (cf. Lk. 24:53).

2. wind is an obvious symbol for the divine Spirit and as such is frequently found both in the *OT* and *NT* (e.g., 1 Kg. 19:11; Ezek. 37:9; Jn 3:8).

3. fire as symbolizing the power of God is also a common biblical usage (e.g. Exod. 3:2). John the Baptist had spoken of the coming messianic baptism as being with the Spirit and with fire, in the sense of judgment and purification (Lk. 3:16). Here the metaphor conveys the idea of the minds of all present being inspired, and their hearts kindled by this powerful visitation of the Spirit.

4. other tongues: glossolalia, or 'speaking with tongues', was a regular phenomenon in the life of the early Church and has never been altogether absent in its subsequent history. Although it is the result of genuine religious experience, it can get out of hand, as Paul found at Corinth. People in the grip of such spiritual ecstasy are known to utter foreign words normally unknown to them, mingled with other unintelligible noises. This is, however, not the point of Luke's statement here. He makes it plain in what follows that he saw in the Pentecostal utterances of the disciples a foreshadowing of the universal mission of the Church, when men of all nations would be brought into a unity of understanding through the preaching of the Gospel in the power of the Holy Spirit. There was added point in this, since it was said that the angels at Sinai had proclaimed the Law to all the nations in their own tongues.

5. men from every nation: Pentecost, because of its occurrence at a more propitious time of the year for travel, induced bigger numbers of Jews from all over the world to make the pilgrimage to Jerusalem than Passover itself. It was also customary for many pious Jews who had spent their lives abroad to return to end their days as close to the Temple as possible.

6. this sound: i.e. the ecstatic cries of the disciples.
each . . . in his own language: apart from Luke's theologizing of the incident referred to above, it would be normal for some of the crowd which gathered to be stirred into a responsive mood by the behaviour of the disciples, just as for others (verse 13) the disciples were no more than a group of men under the influence of drink.

7. Galileans spoke Aramaic with a recognizably broad accent, presumably like Somerset or Ayrshire English, as instanced by Peter in the High Priest's courtyard (Lk. 22:59). Luke's point, however, is that it is the Galilean Gospel that is destined to sweep through the world.

8. native language: the crowd was composed of Jews by race or profession of faith. Those who could not understand Aramaic would have understood Greek. There was therefore no need for a 'miracle of languages'.

9-11. Parthians . . . Arabians: there is probably no more significance in this list of nations represented in the crowd than a general coverage of the known world, possibly based on an astrological catalogue, sweeping roughly from east to west through lands in which the Jews of the Dispersion were to be found.

proselytes were Gentiles who had fully embraced the Jewish faith, involving circumcision (in the case of men), baptism and total obedience to the Law of Moses.

13. they are filled with new wine: Paul, who did not rate 'speaking with tongues' highly among the gifts of the Spirit, speaks of the danger of outsiders concluding that Christians engaged in glossolalia were mad (1 C. 14:23).

PETER'S SERMON **2:14-40**

Whether or not echoes of the first Letter of Peter (assuming that it was written by the chief Apostle) can be detected in Peter's language here, the sermon that follows as the first proclamation of the Gospel undoubtedly reflects an earlier stage in the development of Christian theology than the thought of the *NT* as a whole. On the internal evidence we are entitled to regard it, not only as a type of the missionary preaching in the first stage of the Church's mission, but also to credit Luke with having a reliable tradition of what was said on this particular occasion which he has summarized and edited. We need not press the point, therefore, that the *OT* quotations appear to be based on the Septuagint rather than on the Hebrew version which Peter would have been most likely to use.

The sermon follows the pattern of the other sermon summaries in the first half of Acts, and corresponds with Paul's references to the substance of the teaching that he received when he became a Christian. It is a pattern of which the Gospels themselves are an expansion and the Letters are an inevitable explication. Peter's sermon reflects the basic conviction of the first Christians that all that had happened in the life, death and Resurrection of Jesus was in fulfilment of God's revelation to Israel in the *OT* Scriptures. The age of the Messiah, foretold by the prophets, had dawned: Jesus of Nazareth had been proved by what had happened to be that long-awaited Messiah; he was now exalted as Head of the New Israel, and had given the gift of the Spirit to his followers. All Jews who were willing to enter the new community by repentance for their sins, above all for the sin of crucifying the

Messiah, would receive forgiveness and be filled with the same
Spirit which had so powerfully and visibly come upon the Apostles
and their associates.

14. Peter, standing with the eleven: if the Pentecostal Spirit
seized hold of the whole company of Christians, this suggests that
the Apostles now grouped themselves together facing the crowd,
with Peter as spokesman.

15. the third hour of the day: i.e. 9 a.m.

16. Joel: the name of the prophet is omitted in the Western
text. This was a more common practice in quoting proof-texts
than to specify the author (e.g. Mt. 1-2).

17. in the last days: Peter quotes Jl 2:28-32, where the prophet, in an apocalyptic passage, speaks of the signs of the messianic
age, including a great outpouring of the Spirit of God together
with various natural portents. Peter regards the Pentecostal
experience of the disciples and the miraculous events in Jesus'
ministry, above all the Resurrection, as generally fulfilling the
promise made by God through his prophet and heralding the
beginning of the 'last days'.

all flesh: the international character of the Diaspora Jews
present pointed inevitably in Luke's mind to a mission to the
Gentiles, though neither Joel nor, at this stage, Peter would have
had anything more than Israel in mind.

prophesy: Peter classifies the recent outbreak of glossolalia as
'prophecy' in the correct *OT* sense, which included anything from
the ravings of ecstatics to the inspired utterances of Isaiah or
Jeremiah. Paul distinguished between 'speaking with tongues' and
'prophecy' (1 C. 12:10), but both were equally gifts of the Spirit.
Luke's 'miracle of languages' is not involved.

19. blood and fire and vapour of smoke: omitted by the
Western text, presumably to make Joel's words more apposite.
Minor changes are likewise made in the personal pronouns of
verses 17 and 18 ('their' for 'your', and omission of 'my' before
'menservants' and 'maidservants'), to widen the scope of the
prophecy and to make it cover literally 'all flesh', not merely Jews.

20. the day of the Lord: the *OT* Day of Yahweh became for
the first Christians the Day of Christ, the Parousia, when the
Lord Jesus would return in triumph and judgment (1 Th. 5:2;
1 C. 1:8; 2 C. 1:14; Phil. 1:10).

21. the Lord: in Joel's prophecy this meant Yahweh (or in the
Greek version *Kurios*, 'the Lord'), with whom Peter by implication

equates Jesus. Commitment to Yahweh, in devotion and worship (i.e. to call on the name of Yahweh) is now crystallized and illuminated by the knowledge that God has revealed himself in Jesus. It is this commitment which brings salvation (cf. verse 40).

22. Jesus of Nazareth: although the Greek word *Nazoraios* is not etymologically related to 'Nazareth', it seems more likely that the first Christians connected Jesus with that town (Mt. 2:23), and were called Nazarenes (*Nazoraioi*) for that reason in Ac. 24:5, rather than that the word comes from *Nazir* ('a Nazirite') or *Neser* ('the Messianic Branch' (Isa. 11:1)) or *Nasorayya*, the name possibly given to followers of John the Baptist, which the disciples originally were, according to Jn 1:35ff.

a man attested . . . by God: Peter builds his case in this first essay at Christian apologetics on facts that are known to many of his audience. The **mighty works** of the prophet from Nazareth in the healing of men's minds and bodies must be seen on any reasonable view, Peter claims, to have been done by God through him.

23. plan and foreknowledge of God: the Crucifixion, which on Good Friday seemed to Peter and the other disciples to be the end of everything, is now seen to have been part of God's purpose. The risen Christ himself had guided their thoughts to begin to see in the *OT* Scriptures—and above all in Isa. 53—that the Cross was not a disaster but an act of God's grace for man's salvation. Although it was left to Paul to develop more fully the significance of the death of Christ, by the time of his conversion it was already the established teaching of the Church that Christ died for our sins in accordance with the Scriptures (1 C. 15:3). We can see here, at this early stage in Peter's words, the ripening of this conviction.

lawless men: nevertheless, the Crucifixion was a crime of which all Israelites were guilty, although God had overruled their evil purpose. The sin was the greater, in that they had handed over Jesus for execution to pagan Romans—men to whom the sacred Law of Israel, embodying its covenant with God, meant nothing.

24. pangs of death is an *OT* expression (Ps. 18:4; 116:3 (LXX)). That God had **raised** Jesus from the dead is the climax of Peter's proclamation of the Gospel. Indeed, he claims that the Resurrection was inevitable, since Satan's power of death could not conceivably have proved to be stronger than the power of life in God's Messiah.

25-32. Peter's sermon is built round three scriptural texts, *OT* promises which he asserts have now come true. Having shown that Joel's prophecy of a great outpouring of the Spirit in the messianic age had visibly been fulfilled before their eyes, he now invites his hearers to see in Ps. 16:8-11 a promise of the Resurrection of Jesus. Neither a felon's death on a cross nor a subsequent resurrection formed any part of common Jewish expectation of what would be the nature of Messiah's appearance, hence the refusal of most Jews to accept Jesus as the Messiah. Jesus, by identifying himself with the Servant whose role of victory through suffering could be read out of Isa. 53, had pointed the way towards a messianic explanation of the Crucifixion. The Resurrection was a more difficult problem, and the first Christians were hard put to it to find scriptural evidence for this totally unexpected event, such as would persuade their sceptical countrymen that this too was part of Jesus' fulfilment of messianic prophecy.

The Psalm Peter quotes here was assumed by all present at the time to be Davidic, and it was common ground that Messiah, when he came, would be of David's line. Peter's argument is that the Psalm, which is a thanksgiving for preservation from death, cannot have referred to David himself, who did in fact die and whose place of burial in Jerusalem was common knowledge, but must have been a prophecy referring to the Son of David, the Messiah. Since on this interpretation the Psalm could be taken to mean that God's Holy One, the Messiah, could not be overcome by death and suffer corruption of the body, and since Jesus had risen and left an empty tomb, therefore he must indeed be the Messiah. It should be noted that here and elsewhere the faith of the Church did not depend on rabbinical arguments of this kind, which would be accepted by the Jews of the time as a valid use of the *OT*, however unsatisfactory we find them today. Speakers and writers merely used the Scriptures to support convictions which they had already arrived at on other grounds. In this case the proclamation of the Resurrection was of a historical event to the truth of which the Apostles testified, and scriptural backing was merely introduced for apologetic reasons.

27. Hades: Hebrew *Sheol*, the abode of the dead.

30. with an oath refers to Ps. 132:11. The promise made there that David's descendants would sit upon his **throne** for ever is here applied by Peter to the Son of David, who has taken his seat upon the heavenly throne appointed for him by God.

32. we all: i.e., the twelve Apostles.

33. exalted: i.e., by his Ascension.

poured out this: the ascended Christ is now able to send down the promised Spirit upon his people as evidenced by their power to 'speak with tongues'. Luke heavily emphasizes external manifestations of the Spirit such as this, but does not neglect its inward effect on Christian character (cf. Barnabas, 11:24). Notice the early conception of the Spirit as 'this (thing)'. The neuter gender is used suggesting the experience of a new power, rather than the later conception of the Third Person of the Trinity.

34–5. Peter now adduces his third *OT* quotation, from Ps. 110:1, as a pointer to the exaltation of Christ. This Royal Psalm presumably originally referred to one of the kings of David's line, perhaps at his enthronement; in the Psalm, **the Lord** is Yahweh, and **my Lord** is the king. It is a promise of divine favour and a victorious reign spoken in the name of Yahweh by the Psalmist. The early Christians had no doubt, however, that it was an inspired word of David referring to the future messianic king which had now been fulfilled by the Ascension of Christ. It was used by Jesus himself to refute narrow Jewish views of the Messiah as being merely a king of David's line (Mk 12:35–7), and frequently by *NT* writers—especially the author of Hebrews—as a proof-text of the Lordship of Jesus, exalted and seated at the right hand of God—i.e. sharing his power and sovereignty—until his triumphal return to establish his Kingdom.

36. Lord and Christ: this is the confession of faith of the primitive Church. Jesus whom the Jews, **the house of Israel**, had in their blindness crucified, had proved by what had happened, backed by the testimony of the Scriptures, to be **Lord,** i.e. worthy of worship and loyalty, and **Christ,** i.e. the long-awaited Messiah. That God has **made** the crucified Jesus Lord and Christ does not mean that God adopted Jesus of Nazareth as his Son and made him Lord and Christ by raising him from the dead and exalting him to his right hand, but that by his Resurrection and Ascension Jesus became what, as Luke has already said in his Gospel (2:11), he was destined to be from his birth. As Christian thought developed it was seen that the Lordship of Christ must also involve the pre-existence of the Son with the Father (Phil. 2:5–11; Heb. 1:2).

38. repent: repentance in this case is specifically for the crime of crucifying the Messiah.

and be baptized: baptism was demanded of Gentile proselytes
to the Jewish faith as one of the marks of their incorporation into
the people of God. Repentance for past sins, and baptism as a
symbol of the cleansing power of God's forgiveness, had been the
theme of John the Baptist's mission. Peter's formula was in line
with both of these, except that he invited all present to be baptized
in the name of Jesus Christ, i.e. to acknowledge Jesus of
Nazareth as Lord and Christ and to be incorporated into the new
community of the Messiah.

the gift of the Holy Spirit: repentance and baptism not only
ensured God's forgiveness but his gift of the new power which
Peter's audience has seen at work in the Pentecostal experience
of the Apostles and their associates. It does seem as if, in the
highly-charged emotional atmosphere of the first stage of the
Church's history, the visible and audible manifestation of the
Spirit in glossolalia was primarily regarded as proof that the
Spirit had been received, but it was no less evidenced by the sense
of unity, deepened devotion and the 'glad and generous hearts'
(verses 44–7) which characterized the first believers. It was the
God-given Spirit that brought the Church to life, furthered its
growth, and linked its members collectively and individually with
their ascended Lord and with one another. In the fluid state of
Christian belief and practice in the apostolic age, the variable
relationship between baptism, the gift of the Holy Spirit and the
laying on of hands is faithfully reflected by Luke in the course of
his narrative in Acts (cf. 8:12–17; 10:44–8; 19:5–6).

39. the promise: i.e. of salvation, referred to in verse 21.
and to your children: i.e. to your descendants.
all that are far off: ultimately, of course, this would include
Gentiles, but at this stage the thought is more of the Jews of the
Diaspora.

40. this crooked generation: cf. Dt. 32:5. Peter's words
reflect the conviction of the early Christians that they formed the
faithful Remnant of Israel (cf. Jl 2:32). His invitation to the
crowd is to join this messianic Remnant and accept Jesus as their
Saviour from the wrath to come (1 Th. 1:10) which will fall upon
the mass of faithless Israel. It is a mark of Luke's skill, as well as
of the reliability of his information, that he contrives so convincingly to assemble in this first recorded public proclamation of the
Gospel so many primitive features of Christian belief at a stage
before the great *NT* writers Paul, John and the author of Hebrews

gave their minds to a deeper investigation of the significance of the person of Christ. No less successful is Luke's portrayal of the change that the coming of the Spirit had wrought upon the chief Apostle, transforming him from the timid denier of his Master on Good Friday to such a bold and fearless protagonist of the faith from Pentecost onwards.

THE LIFE OF THE FIRST CHRISTIAN COMMUNITY 2:41–7

41. three thousand souls: Peter's sermon, following on the Pentecostal visitation of the Spirit, moved large numbers of the crowd to acknowledge Jesus as the long-expected Messiah and to associate themselves with his followers. There is no reason to doubt the fact that **three thousand** responded to Peter's invitation to be baptized. The baptism (in the pool of Bethesda?) need not have taken place on the same day, nor need Peter have been the sole officiant. What is unlikely, however, is that the Christian community in Jerusalem expanded so suddenly from a hundred and twenty (1:15) to over three thousand. Such a large number would have involved massive organizational problems not suggested in verses 44–7. What is more likely is that many overseas Jews who were in Jerusalem for Pentecost returned to their own countries as baptized Christians, thus furthering the anonymous spread of the Gospel which is so frequently attested in Acts. The Jerusalem church would seem to have been in its earliest stage a comparatively small and compact body (cf. note on 6:1).

42–7. Luke's vivid picture of the life of the first Christian community can be dismissed as an idyllic reconstruction of what the Church ought to have been; but there is no reason to doubt that in the beginning this is how it was. In the light of the Resurrection and of Pentecost it would be incredible if the tightly knit group of Nazarenes, believing that the last days were upon them, and that the Lord Jesus would soon return in triumph with everlasting blessing for the faithful, did not reach an unrepeatable standard of communal life, compared with which the subsequent history of an expanding Church is a necessary compromise with the world in which it has to live.

42. Luke pinpoints the four foundations on which the primitive Church was built:

the apostles' teaching: this presumably implies a more detailed version of the contents of the sermon which Peter has just preached. Since the qualification demanded of the successor to Judas

Iscariot was that he should know the facts about the ministry of
Jesus from the beginning, we may conclude that it was the words
and works of Jesus as later incorporated in the Gospels that
formed the burden of the Apostles' message. No doubt there was
also constant exposition of *OT* prophecies which had now been
fulfilled.

fellowship: this characteristic word *koinonia*, incorporated in the
trinitarian benediction as 'the *koinonia* of the Holy Spirit', means,
not only the sense of belonging to the community of the new Israel,
but also the practical expression of this fellowship of the Spirit
through the sharing of personal possessions.

the breaking of bread: all meals had religious significance for
Jews, marked by the saying of a prayer of thanksgiving and the
ceremonial breaking of bread; this would be no less true for the
first Christians. There was, however, the additional significance
in their eating together which derived from Jesus' breaking of the
bread at his last meal with the disciples (cf. also Lk. 24:35); Paul
records the repetition of this with sacramental intent as already
established practice before his conversion (1 C. 11:23ff.). It is
therefore no doubt such eucharistic occasions to which Luke
refers here. The 'breaking of bread' is mentioned later in Acts as
having taken place on the first day of the week, the Lord's Day,
the day of the Resurrection (20:7), but in a closely-knit community such as the little group in Jerusalem it may have been a
daily celebration at the main meal of the day. To begin with, the
eucharistic commemoration seems to have taken place before,
during, or at the end of an ordinary meal—the *agapē*, or 'love-
feast'. Later, possibly as the result of abuses such as at Corinth
(1 C. 11:20ff.), the sacrament was celebrated independently.
Whatever relationship existed between the Eucharist as celebrated
by the early Christians and the common meal of the Qumran
community, there is not enough detailed evidence in Acts to
enable any useful comparison to be made.

the prayers: this covers attendance at the public prayers in the
Temple and synagogues, as well as family worship in their own
homes.

43. fear: awe in face of the visible power of God at work through
the disciples, who now by the Spirit were able to perform the
same kind of **wonders and signs** as Jesus had done, as illustrated
in the following chapter.

44-5. all things in common: it is misleading to describe this

as 'Christian communism', or to equate this practice of the early
Church with that of the Essenes of Qumran, where surrender of all
personal property was obligatory. What is described here and in
4:32–5 was a voluntary sharing of possessions based on the deep
sense of fellowship. Property was regarded, not as private and
inalienable, but as held in trust from God to be donated to the
common pool as and when there was need. Barnabas is specially
mentioned for his generosity in doing so (4:36f.) and Ananias is
condemned, not for refusing to part with his property, but for
practising a deception (5:1ff.).

possessions presumably means landed property, and **goods**
personal belongings.

46–7. Luke summarizes the daily practice of the first Christians
as involving loyalty to the established ordinances of Jewish religious
life by their attendance at the **Temple** and also meeting in each
other's **homes** (i.e. house-churches) on specifically Christian
eucharistic occasions; the picture is one of genuinely happy fellowship, shot through with a deep devotional spirit. It is not surprising, therefore, that the little community found **favour with all
the people,** whatever reservations the Jewish ecclesiastics might
have. Ordinary laymen would regard the Nazarenes as a sect
with peculiar convictions, but would judge them mostly on the
splendid quality of their common life. As a result of this, the young
community grew **day by day**, as more and more Jews accepted
Jesus as the Messiah and were thus **saved** (cf. verses 21, 40).

THE HEALING MINISTRY OF THE CHURCH **3:1–11**

1–11. This incident of the healing of a cripple is not necessarily
the first of the **wonders and signs** (2:43) the Apostles were able
to perform in the power of the Spirit. It is recorded as one example
among many others; but a detailed account is given because of
the attention it aroused, and because of its sequel. A similar cure
is attributed to Paul at Lystra in 14:8–10.

1. John: this is most likely John, the son of Zebedee, who
with Peter and James formed an inner circle within the twelve
Apostles during the Galilean ministry, as at the Transfiguration
(Mk 9:2) and in Gethsemane (Mk 14:33). Luke identifies the
two anonymous disciples of Mk 14:13 who were entrusted with
the arrangements for the Last Supper as Peter and John (Lk. 22:8).
Clearly John was overshadowed by Peter, and after this incident
appears in Acts only once more (8:14). This has led to the sug-

gestion that the John referred to here may have been John Mark.
Luke, however, later identifies John Mark by both names in
12:12, 25.

the ninth hour: about 3 p.m. There were three statutory times
for daily prayer observed by loyal Jews, whether they were able to
be present in the Temple or not (cf. Dan. 6:10; 9:21). This
particular 'hour' was the time of the evening sacrifice.

2. Presumably the crippled beggar was in the habit of being
brought by his friends to lie at the Temple gate and ask for alms
when the greatest number of worshippers would be passing by.

gate . . . called Beautiful: it is not clear which gate is being
referred to. The situation would seem to have been to the E. of the
Temple area, since it was adjacent to Solomon's portico (see on
verse 11). Possibly the gate is best identified with the Nicanor
gate of fine Corinthian bronze which led from the Court of the
Gentiles to the Court of the Women.

3. into the temple: into the Temple proper. Peter and John
would have to pass through the Court of the Gentiles to reach the
Court of the Women, the normal place for Jewish worshippers.
The Temple dominated Jerusalem, hence people went 'up' to it
(verse 1). It consisted of a series of terraced courts ascending in
height to the Tabernacle itself, the Holy of Holies. Surrounding
this, and containing the great altar of burnt offerings, was the
court reserved for the priests. Enclosing this court was the Court
of Israel, normally reserved for male Jews wishing to make sacrifices; Gentiles were forbidden on pain of death to penetrate into
the Jewish courts (cf. 21:28).

6. I have no silver and gold: this is probably not so much
intended to imply that Peter had not even a coin for a beggar as
that he wished to stress the greater worth of God's gift of healing.
in the name of: by the power and authority of the Messiah.

7. feet and ankles were made strong: older commentators
tended to find in such phrases evidence of Luke's medical background.

8. walking and leaping: in the picture of the cripple leaping
for joy at his complete cure there is doubtless an allusion to Isaiah's
prophecy of the messianic age when the lame man would leap
like a hart (Isa. 35:6).

11. the portico called Solomon's: it is assumed that the
healed man accompanied the Apostles into the Court of the
Women, joined in the prayers as his special thanksgiving and still

clutched at them as they emerged and made their way to the colonnade on the east side of the Court of the Gentiles, known as Solomon's Portico, which seems to have been the place where the Apostles and their followers congregated (cf. 5:12). Here on this occasion Peter addressed the crowd which was attracted by the spectacular success of the cure.

PETER'S CHALLENGE TO ISRAEL 3:12-26

This second speech by Peter is, like his first speech in chapter 2, of the highest importance for our understanding of how the faith was presented to the Jews in the earliest stage of the Church. In his former address Peter had testified to the power and presence of the Spirit of God at work in a new way in the lives of men through Jesus. Now he proclaims the power and authority of the name of Jesus by which his disciples are enabled to continue his ministry on earth. In both speeches there is a call for repentance for the crime of crucifying the Messiah, but here Peter stresses the role of Jesus as the Suffering Servant of God and as the new Moses who must be obeyed. The chosen people with whom God has covenanted are challenged to acknowledge Jesus as the fulfilment of ancient prophecy and promises, and are given this chance to return to God before Messiah comes again to bring God's purposes to fruition.

12. our own power or piety: Peter will not allow that in this dramatic act of healing the Apostles have been anything more than channels of the power of Christ. It has certainly not been dependent on any claim on their part to personal saintliness.

13. God . . . of our fathers: the solemnity of the ancient title given to God (Exod. 3:6) is designed to emphasize to the full the crime of which the Jews have been guilty.

glorified his servant Jesus: the Greek word *pais* can mean either 'child' (see *RSV mg.*) or 'servant'. Jesus himself by his whole ministry had identified himself with the Servant of Yahweh, who in the thought of Second Isaiah would bring the world to the knowledge of God through giving himself for others. Whether Isaiah had in mind Israel itself, or the faithful minority within it, or a messianic figure yet to come, is less important than that Jesus from his baptism onward adopted this role for himself (cf. Mk 10:45). For the first Christians no *OT* passage was more significant than Isa. 52:13–53:12 (cf. Ac. 8:32). In its words they saw not only the meaning of the Crucifixion as being within the plan of God, but also found there the foundation for a doctrine of Atonement through the death of Christ and a promise of Christ's vindication beyond the Cross. God had **glorified** Jesus—had shown the divine nature of his Servant—by raising him from the dead, and had further confirmed it now by this sign which all had seen of the power of the exalted Messiah.

Pilate: as in Luke's Gospel, Pilate's readiness to acquit the prisoner is stressed, and the blame for the Crucifixion is laid heavily upon the Jews (cf. Lk. 23:22-4).

14. Holy and Righteous One is an early messianic title for Jesus which occurs again in 7:52; 22:14. It no doubt derived from such *OT* texts as Isa. 53:11.

murderer: Barabbas.

15. Author of life: again an early messianic title for Jesus (cf. Heb. 2:10; 12:2 = 'pioneer'), here with the sense that Jesus is the giver of the new life that overcomes death.

16. An involved sentence for which many ingenious solutions have been offered. Its meaning is, however, quite clear: Peter implies now that the cripple had been cured through his faith in the power of Jesus, although this was not explicit in the narrative. Such faith comes itself from Jesus, through his Spirit.

17. in ignorance: the second part of Peter's address is properly more conciliatory than the first. He has declared God's judgment on the collective sin of his countrymen in crucifying Christ. Now, in the spirit of the Christ himself (Lk. 23:34), he stresses God's mercy and holds out the possibility of his forgiveness. What the Jews, both leaders and people, have done to their Messiah they have done through lack of a true understanding of the Scriptures.

18. God foretold . . . that his Christ should suffer: this was precisely what the vast majority of Jews would not admit. Jesus of Nazareth had died a felon's death; as such he was under the curse of the Law (Dt. 21:23; cf. Gal. 3:13), and could not therefore have been the Messiah. Peter is claiming that, on the contrary, the total witness of the Scriptures, **all the prophets,** rightly interpreted, focused on Isaiah's Suffering Servant of Yahweh as the key to the understanding of all that was said elsewhere about the Lord's Anointed.

19. Repent: as in 2:38, repentance, acknowledgment of guilt and change of heart, is what God demands of Israel. His forgiveness is assured.

times of refreshing: it was the teaching of the rabbis that if

Israel as a nation repented, even for a single day, Messiah would
come; it was the teaching of the Church that God had not waited
for national repentance before sending Messiah. The blessings of
the messianic age had already begun to be experienced on earth
with the coming of Jesus. Peter claims that the *full* realization of
these blessings, ('times of refreshing') would be granted by God
if and when Israel turned to him in penitence and, above all,
recognized her monstrous sin in crucifying Christ.

20–1. that he may send the Christ: the first Christians were
faced with the problem that, on the one hand, they believed that
Jesus was the long-promised Messiah; but, on the other hand, the
promised blessings of the messianic age, including the overthrow-
ing of the powers of darkness and the disappearance of evil in all its
manifestations, had not materialized. Jesus himself had spoken of
his vindication beyond the Cross, and of the ultimate triumph of
God's cause; it was natural that this conviction should be expressed both by Jesus and his first disciples in terms which derived
from the *OT* Scriptures, and that the thought of the early Church
should be couched in similar pictorial language. Thus Jesus,
exalted and seated at the right hand of God, would return in
accordance with God's purpose to establish the messianic kingdom
on earth to which the prophets bore witness. It was inevitable in
the light of the Resurrection and Pentecost that the first Christians
should think that this event was close at hand. Peter's words here
reflect this view.

22–3. God will raise up for you a prophet: this quotation
combines Dt. 18:15 with Lev. 23:29. It may have appeared in
this conflated form in a collection of 'testimonies', or *OT* proof-
texts, used by Christian missionaries. The thought that Jesus was
the promised 'prophet like Moses' was common in the early
Church (cf. 7:37). The Jews did not identify the expected new
Moses precisely with the Messiah (cf. Jn 1:20–1; 7:40–1), but
there was a definite association of this new lawgiver with the
messianic age. Peter uses the *OT* words as a warning that only
those who heed the message of Jesus can be regarded as members
of the people of God.

24. Samuel: regarded as the first of the prophets as in 13:20.
these days: the messianic age.

25. sons of the prophets: Peter in his final appeal reminds his
Jewish hearers of their great heritage. They are of the same stock
as the great spokesmen of God, and it was with their forefather

Abraham that God had made his Covenant, appointing Israel to
be the means of blessing to the whole world (Gen. 12:3; 22:18).

   26. to you first: it was fitting, therefore, that God's blessing,
salvation and new life should be offered first of all to his ancient
people through his Servant, Jesus the Messiah, the **posterity** of
Abraham (cf. Gal. 3:16).

raised up in this verse means 'sent'—i.e., to deliver Israel, in line
with verse 22.

THE APOSTLES ARE ARRESTED, EXAMINED AND RELEASED 4:1-22

Luke now describes the beginning of opposition. It comes first
from the Sadducees, the aristocratic priestly party to which most
of the ruling class in Jerusalem belonged. The Apostles are
arrested, ostensibly on a charge of a breach of the peace in the
precincts of the Temple. It would seem, however, that the real
cause for concern on the part of the authorities was the rapid
growth of a movement which they believed they had stifled by
the execution of its leader; any messianic propaganda was viewed
by the Sadducees with suspicion as a threat to law and order and
to their good relations with the Roman government. At this stage,
however, it was felt that no action could be taken, and the Apostles
were dismissed with a caution. Popular support was behind them
as a consequence of the notable cure which they had effected in
the case of the well-known crippled beggar, and no doubt also
as a result of other similar instances of their healing power.
Further, in the eyes of the Pharisees, the larger and more acceptable lay party in the Jewish community, the Nazarenes were still
regarded as zealous, if eccentric, upholders of the Law, punctilious
in the performance of their religious obligations.

   1. as they were speaking: this suggests that John had also
addressed the crowd.

the priests: these would be the particular priests on duty in the
Temple at the time who, no doubt, took exception to this mass
meeting in the precincts.

the captain of the temple: perhaps the *Sagan*, the superintend-
ent of the Temple police, responsible for maintaining order, and
ranking next to the High Priest himself; or possibly one of his
subordinates in charge of the Temple guard.

the Sadducees: together with the above were some members of
the Sadducean party. Deriving their name possibly from Zadok,
the High Priest in Solomon's day (1 Kg. 2:35), the Sadducees

were the religious party in the Jewish state to which most of the
high priestly families belonged, and from which a succession of
High Priests came. Unlike the Pharisees, the other religious party
which features in the Gospels and Acts (see on 5:34), they were
regarded as being more concerned to retain their privileged position in the community, involving collaboration with their Roman
overlords, than to defend distinctive Jewish traditions and to
share popular patriotic and nationalist aspirations. They were,
however, conservative in their theology, regarding as modernist
deviations from the historic faith of Israel such comparatively
recent doctrines as a general resurrection of the dead in the last
days, and belief in angels and demons, together with the corpus
of oral interpretation of the Law which the Pharisees had developed and insisted on as obligatory for all pious Jews (see on
23:8).

2. annoyed: the grounds for intervention are given as resentment against unauthorized preaching by unprofessional preachers
taking place within the Temple area, and, in particular, objection
to any teaching about the Resurrection of Jesus since this would
support the doctrine of a general resurrection to which the
Sadducees took exception.

4. five thousand: Luke makes no attempt in the early part of
Acts to give an accurate chronology of events. Presumably he did
not have the materials for doing so. We cannot tell, therefore,
what length of time has elapsed since Pentecost; it may have been
weeks, or even months. The community of the Nazarenes has at all
events grown rapidly, and there is no reason to doubt Luke's
figure as a correct approximation of numbers at the point at which
the Christians began to become a problem to the authorities and
when they began to experience the persecution which Jesus had
foretold (Lk. 12:8-12; 21:12-19). The total population of
Jerusalem about this time has been variously estimated; it may
have been as much as a quarter of a million.

5. on the morrow: when the court could legally be convened.
rulers and elders and scribes: this implies a formal meeting of
the Sanhedrin, the supreme Jewish court in all ecclesiastical
matters and in all civil affairs, subject only to the ultimate
jurisdiction of the Roman procurator—who was at this time, of
course, still Pontius Pilate (A.D. 26-36); it consisted of seventy
members, under the presidency of the High Priest. Luke lists the
three classes from which these members were drawn: **rulers:** the

holders of political office, largely belonging to the few high-
priestly families, and elsewhere called 'chief priests' (e.g., 4:23);
elders: men of high social standing in the community; and
scribes: leading rabbis or teachers of the Law, usually Pharisees.

6. Annas the high priest: Annas had been High Priest in
A.D. 6–15, and therefore was technically no longer in office. He
was, however, the High Priest *par excellence* of his time, since five
of his sons occupied the same office and the reigning High Priest
at that moment was his son-in-law Caiaphas. Throughout the
period of the Gospels and Acts Annas was the power behind the
throne.

Caiaphas: Joseph Caiaphas, High Priest in A.D. 18–36, had, like
Pontius Pilate, played a leading role in the trial and execution of
Jesus.

John: this may be Jonathan, son of Annas, who succeeded
Caiaphas in office in A.D. 36.

Alexander: unknown otherwise, but presumably another member
of the high-priestly caste.

7. in the midst: the Sanhedrin sat in a semicircle. Thus the
prisoners and the witness, in this case the healed cripple, faced
the court from the centre.

by what power: the question at issue is basically the same as that
put to Jesus in the Temple by the Sadducees during Holy Week:
'Tell us by what authority you do these things, or who is it that
gave you this authority?' (Lk. 20:1–2). In the case of Jesus, the
enquiry referred to his 'cleansing of the Temple'; here it is the
apostolic healing of the lame man.

8. Peter, filled with the Holy Spirit: in Acts Luke distinguishes between the permanent indwelling of the Holy Spirit,
which gave men like Stephen and Barnabas their outstanding
qualities of Christian discipleship (6:5; 11:24), and such special
accessions of inspiration as in the case of Peter here, where a simple
fisherman is transformed into a confident and fearless spokesman
for Christ. This was a fulfilment of the promise made by Jesus
himself (Lk. 12:11–12).

11. This is the stone which was rejected: in his reply to the
enquiry of the court, Peter has followed the same line of argument
as in his address to the crowd (3:12–16). Now he adds a further
piece of apologetic, applying Ps. 118:22, which Jesus had quoted
with reference to himself (Lk. 20:17), to the rejection of the
Messiah by the official **builders** of Israel, which regarded itself

as the 'house of God' (cf. Heb. 3:2). The crucified Jesus, the 'stone' rejected by the Sanhedrin, had been vindicated by the Resurrection, and made the **head of the corner,** the keystone which crowns the house (of Israel) and holds its walls together. This would seem to have been a favourite proof-text in the early Church (cf. 1 Pet. 2:7).

12. salvation: Peter uses the word in its fullest sense—deliverance, forgiveness, wholeness and health of body, mind and spirit through Christ alone.

13. boldness: a word used by Luke three times in this chapter to describe the powerful, uninhibited proclamation of the Gospel by the Apostles inspired by the Holy Spirit (cf. verses 29, 31).

uneducated common men: ordinary working men untrained in theology or public speaking.

they recognized that they had been with Jesus: the council presumably already knew that the Apostles were Nazarenes (verse 2). Luke suggests rather that they remembered that Jesus too had been an 'uneducated common man' (cf. Jn 7:15), who had nevertheless impressed the crowds with the 'authority' of his teaching and had been credited with similar cures. These men claimed to have done what they had done in his name; had Jesus therefore been wrongfully condemned? Some members of the Sanhedrin may have felt so (cf. 5:28).

15. commanded them to go aside: Luke does not profess to give a verbatim account of the proceedings. It is therefore not necessary to enquire how the private deliberations of the Sanhedrin became known to the Apostles; the discussion can be inferred from the verdict in verse 18. It is likely, however, that sympathizers such as Nicodemus and Joseph of Arimathea, or simply acquaintances of some of the Christians, may have reported the substance of the discussion both here and in 5:21ff. May Paul, even, have been the informant?

18. charged them not to speak or teach: there was little more that the council could do than to dismiss the Apostles with a ban on any further public speaking; they had committed no crime, and popular opinion was strongly in their favour (verses 21–2). The Apostles' brave rejoinder (verses 19–20) points forward to the occasion of their second arrest shortly afterwards (5:17ff.), when they received harsher treatment.

THE PRAYERS OF THE CHURCH ARE ANSWERED **4:23-31**

The account of the proceedings before the Sanhedrin given by the
Apostles to the inner circle of believers is followed by a solemn act
of supplication. They see in this beginning of persecution the continued fulfilment of Scripture which had been evident in the
Passion of Jesus. In the face of the new threat to the furtherance
of the Gospel, they pray for strength and courage that they might
proclaim the faith undaunted, and for their healing ministry
through the power of Christ to be maintained unabated. They
experience a visitation of the Spirit of Pentecostal intensity in
response to their prayers, confirming that the blessing of God is
upon them and upon their work.

23. their friends: this suggests that Peter and John after their
release returned to 'headquarters', perhaps the upper room of
1:13, where the other Apostles and their associates no doubt had
meanwhile been engaged in intercessory prayer for them.

24. Sovereign Lord: the prayer which begins with these words
and ends at verse 30 is, with its strong *OT* flavour, reminiscent
of the prayers in Lk. 1–2, and probably echoes early Christian
liturgical forms. Its theme reflects the prayer of Hezekiah (2 Kg.
19:15–19; Isa. 37:15–20) transposed into a *NT* setting. The
words in verse 25 prefacing the quotation from the Psalm are confused in the Greek text. In such cases, as in 3:16, it may be the
result of textual corruption or a misunderstanding of original
Aramaic, or it may even be that alternative phrases were left side
by side in Luke's first draft. The *RSV* doubtless gives the correct
sense.

25. Why did the Gentiles rage: quoted from Ps. 2:1–2. No
plainer evidence of the Scriptures being fulfilled in their experience
could have been given to the first Christians than the events of
Holy Week in the light of this text. The whole Psalm possibly
originally referred to the accession of a Davidic king—'the Lord's
Anointed'—and the revolt of his vassals; but it clearly lent itself
to a messianic interpretation, and was so interpreted by Jews in
pre-Christian times as well as by the Christians themselves (cf.
13:33; Heb. 1:5; 5:5).

27. Jesus whom thou didst anoint: as Messiah at his
baptism (cf. 10:38).
Herod ... peoples of Israel are regarded as the Gentiles,
peoples, kings and rulers referred to in the Psalm. 'Gentiles' in this

case are the Romans and 'peoples of Israel' are presumably the tribes of Israel; for Herod (Antipas) and Pilate, see Lk. 23. It is noticeable that Luke faithfully records this condemnation of the Roman authorities, although his own tendency was to show the Romans as being at least impartial, if not sympathetic, to Jesus and his followers contrasted with the attitude of the Jews.

28. predestined: as in 2:23; 3:18, the Passion of the Messiah, God's **holy Servant Jesus** (verses 27 and 30) is now seen as the fulfilment of prophecy and within God's **plan** of salvation.

29. servants: the Greek *douloi* means 'slaves', as distinct from *pais*, used for **servant** as applied to Jesus. David is also called **servant** (*pais*) in this prayer, in the same sense as Abraham (Gen. 26:24) and Moses (Exod. 14:31) were servants of God. The use of 'slave' corresponds to the majesty of 'sovereign Lord' in verse 24.

30. thy hand to heal: it was of course the Apostles' hands that were stretched out to heal, but, as in 3:12, they attributed their power solely to God working through them as they restored men to wholeness in the **name** of Jesus.

31. shaken: not literally by an earthquake, but as a symbol of the presence of God, as in Exod. 19:18; Isa. 6:4. 'Wind' and 'fire' conveyed the power of the divine gift of the Spirit at Pentecost. Similarly here the third symbol of the manifestation of God to Elijah on Horeb (1 Kg. 19:11–12), an earthquake, is used to characterize this renewal of the Pentecostal experience. As a result the Apostles were emboldened to continue to proclaim the faith despite the threats of the Sanhedrin.

This 'second Pentecost', followed by a description of the sharing of possessions within the community and an account of further healings, with their sequel in a second arrest, examination and release of the Apostles, has led to the view taken by some scholars that 2:1–4:22 and 4:31–5:40 are two accounts of the same events deriving from two different sources. There is, indeed, a striking parallelism in these sections of Luke's narrative, but there are equally striking differences and there is an undoubted development in the situation of the Church. It is much more likely that the pattern of events to some extent repeated itself, and that Luke consciously reproduced this in his record.

SAINTS AND SINNERS 4:32–5:16

Luke paints a picture once more (cf. 2:44–5) of the practical expression of the deep sense of fellowship in this first stage of the

Church's history, as a prelude to contrasting the example set by
a man like Barnabas, who emerges consistently from the narrative
as a Christian worthy of his calling, and that of an unsavoury
couple, Ananias and Sapphira, who prove that from the beginning
the Church has suffered from bad characters who are Christians
only in name. The healing ministry of the Apostles continues to
evoke popular support not unmixed with superstitition.

32. the company of those who believed: the Church.
everything in common: as in 2:44, this refers to the attitude
of the first Christians towards personal property based on their
sense of belonging to a closely-knit community, rather than a
literal community of ownership.

33. testimony to the resurrection: the qualifying words
with great power indicate that this was not so much the
historical evidence for the Resurrection as the proclamation of
its signficance.
great grace was upon them all: not only the Apostles, but
the whole community. Nothing but the spirit of God, Luke
implies, could have enabled the Apostles to give such testimony,
or the other believers to show such generosity.

34. not a needy person among them: there must have been
many who needed no help, but those who did could rely on the
richer members.

35. laid it at the Apostles' feet: this seems to be an advance
on the practice described in 2:45, where charity appears to have
been unorganized. Now the Apostles are in charge of the distribution of the money.

36. Barnabas: the derivation of his name is much disputed:
'son of a prophet', 'son of Nebo', 'son of refreshment'. Luke's
interpretation of it has also been variously translated as 'son of
exhortation', 'son of consolation', but the *RSV* 'son of encouragement'—i.e. a man whose nature is to encourage others—is a good
description of Barnabas' character as depicted here and later in
Acts (11:23ff.). He was an overseas Jew from Cyprus, where there
was a large Jewish colony, and a Levite (i.e. of the tribe of Levi).
As such he was entitled to perform minor duties in the Temple,
Levites ranking lower than priests—who, although they themselves were also Levites, claimed particular descent from Aaron,
a grandson of Levi. Barnabas was also a cousin of John Mark (Col.
4:10), whose mother Mary owned the house which appears to
have been the principal meeting place of the Christians in

Jerusalem (12:12) and was probably the house where the Last Supper was held (cf. on 1:13).

37. sold a field: technically Levites were supposed to hold no property (Num. 18:24), but the rule was no longer rigidly adhered to, and would not have applied to those living overseas. If Barnabas' field was in the rich fruit-growing lands of Cyprus, it would no doubt be of considerably more value than a few acres in Judaea. The fact that his action is held up for special commendation indicates that the 'common ownership' of verse 32 is not to be taken literally. Mary, the mother of John Mark, retained her house as her own, but put it at the disposal of the community.

at the apostles' feet indicates, as in verse 35, transfer of ownership, and is reminiscent of such *OT* passages as Ps. 8:6; 60:8; Ru. 4:7.

5:1. Ananias ... Sapphira: this moral tale of the judgment that fell upon a deceitful couple who wrongly claimed credit for the same kind of generosity as Barnabas had shown presumably came to Luke's knowledge in this form. It is a mark of his honesty as a Christian historian that he does not gloss over or omit the fact that there were black sheep in the fold, even in what he clearly regards as the Church's golden age. It is possible that the story records what actually happened, although it attributes to Peter at least a considerable degree of callousness if it does not actually cast him in the role of the Lord's avenging angel. Perhaps, however, the story has grown in the telling, and the sudden deaths of two members of the young community who were afterwards found to have committed a fraud gave rise to this dramatic version as a warning to all that God is not to be trifled with.

2. kept back some of the proceeds: the sin of which Ananias was guilty was hypocrisy, a sin which received from Jesus the most scathing condemnation. Ananias was under no obligation to sell his land at all, or to hand over the proceeds, but having done both he alleged that all the money he had obtained was now being given magnanimously for the relief of the poorer members of the community, whereas in fact he had slyly retained part of it for his own use. His wife was a party to the fraud.

3. Satan: as elsewhere in the *NT* Satan is the personification of evil who constantly seeks to lure men into his service, corrupting their natures and encouraging them to break God's laws.

to lie to the Holy Spirit is the same as to 'lie to God' in verse 4—

i.e. to cheat. Ananias had not only offended against the community, but against God, from whose Spirit it derived its unique
character, in posing as an exemplary benefactor.

4. did it not remain your own? This emphasizes the completely voluntary nature of the sharing of possessions.

5. fell down and died: Ananias' sudden death, presumably
from shock, is regarded as a direct judgment from God (cf. 1 C.
11:30), which creates the same sense of awe (**fear**) as in 2:43 and
verse 11.

6. the young men: lit. 'the younger men', not a distinct group
as opposed to 'elders', but the more able-bodied among those
present. The setting of the story seems to be a lengthy church
meeting.

9. to tempt: or, 'to test', in the hope that the Lord would not
notice or would take no action.

will carry you out: Peter does not bring about Sapphira's
death, but predicts it as an inevitable punishment.

10. she fell . . . and died: the sin of Ananias and Sapphira
with its sequel is reminiscent of the story of Achan (Jos. 7), who
also retained part of property which had been consecrated to God
and had to pay for it with his life.

11. church: this is the first explicit reference in Acts to the
Christian believers as the *ekklesia*. The word is used in the *OT* for
the congregation or assembly of Israel as the people of God (e.g.
Dt. 9:10; Jos. 8:35), and its adoption by the early Christians
indicates their sense of continuity as the new Israel, now the true
people of God, since they acknowledged Jesus, Israel's long awaited
Messiah, as Lord.

12. signs and wonders: the healing ministry of 2:43 continues in answer to the prayer of 4:30.
Solomon's Portico: see on 2:1; 3:11. This would seem to have
been the regular place for the public preaching and teaching of
the Gospel by the Apostles.

13. none of the rest dared join them: this may mean that
'none of the rest', i.e. their opponents, ventured to 'join' (in disputation with) the Apostles; but it is an odd sentence, and there
may be a textual error. 'Rulers' or 'elders' has been suggested as
an alternative to 'rest', i.e. as opposed to the mass of the people
who were well disposed to the new movement.

15–16. Peter . . . shadow: this picture of a massive throng of
sufferers, sick in mind or body, being brought for healing to the

Apostles reflects similar scenes in the ministry of Jesus (e.g. Mk
1:32-4; 6:55-6). The intensity of the faith of their friends is
expressed in the belief that even the shadow of Peter falling upon
them would make them whole. It is not said here that it did so,
although later (19:12) contact with Paul's handkerchiefs and
aprons is claimed to have been efficacious in bringing about
cures. The primacy of Peter is stressed by the use of the same word
as in Lk. 1:35, 9:34 of the 'shadow' of the divine presence of which
Peter is here the channel.

THE APOSTLES ARE AGAIN BROUGHT BEFORE THE SANHEDRIN
5:17-42

The defiance of the Sanhedrin's ban on public preaching, combined with the increasing success of the mission, led to the arrest
of the Apostles for the second time. Released from prison by what
would appear to be the intervention of a sympathetic warder,
they were again apprehended while propagating the Gospel in the
Temple. On being questioned once more before the Sanhedrin,
the Apostles were again uncompromising in their determination to
continue the mission, come what may. They were saved from
death on this occasion by the mediation of Gamaliel, a highly
respected and influential member of the council, whose advice
was to leave the Nazarenes alone; their movement, he said, would
either collapse like other messianic incidents in the past; or, if it
were indeed divinely inspired, the Sanhedrin could do nothing to
stop it. On this occasion the Apostles escaped with a beating. The
relatively mild sentence undoubtedly stemmed from the high
degree of popular support for the mission, and the fact that
Pharisees like Gamaliel were impressed by the loyalty of the
Nazarenes to Jewish tradition and by their zealous observance of
their religious obligations.

17. high priest . . . Sadducees: Luke indicates that the
initiative in the opposition to the mission is still in the hands of the
Sadducees, for the same reasons as were given in 4:2, added to the
fact that they dominated the Sanhedrin whose edict (4:18) the
Apostles had disregarded.

jealousy: because of the success of the mission.

18. arrested the apostles: this time all the Apostles are
arrested, or at all events more than Peter and John (cf. verse 29).
Possibly they were apprehended while teaching in Solomon's
Portico.

common prison: as in 4:3, the Apostles are merely kept in custody overnight until the Sanhedrin could meet on the following day. It is not a prison in our sense, but more likely a guard-room in the Temple precincts.

19. an angel of the Lord: in Acts divine prompting or providential intervention is described in this way (8:26; 12:7, 23). Here the Apostles may have been released by a secret sympathizer among the guardroom staff, who, in retrospect, was no doubt regarded as an 'angel in disguise', as in similar circumstances later (12:7).

20. this Life: as in Jn 11:25, Jesus brings new life or salvation (13:26) through the Resurrection (cf. 3:15). The first Christians may have called the Gospel the 'Life' as well as the 'Way' (9:2, etc.), in accordance with the words of Jesus himself (Jn 14:6).

21. at daybreak: while the Apostles are preaching in their accustomed place in the Temple, the Sanhedrin is summoned to examine them in the senate-house, which, according to Josephus, adjoined the west wall of the Temple.

council and all the senate: the terms are identical; there was only one body involved, 'and' here having the sense of 'even'.

22. officers: of the Temple police.

24. the captain of the temple: see note on 4:1. In this case it was probably the *Sagan* himself.

wondering what this would come to: since they could not trust even the prison guards.

26. without violence: this brings out clearly the popular antipathy towards the Sadducean authorities, and the goodwill of the people towards the Nazarenes.

28. bring this man's blood upon us: this may be simply the High Priest's fear of an insurrection to avenge the Crucifixion. It seems also, however, to imply a guilty conscience on the part of the authorities responsible for the execution of Jesus (cf. Mt. 27:25). Notice the characteristic reluctance to speak of Jesus by name (cf. 4:17).

29. we must obey God rather than men: cf. 4:19. Socrates had said to his judges: 'I must obey God rather than you' (Plato, *Apology*, 29d).

30. raised: probably, as in 3:26, meaning 'sent'.

hanging him on a tree: thus making him accursed according to the Law (Dt. 21:22-3); cf. Gal. 3:13.

31. God exalted him: Peter repeats the theme of God's reversal of man's judgment.

Leader: the same word (*archēgos*) as is translated 'author' in 3:15 but used here rather as in Heb. 2:10; 12:2 ('pioneer'). Jesus, like Moses or Joshua, leads his people into their promised land. He is thus also their **Saviour**, liberator or deliverer.

repentance and forgiveness are both regarded as gifts from God through the exalted Christ.

32. and so is the Holy Spirit: it is no mere human testimony that guarantees the truth of the apostolic message, but the powerful evidence of the presence of the Spirit in the life and work of the believers. In this summarized version of Peter's fourth speech so far in Acts, the main theme as before is that Jesus has come as Messiah to God's ancient people. Crucified by Israel's rulers, he has been vindicated by the Resurrection and exalted as Lord. Israel has still a chance to acknowledge her crime and to fulfil her mission as the people of God.

33. they were enraged: particularly by the apostolic claim that the very activities which the Sanhedrin sought to suppress were in fact the work of God's Holy Spirit.

34. a Pharisee in the council: the Pharisees were the successors of the Hasidim, who combined loyalty to Jewish religious tradition with patriotic fervour in support of the Maccabean revolt against the attack on Jewish institutions by Antiochus IV in the second century B.C. Their name probably means 'the separated ones', and may originally have been a nickname bestowed on them since, once the battle for religious freedom was won, they dissociated themselves from the political and priestly ambitions of the Maccabean dynasty. The reputation they had won as devout and patriotic scholars persisted into *NT* times when, although secular power under the Roman procurators was mainly in the hands of the time-serving Sadducees, the Pharisees wielded far more influence over the people. The hold of the Law over the Jewish community, as exemplified in the dominating role of the synagogues, and the regimentation of daily life, gave the Pharisees (who included in their party most of the scribes—i.e. students and teachers of the Law) a powerful voice, even in the Sanhedrin, where they were greatly outnumbered by the Sadducees.

Gamaliel: the most distinguished rabbi of his day and leader of the Pharisaic group in the Sanhedrin. He was a grandson of Hillel,

founder of the liberal school in the Pharisaic party, as opposed to
the more rigid school of Shammai; his moderate attitude here
would therefore be in character. He had been the teacher of Paul
(22:3) during his rabbinical training, and Paul may have heard of
this private part of the proceedings of the Sanhedrin from Gamaliel
himself (see on 4:15).

35. take care what you do with these men: apart from his
liberal leanings, which would encourage his tolerance of the
Nazarenes as law-abiding and faithful Jews, Gamaliel would be
naturally more sympathetic than were the Sadducees to preachers
of the Resurrection. The Pharisees believed in a future general
resurrection of the dead, a doctrine which the Sadducees did not
accept, since it had no ancient scriptural foundation. Gamaliel's
concluding words (verses 38–9) affirming God's sovereignty over
all human affairs, and the peril of thwarting what might be his
purpose, embody a characteristically Pharisaic viewpoint.

36. before these days Theudas arose: Gamaliel is addressing
the Sanhedrin in all probability within a year of the Crucifixion,
for which a likely date is A.D. 29. He speaks of a movement led by
one Theudas as having caused a stir some time previously. Yet
Josephus (*Antiquities* xx. v. 1), writing towards the end of the first
century, specifically mentions an act of sedition by a certain
Theudas as having taken place during the procuratorship of Fadus
(*c.* A.D. 44–6) i.e., almost fifteen years later than the date of this
meeting of the Sanhedrin. Moreover, Gamaliel goes on to speak
of a rising under one Judas the Galilean as having taken place
after the Theudas affair; yet Josephus confirms Judas' revolt as
having been associated with a census, to which Gamaliel refers,
but identifies the census as that which was carried out by Quirinius in A.D. 6. It would seem, therefore, that if Josephus is to be
trusted Luke must have been misinformed. Josephus is far from
being an infallible historian, but he is unlikely to have confused
the order of two events which happened within his own country
in his own century.

It has been suggested that Luke had read Josephus too hastily,
and had mixed up the order of events, since Josephus goes on to
recount the deaths of the sons of Judas after his account of the
revolt of Theudas. This would however imply that the date of Acts
is later than that of the *Antiquities* (*c.* A.D. 93), which on other
grounds is most improbable. In view of Luke's obvious concern to
get his facts right elsewhere in Acts, it would seem most likely that

the uprising referred to by Gamaliel is not the same as that recounted by Josephus. Indeed apart from the fact that the leader of the revolt in both cases was called Theudas, and that he was put to death, there is no clear correspondence between the two accounts. Josephus himself mentions that, after the death of Herod the Great in 4 B.C., there were 'ten thousand other disorders in Judaea, which were like tumults' (*Ant.* XVII. x. 4), and proceeds to describe the seditious activities at that time of a certain Judas, the son of Hezekiah. If this is not the Theudas referred to by Gamaliel, the names Judas and Theudas being easily confused, Gamaliel's allusion may be to the leader of one or other of Josephus' 'ten thousand' disorders.

giving himself out to be somebody: not necessarily claiming to be the Messiah, but simply to be a man of some importance.

37. Judas the Galilean: he was named by Josephus also as Judas of Gamala, and led an unsuccessful religious rising in A.D. 6 in protest against the Roman census, which was made for purposes of taxation, on the grounds that Israel had no king but Yahweh, and to him alone should true Israelites pay tribute (*Ant.* XVIII. i. 1, XX. v. 2; *Wars of the Jews* II. viii. 1). Although, as Gamaliel says, the revolt was ineffectual, it led eventually to the rise of the party of the Zealots who persisted in opposition to the Romans and were the spearhead of Jewish resistance in the war of A.D. 66, which culminated in the destruction of Jerusalem in A.D. 70. No doubt in A.D. 30 this seemed to Gamaliel an unlikely development, since he regards the whole enterprise of Judas as having been a failure. One of the Zealots, Simon, had become a disciple of Jesus and was now an Apostle (1:13).

census: taken by Quirinius, legate of Syria, on the deposition of Archelaus in A.D. 6, when Judaea was made part of the Roman province of Syria. This is not the census referred to in Lk. 2:1-2: that took place in the reign of Archelaus' father, Herod the Great, who died in 4 B.C.

38. if this plan . . . is of men, it will fail: Gamaliel treats the activities of the Nazarenes as on a par with previous disturbances of a messianic character which alarmed the authorities of the time. He assumes that this too is a 'nine days' wonder', and will come to nothing, but leaves the door open for the possibility that it may be a genuinely religious movement which has the blessing of God. In this case there is nothing that the Sanhedrin can do, or dare do, to stop it.

40. they took his advice: the Sadducean majority acquiesced, no doubt reluctantly and for prudential reasons.

beat them: in addition to repeating the ban on public preaching, the Sanhedrin ordered the Apostles to receive the customary Jewish penalty of 'forty lashes less one' (Dt. 25:3; cf. Ac. 22:19; 2 C. 11:24) for disobeying their previous injunction and then dismissed them.

41. rejoicing: because their situation was as Jesus had predicted (Lk. 6:22-3), and because they gloried in sharing his shame (cf. 16:25).

42. in the temple and at home: in public proclamation and at believers' meetings in the house-churches the theme was the same: Messiah has come in the person of Jesus of Nazareth.

THE APPOINTMENT OF THE SEVEN **6:1-7**

So far Luke's narrative, skilfully woven out of such information as he had been able to obtain, and compressed in a masterly way into a few short pages, has depicted the rapid growth of the Church in Jerusalem from a handful of members to several thousands, based on the teaching and healing mission of the Apostles. Organization is minimal, contributions from the better-off members of the community being used by the Apostles for the relief of hardship as and when required. The Christians are held in high esteem by the citizens of Jerusalem, and the attempt of the High Priest and his Sadducean associates to suppress the movement by threats has foundered on popular support and Pharisaic tolerance. Apart from the occasional backslider like Ananias, the Nazarenes have presented a picture of a tightly-knit brotherhood, exemplary in behaviour and zealous in their public and private devotions. It is indeed such a picture as we should expect in the months that followed Pentecost, when Palestinian Christians found it easy to combine loyalty to the Temple, the Law and the traditions of their forefathers with their new-found conviction that the long-expected Messiah had come, unrecognized by most, but acknowledged as Lord and Christ by those to whom God had given the gift of repentance and faith. They lived a new life in the power of his Spirit, and they eagerly awaited his return.

With the opening of the sixth chapter of Acts, however, a new situation emerges. Greater numbers call for a more developed organization, and we find the membership of the Church divided into two clearly defined groups between whom there is some tension. The Twelve have acquired an even greater authority, and seek to shed some of their burdens. Mention is made of a regular daily distribution of food to needy widows. In short, everything points to a more advanced stage in the history of the Jerusalem church, and we may well think of a lapse of a year or two between the events that have been described and what now follows. It is the prelude to the emergence of a new radical temper in the Church which, although experiencing persecution for the first time, at the same time embarks on that wider missionary enterprise which is in time to lead it into the heart of the Gentile world.

Luke begins with the organizational problems.

1. the disciples: members of the Church, also described as 'saints' or 'brethren'.

Hellenists . . . Hebrews: the 'Hellenists' are Greek-speaking Jewish Christians, normally resident overseas and temporarily living in Jerusalem, or, having been brought up overseas, now permanently settled in Jerusalem. These are distinguished from the 'Hebrews', who are Palestinian-born Aramaic-speaking Jewish Christians. It has been suggested that the distinction may even have been between those who could speak *only* Greek (Hellenists), and those who were able to speak Greek but spoke Aramaic as well (Hebrews). To begin with, the Christian community would appear to have consisted mainly of Hebrews; but it would seem that, with growing numbers, a substantial body of Hellenists had also been attracted into the Church. Some scholars who maintain that there was a direct historical link between Qumran and the Jerusalem church have traced this contact to these Hellenists. Others see it as coming through those who are here described as Hebrews.

their widows: in Jewish practice widows had always been regarded as deserving of special consideration, and naturally this attitude was shared by the young Jewish Christian Church. The two groups of widows, 'Hellenist' and 'Hebrew', would appear to have been looked after separately by their own section of the Christian community.

daily distribution: this would imply a regular dispensation of charity in money or kind, perhaps more probably the right of admission to the common meal, or *agapē*, in the various house-churches. Alleged unfairness in the treatment accorded to the two groups of widows led to complaints by the Hellenists.

2. the twelve: this is the only use of this designation of the Apostles in Acts, but it has been consistently implied by Luke's references hitherto to 'the eleven' (1:26; 2:14), and marks his view of their unique status in the Church. On their authority, the whole body of believers—Hellenists and Hebrews—was summoned to a general meeting; as in modern times, no doubt only a percentage was able or willing to attend.

give up preaching . . . to serve tables: superficially this is simply a statement by the Twelve that the administration of charitable relief as well as the work of Evangelism was proving to be too heavy a burden; the missionary enterprise was suffering in consequence. It would seem from the sequel, however, that more was involved than merely a desire to delegate some of their administrative responsibilities.

3. pick out: the selection of assistants to the Apostles is left to the congregation.

seven men: although seven was a common enough number for the membership of Jewish statutory bodies, it is difficult not to think that the fact that it was also recognized as having Gentile associations would make it appropriate as the number of men chosen to represent the interests of the Greek-speaking section of the Christian community.

4. ministry of the word: although the Twelve claim Evangelism as distinct from administration as their rightful function, it is clear that two at least of the Seven—Stephen and Philip—quickly established themselves as Evangelists in their own right.

5. Stephen . . . Nicolaus: of the Seven, apart from Stephen and Philip, nothing more is said in Luke's narrative. Nicolaus is claimed to have been the founder of the Nicolaitans, the heretical sect of Rev. 2:6, 15. All the Seven have Greek names, and Nicolaus is described as having been a Gentile convert to Judaism.

6. laid their hands upon them: it is not clear from the text whether all present prayed and laid hands on the Seven, or whether it was only the Apostles who did both. There is a precedent for a mass-commissioning to office in Num. 8:10, where the people of Israel are instructed to lay their hands upon the Levites. It seems more likely, however, that the Seven, having been selected and presented by the congregation, were then set apart for their special function by the Twelve with prayer and the laying on of hands.

It has been maintained that this constituted the inception of the order of deacons. Against this it has been pointed out that the Seven are not described anywhere as deacons by Luke, and that he uses the word *diakonia* in this passage both for the distribution of relief and the ministry of the word by the Twelve. In Luke's day, no doubt, deacons were a recognized order as assistants to presbyter-bishops, if we are to judge by Phil. 1:1; but he clearly does not regard the Seven as belonging to this category. Nor, although Stephen and Philip are shortly to be found exercising a highly individualistic preaching ministry, would it appear that this was the first ordination of presbyters. In Jewish Christian communities presbyters or elders seem to have emerged naturally on the Jewish pattern from among the leading members of the community.

Rather, Luke suggests that at this early stage the Seven were appointed as a distinctive body in their own right. They are listed by name, as are the Twelve, and there is no suggestion that when they passed from the scene, either through death—as in the case of Stephen—or by being scattered by the persecution that broke out at that time, any successors were appointed. The office of the Seven, as of the Twelve, is unique, and it seems most natural to regard their appointment as a placatory move to satisfy the Hellenistic party referred to in verse 1. It may well be that it was recognized that Jewish Christians from overseas did not share wholly the attitude of the Palestinian-born Christians, both to Jewish institutions and to the Christian mission. Even if Stephen was more radical than the rest, there may still have been a sufficiently different attitude both to Judaism and Christianity between the two parties in the Church to make it prudent to give the leaders of the more liberal element some official standing.

The laying-on of hands, whether in the *OT* or the *NT*, implies either investing with a particular authority or communicating to the recipient some power which the agent in the laying-on of hands possesses. This applies equally to such incidents as Jacob's blessing of his grandchildren (Gen. 48:13–19), Moses' commissioning of Joshua (Num. 27:18, 23), or the healing acts of Jesus and the Apostles. In Acts it is frequently associated with the gift of the Holy Spirit, as in 8:17 and 19:6. Here, however, the Seven have been chosen because they are already 'full of the Spirit' (verse 3). It is implied, therefore, that they receive no additional *charisma*, but rather a special status in the Church conferred upon them by the Twelve.

7. the number of the disciples multiplied: the implication is that the settlement of the dispute between the Hebrews and the Hellenists, together with a new impetus given by the more active Evangelism of the Twelve, led to a rapid growth of the Church. **priests:** these would be from the lower order of the Jewish priesthood, as opposed to members of the high-priestly families. Some of the priests referred to may have been sectarians from Qumran, but there is nothing here to suggest that an influx of such men at this point was responsible for transforming the Church into a community based on Essene practices.

THE EMERGENCE OF STEPHEN **6:8-15**

Stephen has already been singled out by Luke for special mention among the Seven as 'a man full of faith and of the Holy Spirit' (verse 5). It is in keeping with this that he is now given pride of place in Luke's narrative, and that no less than one twentieth of the whole of Acts is devoted to his very long discourse in chapter 7. Clearly Luke regarded his role in the early Church as having been of unusual significance, and far beyond the fact that he became the first Christian martyr. As Paul is to become Luke's hero, in that he more than any other single man was instrumental in spreading the Gospel throughout the Gentile world, so Stephen here receives honourable recognition as the man who first saw the wider implications of the Church's faith and laid the foundations on which the mission to the Gentiles was built.

8. wonders and signs: Stephen extends the apostolic ministry of healing through the power of the Spirit.

9. synagogue: it is not clear whether only one synagogue is being referred to, or more than one; commentators have argued that the text could imply anything from one to five. There were many synagogues in Jerusalem (traditionally 480), and each of the groups mentioned in this verse may have met in a separate place. It could also be that three synagogues are intended—one attended by Freedmen, one by Jews from North Africa (Cyrenians and Alexandrians), and one by Jews from Asia Minor (Cilicia and Asia). It has been suggested that for 'Freedmen' (*Libertinōn*) we should read 'Libyans' (*Libustinōn*), in which case the North African synagogue might have included these as well, giving a total of two. On the whole, it seems most likely that one synagogue is intended, frequented by a mixed group of Jewish Freedmen or their descendants from overseas.

Freedmen: these were probably descendants of Jewish captives who had been taken to Rome by Pompey in 63 B.C. and subsequently liberated by their Roman masters.

Alexandrians: it has been suggested that Stephen himself came from Alexandria.

Cilicia and Asia: Cilicia lay in the south-east of Asia Minor, with Paul's native city of Tarsus as its capital. 'Asia' was the name given to the Roman province at the western end of Asia Minor.

arose and disputed with Stephen: thus Luke pinpoints the new note in the missionary activity of the Church. Stephen carries the war into the enemy's camp. Public disputation in the synagogues may have happened before, but it has not been mentioned; it was to become a major feature of Paul's technique of evangelism. We may well suppose that among those who engaged Stephen in argument in this synagogue of Dispersion Jews was Rabbi Saul of Tarsus himself.

10. wisdom and the Spirit: a formidable combination of a brilliant mind and passionate conviction made Stephen a doughty protagonist of the faith.

11. blasphemous words: if Stephen's advocacy of the Gospel is correctly reflected in his address to the Sanhedrin in chapter 7, the Jews would be entitled to treat this as blasphemy. From this point Luke clearly sees a parallel between Stephen's trial and death and that of his Master; false witnesses and the charge of blasphemy also featured in the trial of Jesus (Mk 14:56ff.).

12. stirred up the people: despite Stephen's powers of healing which would commend him to the ordinary citizens of Jerusalem, his opponents among the Jews from overseas were able to persuade them that Stephen's views on the relationship between the faith of old Israel and the faith of the Nazarenes were a threat to their Jewish heritage. The more conservative Apostles had made it possible for a moderate Pharisee like Gamaliel to see no danger in their delusion that Jesus was the Messiah. Stephen's radical approach, however, as will be apparent from his speech, made it clear that he was attacking the very foundations on which Judaism rested. Thus both popular feeling and the Pharisaic party, consisting of **the elders and the scribes,** united in opposition and brought about his arrest.

council: the Sanhedrin.

13. this holy place: referring to the Temple to which the council chamber of the Sanhedrin was adjacent. If the charge had been wholly true that Stephen incessantly denounced both Temple and Law, he would have been disowned by his Palestinian-born fellow-Christians as well. At this stage their loyalty to both was complete. There was doubtless some substance in the charge, in so far as Stephen had been critical of certain strongly held Jewish beliefs and cherished practices, if we are to judge by his speech.

14. we have heard him say: whatever Stephen had said was deliberately twisted by the false witnesses, as at the trial of Jesus (Mk 14:58). Several sayings of Jesus could have been distorted into a claim that he would **destroy this place** (e.g., Mt. 12:6; Mk 13:2; Jn 2:19). If Stephen had emphasized the inwardness of worship as opposed to reliance on external ceremonial, he had echoed the thought of Jesus himself (Mk 12:28ff.), and indeed of *OT* prophecy (cf. 7:48-50). If he had criticized Pharisaic interpretation of the Law, again he was faithful to the mind of Jesus (e.g. Mk 2:23ff.). There was thus substance in the charges brought against Stephen, although his actual words were misrepresented.

15. like the face of an angel: if Saul of Tarsus was present at this meeting of the Sanhedrin, which is more than likely (cf. 7:58, 8:1), this striking comment may have come to Luke from him. Moses' face is said to have shone as he came down from Sinai where he had communed with God (Exod. 34:29ff.). Here, in Stephen's case, it is the prelude to a similar vision of the glory of God, which is referred to in 7:55-6.

STEPHEN'S SPEECH 7:1-53

On the basis of this speech, Stephen has been variously described as an Essene, an ultra-orthodox Jewish–Christian supporter of James the Lord's brother, a radical Hellenist, or as the real founder of the mission to the Gentiles. The speech itself has been regarded in equally divergent ways ranging from a martyr's apologia to a fictitious literary creation. It has been argued that it marks Stephen out as a 'towering theological genius' who is pleading for the rejection of the Jerusalem Temple and its cult as the essential prelude to a Christian mission to the Samaritans. On the surface it appears to be a rather tedious recital of Jewish history which has little relevance to the charges on which Stephen has been brought to trial; on closer study, however, it reveals itself as a subtle and skilful proclamation of the Gospel which, in its criticism of Jewish institutions, marks the beginning of the break between Judaism and Christianity, and points forward to the more trenchant exposition of the difference between the old faith and the new as expressed by Paul and the author of the Letter to the Hebrews.

1-8. The charge against Stephen was that he had attacked the most cherished institutions of Judaism, the Temple and the Law. Invited by the High Priest to defend himself against the charge, Stephen first reminds the Sanhedrin that God's covenant relationship with Israel began long before the giving of the Law to Moses or the building of the Temple by Solomon. It depended on God's call to Abraham, which came to him in far-off Mesopotamia, while the sacred soil of the Holy Land was still in the hands of Canaanites, and on God's promise that one day, not only would Canaan become the home of Abraham's descendants, but that through them the world would be brought to the knowledge of God (Gen. 12:1-3). Less explicitly than Paul in Gal. 3:16, Stephen sees the promise to Abraham as having its fulfilment in his offspring Israel's Messiah, who for both Paul and Stephen was, of course, Jesus. From Abraham's day the whole of God's redemptive purpose for the world through Israel pointed to and focused on the coming of the Messiah.

2. The God of glory: the glorious God (Ps. 29:3).
appeared . . . in Mesopotamia: according to Gen. 12:6-7, God appeared to Abraham at the terebinth of Moreh in Shechem in Canaan, and not in Mesopotamia. This is the first of a number of minor differences between Stephen's review of Israel's history and the *OT* narrative, both in the Hebrew and Greek texts. None of them is material, and they reflect the fact that in Stephen's day the *OT* text was still fluid, discrepancies involving dependence on varying traditions being common before the text was finally established. Philo and Josephus in their allusions to events in ancient biblical history likewise display variations from the standardized form of the *OT* narrative.
Haran: in the account of the migration of the family of Abraham given in Gen. 11:27-32, Ur of the Chaldeans in southern Mesopotamia is referred to as the original home of the tribe. From there under the leadership of Terah, the father of Abraham, they moved through the Fertile Crescent to Haran in northern Mesopotamia, where for a time they settled, and where Terah died. Some scholars believe that Haran rather than Ur was the more likely place of origin of the patriarchal family, but Stephen's

location of God's call to Abraham in Ur is supported by Gen.
15:7; Jos. 24:3; Neh. 9:7.

5. not even a foot's length: Stephen stresses that the father
of the Israelites had no settled home in the Promised Land by
which the Jews set so much store. The author of Hebrews makes
the point that Stephen hints at here, when he claims that Abraham
knew that the true promised land of the people of God was not an
earthly but a heavenly home, in which the saints of old Israel
and of new Israel are gathered together before God through the
work of Christ (Heb. 11:8-16).

6. four hundred years: roughly the traditional period during
which the Israelites were in Egypt (Gen. 15:13; Exod. 12:40).

8. covenant of circumcision: Stephen's point is that Israel
had become the people of God through the promise to Abraham
before the rite of circumcision—which was all-important to
Judaism—was instituted, and before Palestine had become their
Holy Land.

9-16. The Egyptian bondage of the people of God, ending in
their liberation and entrance into their promised inheritance,
would suggest to the Christian apologist, if not to the Sanhedrin,
a parallel with the rejection and suffering of Jesus before his
exaltation to the right hand of God. Even more clearly, the story
of Joseph, betrayed by his jealous brothers and sold into slavery,
but raised to high distinction by the hand of God, has always been
seen by Christian writers as a foreshadowing of the experience of
Christ. The **second visit** referred to in verse 13 has been thought
by some to be an allusion to the Second Advent. This is less likely
than that, in drawing attention to the burial of the patriarchs at
Shechem, Stephen was underlining that it was in Samaritan
territory, which was anathema to Jewish orthodoxy, that the
first fathers of the race had found their last resting place.

14. seventy-five souls: the more usual number given in the
OT is seventy (Gen. 46:27; Exod. 1:5; Deut. 10:22). In the first
two references LXX, however, has seventy-five.

16. the tomb that Abraham had bought: the *OT* locates
at Hebron the tomb that Abraham bought (Gen. 23), in which
Jacob was later buried (Gen. 50). Jacob had purchased a plot of
land at Shechem (Gen. 33:19), in which Joseph was buried (Jos.
24:32); no mention is made of the burial place of Jacob's other
sons. Stephen's version is apparently based on a tradition that
makes Shechem the burial place of the whole family.

17–38. More specifically than in the life of Joseph, Stephen sees in the story of Moses a type of the new and greater Moses—Christ himself. There is, of course, no exact correspondence in the actual course of events, but the manner in which Moses is described and the features of the *OT* narrative emphasized make it plain that in Stephen's mind the experiences of the saviour of his people at the time of the Exodus pointed forward to those of the greater Deliverer, Jesus the Messiah. Moses came **as the time of the promise drew near** (verse 17), in the same way as Christ came 'when the time had fully come' (Gal. 4:4). The infant Moses narrowly escaped death at the hands of the Pharaoh (verse 19), as the infant Jesus was saved from the Massacre of the Innocents ordered by King Herod. Moses as a child **was beautiful before God** (verse 20) and **instructed in all the wisdom of the Egyptians** (verse 22), as the young Jesus 'increased in wisdom and in stature, and in favour with God and man' (Lk. 2:52). Jesus like Moses **was mighty in his words and deeds** (verse 22; Lk. 24:19).

When Moses was **forty years old,** after the years of preparation for his task, **it came into his heart to visit his brethren** (verse 23) and to become God's instrument for their **deliverance** from the Egyptians (verse 25). So Jesus, after the 'Hidden Years' of preparation, when he was about thirty years of age, began his ministry among his fellow-townsmen of Nazareth with a message of deliverance from bondage (Lk. 3:23; 4:16–19). Both Moses and Jesus were misunderstood and driven away (verses 25, 27; Lk. 4:28–9). But God, despite the rejection of Moses by his people, made him **both ruler and deliverer** to lead them from the death of slavery in Egypt to new life and liberty in the Promised Land (verses 35–6). So by the Resurrection, greatest of all **wonders and signs,** God made Jesus, rejected and crucified, both Lord and Christ, and Saviour of his people from the slavery of sin and from the power of evil and death.

Moses himself had recognized that a greater prophet than himself was still to come (verse 37), although in his day, while on the one hand a member of the people of God, on the other hand he was himself a mediator between God and his people and communicated to them God's word of life contained in the Law (verse 38). For Stephen, as for all Jewish Christians, there was no question but that Jesus was this prophet to come of whom Moses spoke, the new Moses (see on 3:22), made like his brethren in every respect (Heb. 2:17), but, as Son of God, being also the perfect mediator between God and man, and the giver of new life through the Spirit (see on 2:33).

21. Pharaoh's daughter . . . brought him up: thus the pillar of the Law was reared in a foreign land and in a Gentile court.

22. all the wisdom of the Egyptians: Jewish writers such as Josephus and Philo stressed the vast learning and great wisdom of Moses.

mighty in his words: This would appear to conflict with Moses' modest disclaimer in Exod. 4:10, but it could refer to his written words.

23. forty years old: Moses' age at this time is not given in the *OT* (cf. Exod. 2:11: 'when Moses had grown up'). Rabbinical writings, however, agree with this statement, dividing his total age of one hundred and twenty years into three equal parts, the two stages mentioned here (cf. verse 30 and Exod. 7:7), and the forty years in the wilderness.

29. Moses fled: here it is implied that his flight was the result of his rejection by his own people. This preserves the parallel with Jesus as the deliverer who was not accepted, but the *OT* attributes Moses' flight to fear of the Pharaoh's wrath (Exod. 2:15).

30. an angel: as in Exod. 3, the angel is identified with God. In Christian thought Christ was regarded as having been present throughout Israel's past history (1 C. 10:1–4; Jn 12:41; Heb. 11:26). It may be that here, as in verses 35 and 38, the angel is seen as Christ, **the Lord** (verse 33). Probably also Stephen thinks of God's call to Moses at the Burning Bush as a parallel with the divine voice at Jesus' baptism.

Sinai: called Horeb in Exod. 3:1. But Mount Horeb is identified with Mount Sinai by implication in the Exodus story (cf. Exod. 3:12; Dt. 1:6; Exod. 19:11–20). Stephen would see additional strength for his case, in that God's call to Moses and later the giving of the sacred Law took place, not in the Holy Land, but on foreign soil. Not only the Temple was a 'holy place' (6:13); wherever God chose to reveal himself was **holy ground** (verse 33).

36. Egypt . . . the Red Sea . . . wilderness: Jesus too had been brought out of Egypt by Joseph and Mary, had passed through the waters of Jordan at his baptism (**the Red Sea**), and had been tempted in the wilderness for **forty** days.

37. a prophet (like Moses): based on the words of Dt. 18:15,

18, this was a common description of Jesus in early Christian apologetic (3:22, and cf. Lk. 24:19 with 7:22). It has been pointed out that the central section of Luke's Gospel (9:51–18:14) seems to treat Jesus' last journey to Jerusalem as the new Exodus. Luke, convinced that Jesus was the prophet of whom Moses spoke, arranges the events and topics of his last journey on parallel lines with Deuteronomy. The new Moses goes to Jerusalem to effect a greater deliverance of God's people, and to lead them to their true Promised Land.

38. the congregation (*Gr. ekklesia*) **in the wilderness** (Dt. 18:16) is seen as the type of the Christian *ekklesia* where Jesus replaces Moses.

39–53. Stephen has just made it plain that, whatever he was reported to have said about the Law—on account of which he was on trial—he held the Law itself in high esteem as the God-given word of life. Like his fellow Christians, he would see the **living oracles** as now having been incarnated in Jesus, and he would regard the main function of the Law as pointing forward to, and preparing Israel for, the coming of the Messiah. His charge against his countrymen is that, having been given this divine revelation through Moses, they disregarded both the revelation and Moses its mediator. Instead, as their forefathers had preferred idolatry and the worship of the Golden Calf (Exod. 32), so the religious leaders of Stephen's day had made the ceremonial side of the Law a fetish, and its moral side a stranglehold on daily life; thus they were equally guilty of idolatry. Moreover, the historic meeting place of the Israelites with God was the simple tent in the wilderness which accompanied them on their journey to the Promised Land. Even as late as King David, it had been understood that God could not be restricted to one place. Solomon, however, had tried to confine God in a Temple, and this heresy still persisted. In a passionate outburst Stephen accused his fellow-countrymen of having been consistently unfaithful to their heritage, of having rejected all the messengers sent by God, and of finally having crucified the Messiah himself.

40. this Moses: so also the Jews of Stephen's day did not know or care what had become of the new Moses.

42–3. the host of heaven: the narrative of the Exodus in the *OT* makes no reference to the Israelites having worshipped sun, moon and stars during their wanderings, but Jeremiah (19:13) accuses the people of his day of having been guilty of this type of

idolatry. Paul also echoes this Jewish idea, that the punishment
for sin is that the sinner is allowed to sink into even deeper sinful-
ness (Rom. 1:24, 26, 28).

the book of the prophets is the collection of the oracles of the
twelve minor prophets. The quotation is from Am. 5:25-7, where
the prophet, denouncing the traffic in religion in his day, points
to the contrast between the austere, simple faith and practice of
the Exodus wanderings and the elaborate sacrificial rites that had
become the essence of Israel's worship. The second half of the
quotation in Amos is a prophecy that the Israelites will be ban-
ished to exile beyond Damascus, carrying their Assyrian idols
with them. Stephen, however, takes the Amos passage to mean a
condemnation of Israel for not worshipping the true God in the
wilderness as Moses had enjoined them, but for practising idolatry
instead. 'Damascus' in Amos has been changed to 'Babylon' in
Acts, as being the exile that mattered for Jerusalem Jews. The
text has also been corrupted, in that the two Assyrian deities in
the Hebrew of Amos, Sikkuth (Sakkuth) and Kiyyun (Kaiwan),
have been changed by the LXX to **Moloch** and **Rephan,**
probably by assuming that 'Sikkuth' was *sukkoth* ('booths' or
'tents') and that 'king' (*melech*) was 'Moloch'. Rephan is difficult
to account for; it may be an Egyptian name for Saturn.

44. tent of witness: having accused the Jews of having traves-
tied the God-given Law, Stephen now accuses them of having
equally distorted the purpose of the divinely appointed 'tent', or
tabernacle, which had also been part of God's revelation to Moses
at Sinai. The **pattern** of this meeting place of God with his
people had been determined by God himself (Exod. 25:9, 40). The
thought that the earthly tabernacle or Temple was a copy of the
true tabernacle or sanctuary in heaven is expressed in Heb.
8:5, 9:24.

45. brought it in with Joshua: Stephen develops the idea that
the presence of God cannot be restricted to one place. As he had
appeared to Abraham and Moses in foreign lands, so he was constantly present with the Israelites on their journey to the Promised
Land. By mentioning Joshua, which in Greek is the same word as
Jesus, and **the nations,** Stephen (or Luke) may be drawing a
parallel with the Messiah who was to be a light to the (Gentile)
nations (Isa. 42:6, 49:6; Lk. 2:32).

until the days of David: although there were centralized
sanctuaries, the symbolism of the tent to house the Ark of the

Covenant, containing the tables of the Law, was preserved as a reminder of the desert days after the Israelites had settled in Canaan, even when Jerusalem became the capital under David (2 Sam. 6:17).

46. asked leave to find a habitation: according to 2 Sam. 7, David was forbidden by God to build a temple to house the Ark, although, as Stephen implies, David above all might have been expected to get this permission.

47. Solomon: it was, in fact, this ostentatious monarch, who even in the flattering *OT* record of his achievements is criticized for not being as true to the Lord as his father David had been (1 Kg. 11:4), who was in Stephen's view misguided enough to build the first Temple at Jerusalem; this had now, after Herod's reconstruction, become the centre of a perversion of Israel's historic faith.

48. houses made with hands: the phrase suggests pagan idolatry. Even Solomon had acknowledged in his prayer at the dedication of the first Temple, that God could not be contained in any earthly edifice. Presumably the Sadducees of Stephen's day would have agreed; but by their fanatical insistence on the uniqueness of the Temple and its cult they encouraged the belief that this was the very dwelling-place of God.

49–50. Heaven is my throne: this quotation from Isa. 66:1–2, whom Stephen calls **the prophet,** and therefore as much worthy of attention as Moses, is a forthright condemnation of the Temple cult which Isaiah follows with words which indicate that what God wants is rather humility and obedience on the part of the worshipper, and not the performance of ceremonial and ritual. It would seem that these verses form the real thrust of Stephen's speech. In quoting with approval Isaiah's words, Stephen would appear to imply that, as Christ is the new Moses, he is also the new Temple. In him and through him alone can men approach God. This is in line with such passages as Jn 2:19, 21; Eph. 2:19–22; 1 Pet. 2:5. Such a direct attack on the Temple cult may well have caused a commotion in the Sanhedrin that provoked Stephen's final salvo.

51. stiff-necked: as were their ancestors in the time of Moses (Exod. 33:3, 5).

uncircumcised in heart: despite their insistence on circumcision of the flesh as the hallmark of the people of God (cf. Jer. 9:26), they had failed to respond with heart and mind to God's revelation. Like their forefathers who rebelled against Moses and other messengers inspired by God (Isa. 63:10), the Jews had now rejected the latest appeal of God's **Holy Spirit** to Israel through the new Moses and his disciples.

52. killed: the *OT* records that prophets were persecuted, but rarely that they were killed; however, it was common tradition by *NT* times that death at the hands of the people was the normal fate of a prophet (Lk. 11:49-51, 13:34; 1 Th. 2:15).

the Righteous One: the Messiah (see on 3:14). Stephen accuses the Sanhedrin as the supreme judicial authority of the Jews, although with the support of the people, of the ultimate crime of crucifying God's Messiah; this was in character with their past record, in that they had similarly put to death the prophets who **announced beforehand** his **coming.**

53. received the law . . . and did not keep it: if they had taken to heart the revelation of God's redemptive purpose in the Law, they would have known that Jesus had been sent to supersede both Temple and Law.

delivered by angels: as a result of the increasing sense of the remoteness of God which developed in Judaism after the Exile, and arising from the Greek text of Dt. 33:2 ('on his right hand were his angels with him'), the doctrine had grown up that the Law had been given by God to Moses at Sinai by angelic beings. Stephen's words reflect the normal Jewish belief that this enhanced the dignity and importance of the Law. Later Paul and the author of the letter to the Hebrews regard the angelic mediators as an indication of the inferiority of the Law to the direct revelation of God in Christ (Gal. 3:19; Heb. 2:2).

It is impossible to say how much of this speech is a transcript of Stephen's actual words and how much Luke himself has contributed to it. On the face of it, it is unlikely that so allusive and suggestive an oration could be an extempore utterance; on the other hand, there is no good reason to suppose that it does not represent at least the substance of what Stephen said, and that it was because it appeared to Luke to mark a significant development in the history of the Church that he has devoted so much space to it.

The theme of Acts is the progressive detachment of Christianity from its Palestinian setting and its expansion into the Gentile world. Of this swift and dramatic progress Paul was the chief instrument, and because of this the whole of Acts is dominated by his activities. Luke's concern is with the mission to the Gentiles and therefore, while he describes the Jerusalem origins of the

Church with proper care and treats the Twelve and their associates with due respect, his eye is on the future rather than on the past. Accordingly, Stephen's role as the first to challenge Christianity's dependence on Jewish institutions and his radical criticism of traditional Jewish ideology, which until his protest had apparently been complacently accepted by the Palestinian-born Christians as a whole, made him a key figure in Luke's story, and his speech a vital manifesto of the breakaway of the Church from its Jewish moorings.

As a review of Israel's history it lacks the sparkle and élan of the similar recital in the eleventh chapter of Hebrews. Its purpose is different and the argument is more subtle; it is not designed to secure Stephen's acquittal of the charges brought against him, but to proclaim the essence of the new faith. It has been well said that, although the name of Christ is never mentioned, Stephen is all the while 'preaching Jesus'. He is demonstrating that everything in Israel's past history and experience pointed forward to God's culminating act in his plan for the redemption of the world in sending the Christ. The witness of Abraham, Joseph, Moses and David in one way or another underlined the transitory nature of existing Jewish institutions and the hollowness of Jewish claims to have the monopoly of the way to salvation. The presence of God could not be restricted to one Holy Land or confined in one holy Temple, nor could his Law be atrophied in the ceremonialism of the Sadducees or the legalism of the Pharisees. Such a critique, ending inevitably in the martyrdom of its exponent, was under the guidance of the Spirit, the cause of the next great advance in the expansion of the Church. For this reason also it merited the importance Luke has attached to it.

THE DEATH OF STEPHEN 7:54-60

54. they ground their teeth: however completely the finer points of Stephen's tendentious treatment of Jewish history were grasped by all the members of the Sanhedrin, most of those present would bridle at his condemnation of their present attitude to the Law as being tantamount to idolatry and at his dismissal of the Temple cult as a deviation from the ancient practice of Israel. Clearly the prisoner by his own words had admitted that the charges brought against him were only too well-founded. But the whole assembly would find his final sally intolerable when he accused them of being violators of the very Law whose observance by others they so zealously enforced.

55. saw the glory of God: Stephen, faced by the mounting fury of his judges, finds strength through the Spirit in a vision of God enthroned in glory with Jesus at his side.

56. the Son of man: this is the only occurrence in the *NT* of this name for Jesus outside the Gospels. It is reminiscent of the passage in Dan. 7:13 on which Jesus' own words at his trial before the High Priest most probably depend (Mk 14:62; Lk. 22:69). It is more usual to find Jesus spoken of as 'seated at the right hand' of God. Here Stephen speaks of him as **standing**. Both terms are symbolic of the authority conferred on the exalted Christ. In Stephen's vision there may be the thought that Christ is standing to welcome him into his presence.

If on the other hand, as has been suggested, Stephen's vision of Jesus as Son of Man connects directly with the vision of Daniel, where 'one like a son of man' stands before God (the Ancient of Days), and is given 'dominion and glory and kingdom, that all peoples, nations and languages should serve him' (Dan. 7:13-14), something more rofound is intended. Was Stephen indeed the first Christian to see Jesus, not merely as the Jewish Messiah, but as the universal Saviour of mankind? Did he at the same time see that this inevitably implied that for Christians God's call was to embark on world mission, to leave behind them the static institutions of their Jewish heritage, and to become a pilgrim people as Israel at its best had been? If this is so, it gives added point to the repeated emphasis in Stephen's speech on Israel's past involvement with the nations of the world, on the journeyings of Abraham and Moses ever questing for the Promised Land, and on the 'tent of witness' as the symbol of the presence of God with the people of his choice as they move ever onwards in fulfilment of their destiny as the messengers of his truth in all the nations.

Stephen could thus have had close kinship with the author of the letter to the Hebrews, who would seem to have sought to persuade conservative Jewish Christians, seeking to substitute the alleged certainties of the old faith for the unpredictable guidance of the Holy Spirit, that for Christians the only certainty is Christ, and that their place is with him 'outside the camp' of Israel, 'bearing abuse for him' among the Gentiles (Heb. 13:13). Such an interpretation of the meaning of Stephen's words would give added justification for the significance that Luke undoubtedly sees in his contribution to the story of the Church.

57. stopped their ears: however Stephen's words were

interpreted by the Sanhedrin, it was clearly blasphemy in their eyes to identify the figure of the Son of Man in glory with the crucified malefactor Jesus of Nazareth.

58. stoned him: stoning to death outside the city walls (i.e. outside the camp) was the punishment for blasphemy (Lev. 24:10ff.). It is not clear whether Stephen's death was the result of judicial action by the Sanhedrin or of mob violence. The Sanhedrin may have pronounced sentence, which would presumably have to be ratified by Pilate as head of state; Pilate, however, would be at Caesarea and not in Jerusalem, and if he eventually heard that one more Jewish trouble-maker had been despatched by an angry crowd he would not be too concerned.

witnesses: their presence implies that those who had given evidence against Stephen threw the stones in accordance with legal practice (Dt. 17:5–7). The prisoner was stripped, thrown into a pit, and stoned from above. The cumbersome outer robes of the executioners would be discarded for ease of movement.

a young man named Saul: this is the first mention of Paul in Acts, and it is not merely a superb dramatic touch that makes Luke introduce his hero in this repulsive role, the memory of which haunted him (22:20); according to Augustine, it was the sight of Stephen praying for his murderers that sparked off the questions in Paul's mind that ended in his conversion. Whether Paul was a full member of the Sanhedrin or not, he was a prominent Pharisee. His age at the time may have been just over thirty, in which case Jesus and Paul were roughly contemporaries.

59. Lord Jesus: in his dying prayer the first Christian martyr addresses to Jesus words which his Master on the Cross had addressed to his Father (Lk. 23:46).

60. do not hold this sin against them: these words likewise echo another saying from the Cross recorded by Luke (Lk. 23:34); he undoubtedly saw the trial and death of Stephen in the light of Jesus' own Passion. Augustine's words are worth recording: if Stephen had not prayed, the Church would not have had Paul. **he fell asleep:** a characteristic *NT* expression for death (13:36; Jn 11:11; 1 Th. 4:14).

THE EXPANSION OF THE CHURCH 8:1–12:25

Stephen's martyrdom was not in vain. After his death, the Jewish ecclesiastical authorities took strong measures to suppress the subversive tendencies among the hitherto law-abiding Nazarenes

which his teaching had encouraged, and the more radical hellenistic elements within the Church had to flee from Jerusalem to
escape persecution. This proved, however, to be the beginning
of the mission of the Church to the world: unknown refugees made
their way to various centres up and down the Levant, in Palestine,
and beyond it; wherever they went, they proclaimed the Gospel
so that, not for the last time, the blood of the martyrs became the
seed of the Church.

But the message reached not only Jews. Luke skilfully shows how
one barrier after another was broken down by the reconciling
power of the Spirit. Philip, one of the Seven, conducts a mission
among the despised Samaritans, and baptizes an African eunuch
into the Faith; Peter under pressure from the Spirit admits an
officer of the hated Roman occupying power into the Church; the
Gospel spreads to Damascus, Phoenicia and Cyprus; and Antioch,
the metropolis of Syria, becomes the great centre of Gentile
Christianity. Most important of all, Antioch becomes the spearhead of a missionary enterprise which is to reach through Asia
Minor and Greece to the capital of the Roman Empire itself,
under the leadership of Saul of Tarsus, the instigator of the
first persecution of the Christians, who by his conversion to
Christianity becomes its most doughty advocate.

THE FIRST PERSECUTION 8:1-3

1. Saul was consenting: Stephen's death had Paul's full
approval (cf. 22:20).

a great persecution: this was not an official matter which would
concern the Roman authorities, but more of a campaign of in-
timidation, instigated by bigots like Paul and directed against all
who were known or thought to share Stephen's views. For their
own safety such Hellenists sought refuge in remoter parts of the
country out of reach of the Jerusalem fanatics. This was the
beginning of the Dispersion of the new Israel.

except the Apostles: Luke makes it plain that the persecution
was directed against the radical hellenistic section of the Church,
and not against the 'Hebrews' (see on 6:1), among whom were
the more conservative Twelve and presumably their supporters.
In the eyes of the Jewish ecclesiastics such Nazarenes were still
harmless. Probably the Twelve and their associates also felt that
Stephen had gone too far.

2. Devout men: these are more likely to be secret sympathizers with Stephen or shocked moderates among the Jews themselves than Christians, for whom such a public display in support of Stephen would have been too dangerous; if so, the episode would provide a parallel with the actions of Joseph of Arimathaea and Nicodemus after the Crucifixion. The reference to **great lamentation** supports the view that Stephen was lynched by a mob rather than judicially executed, since public mourning was forbidden in the latter case.

3. Saul laid waste the church: it would not be difficult in the tortuous streets of Jerusalem, and at a time when religious passions ran high, for a band of bigots, headed by one so able and determined as Paul, to carry out such a programme as Luke describes without attracting Roman attention. Paul later refers to this shameful chapter in his life in his speeches in 22:4f. and 26:10f., and in his letters (1 C. 15:9; Gal. 1:13, 23; Phil. 3:6).

PHILIP AND THE SAMARITANS **8:4–25**

4. preaching the word: although Luke highlights the major evangelistic achievements of Philip, Peter and above all Paul, he does not allow us to forget the countless anonymous missionaries who like the Apostles could not but speak of what they had seen and heard (4:20).

5. Philip: next to Stephen the most outstanding of the Seven (6:5).

a city of Samaria: lying between Judaea and Galilee, Samaria was for various reasons suspect to orthodox Jews. It had a population of mixed ancestry, dating back to the ravaging of the old kingdom of Israel and the sack of its capital, Samaria, by the Assyrians in 722 B.C. At that time many of the inhabitants had been carried off to exile, and the land had been resettled with a heterogeneous collection of subject peoples from other parts of the Assyrian Empire. There was further bad blood between the Jews and the Samaritans in the time of Nehemiah, when the Samaritans tried to prevent the rebuilding of Jerusalem, laid waste by the Babylonians in 587 B.C. The Samaritans themselves claimed to belong to the true stock of Israel and to be worshippers of Yahweh; they observed the Sabbath, and practised circumcision. But they had their own temple on Mount Gerizim, and recognized only the Pentateuch as holy Scripture. They were therefore regarded by the Jews as heretics and schismatics rather than as heathens; it

would be too much to say that the Jews had literally 'no dealings
with Samaritans' (Jn 4:9), but dealings were not encouraged.

It was thus a break with Jewish tradition for a Jewish Christian
like Philip to embark on a mission among them. His hellenistic
upbringing would no doubt make him less rigid in his attitude
than were the 'Hebrews'. The 'city' which he made the centre
of his activities may have been Sebaste, the old capital of Samaria,
rebuilt and renamed by Herod; or it may have been Gitta, which
is said to have been the home of Simon who is referred to in verses
9ff. Philip's ministry, like that of Stephen, was a combination of
preaching and healing, and his proclamation of **the Christ** was
to people who were expecting the Messiah (Jn 4:25, 29) whom
they called the *Taheb*, or 'restorer', and whom they identified
with the 'prophet like Moses' who was to come.

9. Simon is generally considered to be the Simon Magus, or
Simon the Sorcerer, who features largely in the works of second-
century Christian apologists as the first heretic, the arch-enemy
of Peter, and the founder of Gnosticism. Justin Martyr, himself a
native of Samaria, credits him with having done great damage to
the Faith, not only in Samaria, but later in Antioch and Rome.
His followers, the Simonians, were still active in the third century.
So much legend has gathered round his name that it is difficult
to assess his real importance. The ancient Near East at this time,
due to the decline of official pagan religions and the impact of
popular philosophy on the oriental cults, had produced a crop of
astrologers, wizards, healers, exorcists and magicians who claimed
in one way or another to meet the needs of an age that was questing
for truth, and for power to cope with the changes and chances of
ordinary life. Some of these were no doubt men of high principle,
like Apollonius of Tyana, whose activities were later compared
with Christ's; most were frauds and charlatans who preyed on a
gullible and superstitious public.

somebody great: Simon had apparently successfully persuaded
the Samaritans by his magical skill that he was some kind of
messianic figure, cf. Theudas in 5:36.

10. that power of God which is called Great: he was
acclaimed by the people as being in some way the special channel
of the power of God or the supreme emanation of God himself.

13. Simon himself believed: Philip's mission among the
Samaritans was successful in winning many converts from Simon's
occult practices. Among those who professed their faith in the

Gospel and were baptized was Simon himself, who would appear, however, to have been more impressed by Philip's healing powers than by his message.

14. the Apostles ... sent ... Peter and John: the success of Philip's mission among the Samaritans must obviously have gratified the Jerusalem Apostles. It was a new departure, and in line with Jesus' own injunction (1:8); though as 'Hebrews' the Twelve might have hesitated to embark on such an enterprise themselves. There is no suggestion that they sent Peter and John to criticize, or to satisfy themselves that the Gospel was being properly preached—still less that it required an apostolic visit with the laying-on of hands to ratify the baptism that had taken place; it was primarily a mission of goodwill, and a token of the solidarity of Christian believers, whether Jews or Samaritans. Peter was an obvious choice as the chief Apostle and, on the assumption that John is the son of Zebedee and not John Mark, it would be particularly fitting that a disciple who had at one point wanted to call down fire from heaven on a Samaritan village (Lk. 9:54) should now go to welcome Samaritans into the Church.

15–16. the Holy Spirit ... had not yet fallen: it would seem that, although those Samaritans who had responded to Philip's preaching had been baptized, they had not experienced the characteristic Pentecostal fervour accompanied by glossolalia.

17. they laid their hands on them: after prayer and the imposition of hands by the Apostles, the Samaritan converts became ecstatic in a way that was already familiar to the Jerusalem Christians (cf. 2:4; 4:31). It is wide of the mark to see in this any suggestion that Luke regards the gift of the Spirit as dependent on the apostolic laying-on of hands, as in the later practice of episcopal confirmation. In the case of Cornelius, a little later in the story (10:44), the Spirit is given even before baptism. The evidence of Acts—and indeed of the rest of the *NT*—is that baptism was regarded as the all-sufficient act of incorporation into the Christian fellowship, and except in the few cases—as here—to which Luke draws attention (cf. 19:1ff.), the gift of the Spirit was regarded as having been conferred in that rite (cf. 1 C. 12:13). In laying hands on the Samaritans, the two Apostles were identifying the mother church in Jerusalem, which they represented, with their long-separated brethren in Samaria; so significant an event would be properly blessed by a repetition of the Pentecostal experience. Luke is thus not concerned with anchoring later

ecclesiastical practice in the fluid and 'irregular' form and order
of the primitive Church; he is more interested in the effect of the
Samaritan Pentecost on Simon Magus.

18. he offered them money: Simon sees the power of the
Apostles to bring about an outburst of glossolalia as a commercial
asset which would make a good investment; his desire to buy and
sell the power to confer spiritual gifts has given rise to the word
'simony'. Clearly his conversion had been no more than skin-deep.

20. your silver perish with you: Peter as chief Apostle
exercises the authority of the Church to discipline sinners (Mt.
16:19, 18:18; Jn 20:23; 1 C. 5:3f.).

21-3. Peter's words have a strong *OT* flavour (cf. Dt. 12:12;
Ps. 78:37; Dt. 29:18; Isa. 58:6). Simon is excommunicated, but
repentance and forgiveness are still possible.

24. The Western text adds that Simon 'went on for a long time
weeping greatly'.

25. they returned to Jerusalem: the two Apostles and Philip.
This evangelistic work among the Samaritan villages confirms that
the apostolic delegation to Samaria had been on a mission of goodwill, and not to conduct a court of inquiry.

PHILIP AND THE EUNUCH **8:26-40**

26. an angel of the Lord said: the phrase means that Philip
received what he believed to be divine guidance to undertake this
particular journey. Another way of expressing the same idea in
terms of the Spirit is found in verse 29.

go toward the south: the words could also mean: 'towards
noon', but this is less likely.

Gaza had been one of the five towns of the Philistines on the
maritime plain. Destroyed in 93 B.C., it had been rebuilt nearer
the sea. The old town was referred to as 'Desert Gaza', and this is
probably meant here rather than **a desert road,** which properly
begins only at Gaza on the way to Egypt.

27. and he rose and went: Philip's behaviour in this incident
is reminiscent of that of Elijah, following impulses which he
recognizes as divine prompting, appearing in unexpected places,
and disappearing equally unexpectedly. It has also often been
noted that there are curious correspondences between Zeph. 2-3
and this passage—among other similarities Gaza, Ethiopia and
Azotus are mentioned in both.

an Ethiopian, a eunuch: it was the second aspect of the traveller whom Philip now encountered which was more significant for Luke's story. Philip had been instrumental in bringing Samaritans, despised by Old Israel, into the community of the New Israel; now he disposes of another barrier, and welcomes into the Church a eunuch, who according to Jewish law was not eligible to belong to the old *ekklesia* (Dt. 23:1), although Isa. 56:3ff. advocates a more liberal view. By Ethiopia is meant not the present-day Empire, otherwise known as Abyssinia, but modern Sudan, farther west and to the south of Egypt.

Candace: the generic title given to the queen-mothers in Ethiopia, who were the real rulers of the land. The eunuch, who was apparently the court chamberlain, was returning from a pilgrimage to **worship** in Jerusalem. This implies that he was a 'God-fearing Gentile', i.e. an adherent of the Jewish faith but unwilling (or, in this particular case, unable) to become a full proselyte (see on 2:10).

28. seated in his chariot . . . reading: the chariot was probably a covered waggon, and the normal practice in ancient times was to read aloud.

29-35. Philip responds again to divine prompting, and, as he runs alongside the chamberlain's coach, recognizes the words as the Greek version of Isa. 53. No passage in the *OT* is more frequently referred to by *NT* writers than this last of the Servant Songs; the early Church saw Isaiah's Servant, who was to bring the world to the knowledge of God through his suffering, as perfectly pre-figuring Christ. This is the earliest explicit reference to this belief in Acts, although mention has already been made of it in 3:13, 26; 4:27, 30. Jewish interpretation of the Servant in Isaiah's prophecy varied between identifying this mysterious figure with the Messiah and with Israel itself. For Jesus, however, the role of the Servant was the key to his ministry, and it was in this way that he chose to fulfil his mission as Israel's Messiah from his Baptism and Temptation onwards.

Invited to join the chamberlain in his carriage, Philip is asked by the puzzled Ethiopian to explain Isa. 53:7–8. For Philip they meant the silence of Jesus at his trial, his cruel death and his Resurrection. With these verses as his starting-point, Philip went on to expound the faith of the Church.

36. what is to prevent my being baptized? The Western text adds verse 37: 'And Philip said, "If you believe with all your heart you may". And he replied, "I believe that Jesus Christ is the

Son of God".' This is probably not original, and may have been
added to overcome the difficulty that the eunuch is baptized
without making any kind of confession of faith. It does, however,
represent an early form of a Christian creed, as do 11:17 and
16:31. Some scholars think that the eunuch's words in verse 36
constituted an early baptismal formula, and draw attention to
a similar use of the Greek *kōluō* (**prevent**) in 10:47 and 11:17 in
connection with the baptism of Cornelius and his household.

38. Baptism at this stage was normally by total immersion, and
where possible in running water, as in the case of Jesus (Mk
1:9–10).

39. Some MSS. read: 'And when they came up out of the water,
the Spirit fell on the eunuch but the angel of the Lord caught up
Philip . . .' This is possibly an addition by some scribe who felt that
the eunuch must be shown to have received the Spirit in line with
the Samaritans in verse 17. Philip mysteriously disappears from
the scene like Elijah; but the eunuch continues on his way
rejoicing, a word reflecting the frequently attested spiritual joy
of believers after baptism (cf. 16:34).

40. Azotus, where Philip again suddenly reappears, is the old
Philistine city of Ashdod. Philip ends his mission at **Caesarea,**
(see on 10:1), where we find him settled with his family more than
twenty years later (21:8–9). As Paul's associate during the
Apostle's enforced captivity in Caesarea which lasted for two
years (24:27), Luke would doubtless make full use of such information as Philip could give him in compiling the early chapters of
his narrative in Acts.

THE CONVERSION OF PAUL **9:1-9**

Having described some of the missionary activity which resulted
from the persecution of the church in Jerusalem chiefly instigated
by Paul, Luke now returns to the grand inquisitor himself. Not
content with his assault on the new heresy in Jerusalem, Paul was
determined to root it out wherever it might be found. It was while
he was on his way to Damascus bent on this vindictive enterprise
that, as he says himself, God 'was pleased to reveal his Son' to him
(Gal. 1:16) and he became thenceforward 'a man in Christ' (2 C.
12:2). No conversion has been more significant in the history of
the Church and Luke underlines this by giving no fewer than
three accounts of it, here and in chapters 22 and 26—in Paul's
speeches after his arrest in Jerusalem and in his own defence before King Agrippa.

Like Paul himself in these two speeches and in his letters, Luke does not disguise the dark side of his hero's character. So far we have seen him as a bigoted fanatic, the merciless persecutor of any who questioned the divine authority of the Jewish law. Stephen's brilliant analysis of the irreconcilable differences between orthodox Judaism and the faith of the Nazarenes in his speech before the Sanhedrin had finally made it clear to Paul that this new teaching was no innocuous delusion which had possessed a handful of simple Galilean fishermen and their supporters, inducing them to believe that the mad carpenter of Nazareth had been the Messiah. On the contrary, this was a blasphemous heresy which threatened to undermine the authority of the Temple and the Law, which perverted the Scriptures, which was leading gullible people astray, and which therefore must be stamped out.

Saul, more generally known by his Roman name Paul, had been born in Tarsus in Cilicia in Asia Minor (21:39), son of a strictly orthodox Jewish father, 'a Hebrew born of Hebrews' (Phil. 3:5), 'a Pharisee, a son of Pharisees' (23:6). Although he had been born in a Greek city, and was therefore like his chief opponent Stephen technically a Hellenist, a Greek-speaking Jew, it was the Jewish synagogue of Tarsus rather than the Greek university which had shaped his future. An equally minor role in his upbringing was played by his Roman citizenship, which he inherited from his father (22:28). Trained as a rabbi in Jerusalem under Gamaliel, he absorbed more of 'the strict manner of the law' (22:3) than of his teacher's tolerance and moderation (5:34ff.). 'I advanced in Judaism beyond many of my own age among my people, so extremely zealous was I for the traditions of my fathers', he wrote later to the Galatian Christians (Gal. 1:14).

Having possibly returned to his native Tarsus as a rabbi, Paul may have gone back to Jerusalem after Pentecost. He could hardly have been in Palestine during the ministry of Jesus without either becoming a disciple or, more likely, becoming involved in the Crucifixion. Presumably until the advent of Stephen he regarded the Nazarenes as harmless illiterates. Perhaps the disputations in the synagogue of the Freedmen (6:9), in the course of which he found himself matched by a mind as incisive as his own, but certainly Stephen's speech to the Sanhedrin, convinced him that the survival of Judaism depended on the extermination of these new radicals among the Nazarenes.

1. Saul . . . went to the high priest: connecting back with
8:3. If Paul's conversion took place in A.D. 32, as is probable,
Caiaphas was still High Priest (see on 4:6).

2. synagogues at Damascus: there was at this time a large
Jewish element in Damascus, including the strict 'Covenanters of
Damascus', who produced the Zadokite Fragments and were
connected with the Qumran community. Paul's concern would be
to prevent similar trouble from breaking out in the synagogues of
Damascus as had already been caused by Stephen in Jerusalem.
Radical Jewish Christians, sharing Stephen's views, who had fled
from Jerusalem to Damascus, must be identified and apprehended.
It has been questioned whether it would be likely that the writ of
the High Priest at Jerusalem would extend to the synagogues of
Damascus, entitling him to authorize Paul to arrest and deport
any Jews found guilty of spreading radical Christian propaganda.
Against this it must be said that the Roman authorities under-
wrote the jurisdiction of the Sanhedrin over Jewish citizens in
general. Moreover, according to 1 Mac. 15:15ff., Rome had
sanctioned the extradition of Jews who had fled to Egypt, ordering
King Ptolemy to hand them over to Simon Maccabaeus, who was
then High Priest. The Jews in the time of Paul were, however,
considerably less powerful politically than they had been almost
two centuries before in the time of Simon, and it may well be that
Paul's instructions from the Sanhedrin were to lay hands on as
many trouble-making Christians as he could without attracting
the attention of the Roman authorities.

the Way is a common description of Christianity in Acts (19:9,
23; 22:4; 24:14, 22). It may have been used by Christians of
themselves following the words of Jesus: 'I am the way' (Jn
14:6); cf. 'this Life' (Ac. 5:20): his was *the* way of life. The
members of the Qumran community likewise described their mode
of life as 'the Way', meaning the way of obedience to the Law of
Moses.

3-9. The account Luke gives here of the experience which
transformed the life of a bigoted Pharisee and changed him into
a slave of Christ (Rom. 1:1) differs only in minor details from
Paul's own version of the event in his two speeches later in Acts.
All three narratives are confirmed by Paul's references to his
conversion in his letters: he speaks of an appearance of the risen
Christ to him, as real as the Lord's appearances to the disciples
after his Resurrection (1 C. 15:5-8); he had 'seen Jesus our

Lord' as plainly as had they (1 C. 9:1), when God 'was pleased to reveal his Son' to him (Gal. 1:16). In the light of Paul's subsequent career, his single-minded devotion to Christ, his tireless efforts to bring Jews and Gentiles alike face to face with the same Lord as he had encountered on the Damascus road, his remorse for his vindictive cruelty, his atonement for it in selfless service of the Church he had tried to crush, it is frivolous to attempt to explain away Paul's conversion as a hallucination, an attack of sunstroke, or an epileptic fit. It was as is every genuine conversion experience a miracle of the grace of God.

This is not to say that psychology cannot help us to understand how sudden conversions come about. Augustine was a good psychologist when he suggested that the effect of Stephen's martyrdom and his dying prayer for his persecutors may have sown the seeds of doubt as to the pernicious nature of the Nazarene heresy in Paul's mind. The redoubled fury of his campaign against the Christians may well have been an attempt to kill a guilty conscience (cf. 26:14). But could the harrying of helpless men and women be in fact the will of God? May not Isaiah's picture of the Servant of God who, through humiliation and death, was crowned with glory have been fulfilled in the rejected Jesus of Nazareth? Did rigorous obedience to the Law make a man at peace with God? The seventh chapter of his letter to the Romans—assuming that it is autobiographical—would suggest that Paul had found that it did not. All this is largely conjectural. What is beyond question historically is that the fanatical oppressor of the Nazarenes, who left Jerusalem 'breathing threats and murder' (verse 1), entered Damascus mentally shattered and physically blinded, and became on his recovery the foremost protagonist of the beliefs he had set out to extirpate and the most devoted follower of the Jesus he had despised.

3. a light from heaven: in 26:13 the heavenly light shone round both Paul and his companions. This is no doubt the light of revelation to which Paul refers in 2 C. 4:6 as 'the light of the knowledge of the glory of God in the face of Christ.'

4. heard a voice: the heavenly voice, as in 7:31, 10:13. **Saul, Saul:** the words are the Semitic form of Paul's name, *Saoul, Saoul,* 'in the Hebrew language' (26:14). Jesus addresses him in Aramaic.

why do you persecute me?: Paul had not persecuted Jesus, but in persecuting the Nazarenes he had been persecuting the body of which Jesus is the head (Rom. 12:4, 5; 1 C. 12:12–27; Eph. 5:30; and cf. Mt. 25:34–45).

5. Lord in this case is a title of respect, meaning 'Sir', since Paul could hardly believe who was speaking. In Paul's own account, after Jesus has disclosed his identity he calls him **Lord,** with the full significance of the term (22:10).

6. you will be told: here Paul is merely called into the service of Christ. In his own account of his vision in 26:16–18, he is given his commission as the Apostle to the Gentiles by the risen Christ.

7. hearing the voice but seeing no one: this seems to contradict 22:9, where we are told that Paul's companions 'did not hear the voice of the one who was speaking to me'. It may be that they heard the sound without distinguishing the words, or, more likely, it was Paul's voice they heard but could not see to whom he was speaking.

8. Saul arose . . . and . . . could see nothing: Christian artists have depicted Paul falling from horseback or from the back of a mule. There is nothing about this in the narrative. When he picked himself off the ground he discovered that he was blind, and the proud Pharisee, stripped of all his pride, had to be led by the hand into Damascus.

9. three days . . . neither ate nor drank: it has been suggested that this was either penitence or fasting before baptism; more probably the blindness and the inability to eat were both the result of total shock. In this sudden overpowering revelation that Jesus the crucified malefactor was God's Messiah, that the Nazarenes were right and that he, Paul, had been catastrophically wrong, the foundations on which his whole life had been built collapsed under him.

PAUL AND ANANIAS **9:10–19a**

10. Ananias is described more fully in Paul's own words in 22:12 as 'a devout man according to the Law, well spoken of by all the Jews who lived there'. This would suggest that he was not one of the recent fugitives from Jerusalem, but an earlier Christian convert. His good standing with the Jews would imply that he was one of the conservative type of Jewish Christians who found it possible to combine the practice of Judaism with the belief that Jesus was the Messiah. How Christianity reached Damascus is unknown; it may have come through Jews who had been to Jerusalem on pilgrimage at Pentecost and had been converted

then; or through travelling merchants, since Damascus was easily
accessible from Judaea; or even through Galileans from the time
of Jesus' ministry there. The size of the Christian community in
Damascus is not stated, nor is it clear whether Ananias was head
of the community or merely an ordinary member. Like all
Christians in Damascus, he would, however, be alarmed at the
report that the chief persecutor of the Church was on his way to the
city on a mission that threatened the safety of the whole community. The story of how he learned of Paul's conversion and of
how he was moved to welcome Paul into the Church is told in
terms of a vision of Christ in which Ananias is given instructions
as to what he must do. This account, probably written up by Luke
for dramatic effect, should be compared with the simpler version
in Paul's own words in 22:12–16. The basic fact would seem to be
that Ananias despite his natural reluctance responded to a God-
given impulse to welcome into the Christian community the
dreaded inquisitor of whose conversion he had heard.

11. the street called Straight, or Straight Street, is still a
main thoroughfare in Damascus.

the house of Judas: Paul had been taken to this house by his
companions, presumably officers of the Sanhedrin. Luke carefully records the addresses at which Paul stayed, no doubt having
noted them as he heard of them, or remembering them if he had
been there himself—e.g. at the house of Lydia in Philippi (16:15);
of Jason in Thessalonica (17:6–7); of Aquila and Priscilla in
Corinth (18:2–3). Likewise he notes that Peter lodges with
Simon, a tanner, whose house was by the seaside (10:6).

a man of Tarsus: the first mention of Paul's native city.

he is praying: prayer and vision are closely associated in Acts
(10:9f.; 22:17). Here Paul is given a vision of Ananias, a vision
within a vision.

13. So far Ananias knew of Paul only by hearsay.

saints: Paul's normal word for Christians is appropriately used
in Acts only in this chapter and in Paul's speech in 26:10.

14. chief priests: Paul's documents were officially from the
High Priest (verse 1), but in the eyes of ordinary citizens the high
priestly families acted as a corporate body.

15. a chosen instrument: this was certainly how Luke regarded Paul, and how Paul regarded himself (Rom. 1:1; Gal.
1:15). He had been 'set apart' by God to be his agent in bringing
the Gospel to the Gentiles as well as to the Jews.

kings: such as King Agrippa (25:23ff.) and Nero (27:24).

16. Paul had himself brought suffering upon the 'saints at Jerusalem' (verse 13). In the course of his missionary campaigns he would more than expiate his crimes in his own body (2 C. 11:23ff.), which he regards as sharing the sufferings of Christ (Phil. 3:10).

17. laying his hands on him: as in 8:17, the laying-on of hands is a token of welcome into the Christian fellowship, lending support by an action to the word **Brother** with which Ananias addresses Paul, whom he calls by the Aramaic form of his name, *Saoul*, as in verse 4. We are probably meant to understand that, in receiving the gift of **the Holy Spirit,** Paul experienced the Pentecostal ecstasy.

18. scales: the word is used figuratively rather than technically. Paul receives his physical sight, which in its turn is the symbol of enlightenment (Heb. 6:4) through being **baptized**. The actions are all interrelated. By baptism and the gift of the Spirit Paul, who had been spiritually as well as physically blind, can now truly see.

19a. took food: as a sign of his complete recovery (cf. Mk 5:43).

AFTER PAUL'S CONVERSION 9:19b–31

Luke's account of what happened between Paul's conversion and his departure for Tarsus in verse 30 implies that he embarked at once on missionary work in Damascus. Driven from that city by Jewish opposition, he went on to Jerusalem, where, after a hesitant reception by the Christian community, he engaged in a further evangelistic campaign which ended, like that in Damascus, in his having to leave the city for his own safety. In his own version of this period in his life in Gal. 1:11–24 Paul states that after his conversion he 'did not confer with flesh and blood', but 'went away into Arabia, returned to Damascus' and only 'after three years' (i.e. in the third year) 'went up to Jerusalem' on what appears to have been a private visit. There he stayed for a fortnight, seeing only Peter and James the Lord's brother among the Apostles before going off to Syria and Cilicia.

Obviously Paul knew better than Luke what had happened; and, if it were the case that the two accounts were contradictory, we should have to say that Luke had got his facts wrong. On closer examination, however, and remembering the different purposes in the minds of the writers, it would appear that the two

versions of these events are complementary rather than contradictory. Paul's primary concern was not to tell the story of his life
for the benefit of the Galatian Christians, but to establish the fact
that his claim to be an Apostle rested on his direct commission
from Christ at his conversion, and did not depend on any delegated authority from the Twelve; in that argument his early
missionary activities in Damascus and Jerusalem were irrelevant.
Luke, on the other hand, is telling the story of the expansion of the
Church, and for this Paul's excursion into Arabia was as unim-
portant as was the number and identity of the Apostles whom Paul
met in Jerusalem.

When Paul claims that, following his conversion, he 'did not
confer with flesh and blood', he cannot have forgotten the part
played by Ananias and the Damascus Christians. He must have
been baptized at this time (Rom. 6:3); where else except from
Ananias and his friends did he receive his early instruction in the
faith which he refers to in 1 C. 11:23–6; 15:3–7? His account of
his movements at this time in his letter to the Galatians is as full
of question marks as Luke's story in Acts. He goes 'into Arabia',
he returns 'to Damascus'; three years after his conversion he
spends a fortnight with Peter in Jerusalem, then goes off to
'Syria and Cilicia'; apart from the specified fifteen days with
Peter, Paul does not tell us how long he spent in Arabia or
Damascus, what he did in either place, or how long it was after his
stay with Peter that he left for Syria and Cilicia, or why he went.
If Luke's accuracy is in question, Paul's vagueness is equally
unsatisfactory. In the first half of the book of Acts Luke is not
concerned with detailed chronology. Presumably he did not have
the requisite information, and he is too good a historian to invent
what he does not know. In this passage, apart from Paul's claim
to have visited Arabia, Luke's version tallies in general with what
Paul tells us in Galatians, and supplements the rather bare
outline of his movements which Paul gives there.

19b. for several days: this may mean until Paul was physically able to travel.

20. immediately he proclaimed Jesus: we may take it
either that Luke did not know of Paul's Arabian visit, or that he
was telescoping events for the sake of brevity. Psychologically it
would seem more likely that Paul went off into the Syrian desert
E. of Damascus, which was called Arabia, than that he at once
engaged in missionary activity in Damascus; like an O T prophet,

or Jesus after his Baptism, he sought to know God's will in solitude. It was no doubt there that he began the re-thinking of his faith in the light of his conversion experience, which ultimately crystallized into the 'Gospel according to St Paul' as we find it expressed in his letters. However long this period of wrestling with his problem lasted, he eventually came back to Damascus, although he may have even begun missionary work among Jews in Arabia before his return.

He is the Son of God: for Luke the miracle of Paul's conversion was that the man who came to Damascus to suppress the Nazarene heresy now proclaims the felon who had died under the curse of the Law (Gal. 3:13) as 'the Son of God'. This, as is evidenced in Paul's letters, was his basic conviction about Jesus, as Luke well knew. The title occurs nowhere else in Acts. In *OT* use it could refer to Israel as a nation or to its king as God's anointed; out of this developed the thought of the ideal king, the Messiah, as being Son of God. This is the sense in which it is used here, as is the title occurring in verse 22.

22. proving that Jesus was the Christ: citing scriptural evidence which he claimed to have been fulfilled in Jesus, Paul has now donned the mantle of Stephen with whom he had previously disputed the same issue (6:9).

23. many days: according to Paul (Gal. 1:18) it was anything up to three years from his conversion before he returned to Jerusalem.

24. were watching the gates: Luke attributes Paul's hasty departure from Damascus to the hostility of the Jews who, in their determination to kill him, posted assassins at the city gates. Paul himself in 2 C. 11:32 attributes this watch on the gates to the Ethnarch of King Aretas; it may be that the Jews had enlisted his aid. Aretas was ruler of the Nabataean Arab kingdom, which stretched from the Euphrates to the Red Sea and had its capital at Petra; at one time it had included Damascus, which was now, however, within the Roman province of Syria. If Paul's sojourn in Arabia had included evangelistic activity and had caused trouble among the Jews there, he may have aroused the displeasure of Aretas. The Ethnarch may have been the king's representative in Damascus, with oversight of the Arabs resident in that city.

25. his disciples: Paul had been long enough in Damascus to attract devoted followers.

over the wall . . . in a basket: this ignominious escape, confirmed by Paul in 2 C. 11:33, was apparently for him, as a Roman citizen, the crowning humiliation of his career; he treats it as the nadir of his tale of sufferings for Christ (2 C. 11:23–33).

26. disciples: these were presumably the more conservative Jerusalem Christians, the 'Hebrews' of 6:1. They may have judged Stephen and his supporters to have been too liberal, but they were all Christians, and were naturally suspicious of Paul's motive in view of his past record.

27. Barnabas reappears in Luke's narrative, again in a praiseworthy role (cf. 4:36f.).

the apostles: Luke is not concerned with Paul's problem of his apostolic status in Gal. 1:18f. By the time he wrote Acts, this particular issue was a dead letter, and he treats the Twelve with the respect that is due to their unique office. Later in 14:4, 14 he accords the title of Apostle to both Paul and Barnabas, but here they are distinguished from the Twelve. According to Paul in Gal. 1:19, he saw none of the Twelve on this visit apart from Peter and James the Lord's brother, whom he also appears to classify as an Apostle. Barnabas, who seems to have known Paul well, vouches for his integrity, both in the sincerity of his conversion and in his subsequent missionary activity in Damascus.

28. at Jerusalem: Paul's evangelistic work, presumably after his fortnight's stay with Peter (Gal. 1:18), which no doubt he used to get first-hand information about the words and works of Jesus, was confined to Jerusalem. For this reason he was 'still not known by sight' to the other Christian communities scattered about Judaea (Gal. 1:22).

29. Hellenists: as a Greek-speaking Jew of the Diaspora, Paul was himself a Hellenist, although his training and sympathies made him regard himself as 'a Hebrew born of Hebrews' (Phil. 3:5). The Hellenists with whom he **disputed** in Jerusalem were of the same type and perhaps the same people as those with whom Stephen had argued (6:9). Like Paul himself before his conversion, they appear to have been more fanatically Jewish than the native Palestinians, and their venom, previously concentrated on Stephen and now homicidally directed against the man whom they regarded as the arch-traitor, pursued him throughout his missionary career.

30. the brethren: a name commonly used for Christians in Acts and in Paul's letters. Paul's acquiescence in the concern of the Jerusalem Christians for his safety was, according to his statement in 22:17-21, reinforced by a vision he had in the Temple at this time, in which Christ commanded him to leave Jerusalem and evangelize the Gentiles 'far away'.

Caesarea: the home of Philip (see on 8:40) and a possible port of departure for **Tarsus,** Paul's own city. This is the last we hear of Paul until, almost ten years later, he is brought back by Barnabas to Antioch, which had meantime become an important centre of Gentile Christianity (11:25-6). Presumably it was in these years that Paul engaged in missionary work in 'the regions of Syria and Cilicia', of which latter area Tarsus was the capital, and to which he refers in Gal. 1:21. It was no doubt also in these years that he encountered many of the hardships which he recounts in 2 C. 11:23ff. but which Luke does not include in his narrative.

. **31. the church:** this means the whole Church, consisting of the groups of Christians in **Judaea and Galilee and Samaria.** Missionary activity in **Galilee** so far has not been mentioned; we may connect the existence of Christian believers there with Jesus' own ministry and such references to appearances there of the risen Christ as Mk 14:28; 16:7, together perhaps with the reference to the five hundred brethren of 1 C. 15:6.

peace: as a prelude to the admission of a Gentile into the Church by Peter, the chief Apostle, which opens the next stage of expansion, the mission among the Gentiles, Luke rounds off the first stage, the mission among the Jews, with a picture of the Church in Palestine, for the time being unmolested and growing in numbers **in the comfort of the Holy Spirit.**

THE MINISTRY OF PETER 9:32-43

32. Peter: last heard of on evangelistic work among the Samaritans (8:25), Peter is brought back into Luke's narrative and is shown exercising a pastoral ministry among the Christian communities in western Palestine.

Lydda lay between Jerusalem and Joppa. The **saints** there need not necessarily have been driven from Jerusalem by the persecution; there must have been many small groups of early believers originating from the time of Jesus' own ministry or from Pentecost.

33-4. Aeneas: his cure parallels Jesus' own healing of the paralytic in Lk. 5:18-26, as the restoration to life of Tabitha (verse 36ff.) corresponds with the similar Gospel incident in the case of Jairus' daughter (Lk. 8:49–56). No doubt Luke saw in these events the pattern of Jesus' healing ministry now taking shape in the ministry of his chief Apostle. It is not said that Aeneas was a Christian, but his plight was apparently well known. Peter heals him in the name and in the power of Christ, and, as proof of his cure, bids him get up and either make his bed or get ready for a meal. The Greek could mean either (lit. 'spread your couch'—to sleep on or recline at table).

35. Sharon was the plain that stretched up the coast from Lydda to Mount Carmel. It was a semi-Gentile area, thus marking a further stage towards the mission to the Gentiles. We need not assume that **all** means a mass conversion.

36. Joppa (mod. Jaffa), the port of Jerusalem, was the home of **Tabitha**, a good Christian woman whose name in Greek was **Dorcas,** both words meaning **Gazelle**.

39. widows: the beneficiaries of Dorcas's charitable activities who particularly mourned her death and who point to the clothes they are wearing which she had made for them.

40. Tabitha, rise: in Mark's account of the restoration to life of Jairus' daughter (5:35–43), he quotes the Aramaic words which Jesus used: *Talitha, cumi* ('Little girl . . . arise') (5:41). Here Peter's words would be: '*Tabitha, cumi*', which has given rise to the suggestion that the two incidents may have been confused. No doubt the story here has been influenced by the form of the Jairus story, with echoes also of similar *OT* narratives in 1 Kg. 17:17ff. and 2 Kg. 4:32ff. On the other hand, the raising of the dead to life was included by Jesus as part of the healing ministry of his twelve disciples (Mt. 10:8), and there is no reason why Peter should not have exercised in this way the power and authority given to him by Jesus.

43. Simon, a tanner: this man's trade is mentioned, not merely to distinguish him from Simon Peter, but perhaps also to point to another break with the restrictions of rigid Judaism: Peter lodges with a man who handled skins of animals which were technically unclean. Simon lived **by the seaside** (10:6), segregated against any possible contamination of orthodox Jews.

THE STORY OF CORNELIUS **10:1–48**

The importance which Luke attaches to the next development in his account of the early Church is indicated by the fact that he devotes to it the whole of chapter 10 and much of chapter 11, and refers to it again in chapter 15. Although Paul is the primary agent in the mission to the Gentiles, Luke wishes to make it plain, not only that Peter was in full sympathy with his position, but that, as head of the Church, Peter was the first to give its official blessing to the admission of Gentiles as full and equal members of the New Israel by his action in the case of a Roman centurion and his friends, as is now related.

1. Caesarea had been an insignificant place called 'Strato's Tower'. The Emperor Augustus gave it to Herod the Great, who rebuilt it, equipped it with an artificial harbour, and renamed it after his patron. It had become the administrative capital of Judaea under Roman rule, headquarters of the procurators and a garrison town.

Cornelius is identified by the second of the three names which Roman citizens normally bore at this time. It has been pointed out as evidence of Luke's historical accuracy that by the middle of the first century it was only in such a conservative stratum of Roman society as the army that this brief old-fashioned way of identifying a Roman survived (cf. 27:1).

a centurion was equivalent in status to a modern warrant officer; he had charge of 100 men. It has been noticed that the centurions mentioned in the *NT* generally appear in creditable roles (e.g. 27:1ff.; Lk. 7:2ff., 23:47). Cornelius may have retired from the army and made his home in Caesarea, in view of the reference to his **household** in verse 2. His retinue referred to in verse 7 may sound lavish for a retired sergeant-major, but it should be remembered that a centurion in charge of 100 men was in some respects more like a modern company commander, and that service in the Roman army afforded more opportunities for affluence than the army of today.

Italian Cohort: a cohort consisted of 600 men, the tenth part of a legion. There is evidence on an inscription of the presence of an Italian cohort in Syria later in the century.

2. a devout man: the description of Cornelius indicates that he was a 'God-fearing Gentile', i.e. an adherent of the synagogue, but not a 'proselyte' to the Jewish faith, which involved circumcision (see on 2:10). It has been suggested that Luke himself may have been a 'God-fearer' before he encountered Paul. The **people** to whom Cornelius gave **alms** were Jews.

3. the ninth hour: 3 p.m., one of the statutory Jewish hours of prayer (see on 3:1).

vision: as in the visions of Paul and Ananias in the previous chapter the main point Luke wishes to emphasize is that the hand of God is in the affair; it is no chance whim that induces Cornelius to send for Peter, as it was no coincidence that sent Ananias to Paul. The story must originally have come from Peter, but Luke has written it up with dramatic effect.

an angel of God: as in 8:26 and 27:23 a message from God is described in this way.

4. Cornelius' **terror** was caused by the unexpected appearance of this supernatural being whom he addresses as **Lord** ('Sir').

memorial: Cornelius is assured that his prayers and good works are accepted by God as the equivalent of a sacrificial offering in the Temple, which is called a 'memorial portion' in Lev. 2:2, 9, 16, (cf. Ps. 141:2; Phil. 4:18; Heb. 13:15–16).

5. send men: Cornelius, as a deeply religious man who had found in the faith and practice of Judaism what he had sought in vain in pagan cults, had no doubt also heard with interest of the beliefs of the Nazarenes. The reported presence in Joppa, only thirty-odd miles distant, of the chief spokesman of this new off-shoot of Judaism would make Cornelius anxious to hear of it from Peter himself, and to respond to an inward prompting to send for him.

6. Simon, a tanner: see on 9:43.

7. a devout soldier: Cornelius' batman is also a 'God-fearer'.

9. about the sixth hour: noon. Assuming that the messengers set off on horseback early the following morning, they would reach Joppa about midday.

on the housetop: the flat roofs of oriental houses were used for privacy, sleep or taking the air. Peter had gone up to the roof of Simon's house to pray (Ps. 55:17).

10–16. Peter presumably fell asleep and had a dream (**trance**) which he regarded as a divine revelation. The curious character of his vision may have been influenced by local circumstances: an awning on the roof, or the memory of a ship's sail being lowered in the harbour, may be responsible for the **great sheet** (verse 11) of his dream. The command to **kill and eat** (verse 13) would come not unnaturally from his hunger (verse 10), while the distinction between what is ceremonially 'clean' and what is 'unclean', which he took to apply to the relation between Jews and Gentiles (verse 28), must have been much in his mind as a result of the expansion of the Church.

17. what the vision . . . might mean: in the sequel it transpires that the vision involved a variety of problems connected with
the movement of the Church from its Jewish setting into the
Gentile world. On the basis of Jewish ritual law, which specified
certain types of food permissible for Jews, the vision raised the
question of whether such laws were now obligatory for all
Christians. It also raised the question of whether Jewish Christians
should associate with Gentile Christians who had no such scruples
about dietary regulations. More important, since Gentiles, who
were in orthodox Jewish eyes unclean in any case, did not practise
circumcision, which was a major demand of the Law, it became a
burning issue as to whether they could be admitted to the Church
without being circumcised. All these questions were interrelated,
and bedevilled Paul's missionary work among the Gentiles, since
the conservative Jewish Christian sector of the Church tended to
insist that the practices of Judaism should be accepted also by the
larger Gentile Christian sector. Paul resisted this attitude with all
the vigour he could command, as can be seen from his letter to the
Galatians, and it became the subject of the first General Council of
the Church, which was held at Jerusalem and which is described
in chapter 15; on that occasion he received wholehearted support
from Peter, who based his attitude on this vision and its sequel,
which he held to be a revelation of God's will for the Church.

19. the Spirit said: as a good Jew, Peter in his dream had
refused to eat ritually contaminated food. He had been rebuked
by the divine 'voice' (verse 13), whose command to 'kill and eat'
had pronounced all things clean (cf. Mk 7:14–23). The vision had
been repeated three times to emphasize its divine origin (verse
16). Now he is directed by **the Spirit,** as Cornelius was directed
by the 'angel' (verse 3). There is no point in trying to distingish
between the 'voice', the 'angel' and the 'Spirit'; both Cornelius
and Peter, Luke is saying, were being impelled towards a confrontation which would be vital for the future of the Church by
irresistible signs of God's mighty purpose in Christ.

23. the next day: on the third day after the vision of Cornelius,
arriving in a party of ten (cf. 11:12) at Caesarea on the fourth day.

25. worshipped him: Cornelius treats Peter with the defer-
ence due to a prophet who has a message from God (verse 33).
Peter rejects this homage, as Paul and Barnabas were later to do at
Lystra (14:12ff.; cf. Rev. 19:10; 22:8–9).

28. Peter, whose companions are Jewish Christians from Joppa (verse 45), makes it plain that only the divine revelation which had been granted to him in his vision impelled him to enter the house of a Gentile, which for a law-abiding Jew meant that he became technically unclean.

30–3. Having recounted his own remarkable experience for the benefit of Peter's companions, Cornelius invites Peter to address the gathering of his Gentile relatives and friends.

34–43. In this first recorded sermon to a Gentile audience, Peter adapts the form of the primitive *Kerygma* (which Luke has summarized already in 2:14ff. and 3:12ff., as he does more fully here) to meet the situation and needs of the non-Jewish world. He stresses that God shows no favouritism, but accepts men in all nations who do his will. Israel was indeed chosen as his special channel of revelation, but the Gospel of Christ is a message of reconciliation for all men and Jesus is Lord of all, and Judge of all; through him forgiveness, too, is open to all. Peter's speech is appropriate for 'God-fearing' Gentiles like Cornelius, and presumably his friends, who were not only familiar with the Jewish scriptures, but also may be assumed to have heard something of the beliefs of the Nazarenes, perhaps from Philip if he was now resident in Caesarea (8:40); therefore it differs in character from such other addresses to purely Gentile gatherings as Paul's two speeches at Lystra and Athens (14:15–17, 17:22–31).

38. anointed: at Jesus' Baptism.

41. ate and drank with him: an important proof that the appearances of the risen Christ were no mere subjective visions (cf. Lk. 24:41–3).

42–3. Jesus as Son of Man (Jn 5:27) is appointed to be Judge of all men (Dan. 7:9ff.), Jews and Gentiles alike, 'the living and the dead' (cf. 1 Pet. 4:5). In face of this, men's common need is for **forgiveness** of their **sins,** which is granted to all who commit their lives to Christ.

44–6. the Holy Spirit fell: this is the climax to which the Cornelius story has been leading. Peter's sermon was interrupted by a repetition of the Pentecostal gift. Now, to the amazement of Peter's Jewish-Christian companions, **the believers from among the circumcized,** this group of Gentiles experienced the same fervour, **speaking in tongues** with ecstatic cries of praise. The Gentile Pentecost was clear evidence that the blessing of God was upon Gentiles as much as upon Jews. The external manifestations implied that both had received equally the same inward gift.

47. forbid: see on 8:36.

baptizing: the gift of the Spirit was normally associated with baptism. Here uniquely, except for the Jewish Pentecost, the Spirit is given independently and unmediated. Baptism now follows as the mark of the full incorporation of Gentiles into the New Israel.

48. he commanded: Peter does not himself baptize the converts. Some confession of faith may be implied by the words **in the name of Jesus Christ.** The Trinitarian formula is not yet in use.

some days: Peter remains in the Gentile household in confirmation of the new relationship.

PETER DEFENDS HIS ACTION **11:1–18**

Luke now recounts how Peter was taken to task by the right-wing Jewish Christians in Jerusalem for mixing with Gentiles in Caesarea. This charge he answers by a full recital of the Cornelius story, stressing the unmistakable signs of divine guidance culminating in the repetition of the Pentecostal gift of the Spirit. Convinced by his testimony, the ultra-conservative element in the mother church of Jerusalem acknowledged the right of Gentiles to be included in the New Israel. That this was more a recognition in principle than a final settlement of the problem is clear from the following chapters.

1. the Apostles and the brethren: the rest of the Twelve may have been engaged, like Peter, in pastoral and evangelistic work in various parts of Palestine. The 'brethren' represent the ordinary Jewish Christian membership of the Church, some of whom, Hellenists like Stephen, would no doubt be sympathetic to the new development; others who adhered strongly to Jewish tradition would hear the news with deep misgiving.

2. when Peter went up to Jerusalem: although it is not stated that Peter was recalled to Jerusalem to account for his actions, he obviously expected criticism, since he took with him the six men who had been witnesses of the Gentile Pentecost to support his story (verse 12). Perhaps in order to avoid the impression that the chief Apostle was summoned by the others, the Western text rephrases, and reads: 'So Peter after some time wished to go to Jerusalem . . .'

the circumcision party: the Greek is the same here as in 10:45 and, on the face of it, is simply an expression meaning Jewish Christians. But, since the Church in Palestine at this time

consisted of no one else, apart from Cornelius and his friends, the
meaning must be, as *RSV* suggests, the extremists among the
Jewish Christians who were so deeply attached to the historic
institutions and traditions of their forefathers that they could not
believe that it was the will of God that they should be abandoned.
There were within the Church some who were still Pharisees
(15:5) and many who had been priests (6:7); these were not
likely to share Stephen's views about the transitory nature of the
Law and the Temple. When the extremists **criticized** Peter, Luke
is drawing attention for the fourth time to the human frailty that
has always marred the Church, even in these early days; the
hypocrisy of Ananias (5:2), the resentment of the Hellenists (6:1),
the attempted bribery of Simon (8:18), and now partisanship.

3. Why did you . . . eat with them?: the most heinous
offence of which Peter had been guilty, in the eyes of the extremists, was not that he had baptized Gentiles, but that he had
associated with them and sat at their table; he had broken the Law.
Gentiles ate 'unclean' food; moreover, they were **uncircumcised,**
and therefore outside the covenant relationship with God, which
must be upheld by the New Israel as staunchly as by the Old Israel.

4–17. With minor variations, but with even more vividness,
Peter summarizes the events narrated in the previous chapter.

14. all your household includes, not only the family of
Cornelius, but also his slaves and attendants. It can be argued
that, where a whole 'household' in this sense became Christian,
any children would also be baptized, on the basis of 1 C. 7:14
(cf. 16:15, 33; 18:8; 1 C. 1:16).

15. at the beginning: at Pentecost.

16. see on 1:5.

18. repentance unto life: God has by his grace made it
possible for Gentiles as well as for Jews to share in the new life in
Christ—and to do so without the necessity of first becoming
Jewish proselytes by circumcision. This is the epoch-making
decision of the Jerusalem church authorities which has impelled
Luke to devote so much space to the conversion and baptism of
Cornelius. It opens the door officially to the Gentile mission and,
although it silences the rigorists only for a time (cf. 15:1) and does
not settle the problem which they had raised in verse 3, there can
now in Luke's view be no retreat from the principle that membership of the Church is available to Gentiles, as well as to Jews, by
faith and baptism alone.

THE FIRST GENTILE CHURCH 11:19–26

With the ratification by the Jerusalem mother church of Peter's action in admitting the first group of Gentiles into the Church as his preface, Luke now launches into the main theme of the book of Acts—the expansion of the Church into the whole Gentile world. Again he emphasizes the part played by anonymous believers in spreading Christianity. Without detracting from the massive contribution of Paul or ignoring the significant roles of Peter and Philip, Luke makes it plain, as he has already done in the case of the Palestinian Christian communities, that so also, farther afield in Phoenicia and Cyprus, the Gospel was first proclaimed by men whose names have not been recorded. More important still, taking us back to the point in his story at which the sympathizers with Stephen's radical views were driven from Jerusalem, he shows that it was some of these unknown Hellenists who, without benefit of apostolic approval, laid the foundations of the first Gentile church at Antioch, which was not only to become the springboard for the advance of Christianity into the pagan world, but was also to overshadow the mother church at Jerusalem and become the effective headquarters of the Church in the next stage of its history.

19. those who were scattered: referring back to 8:1, 4.
Phoenicia: the coastal strip N. of Caesarea, containing Tyre, Ptolemais and Sidon, whose Christian communities are referred to later in Acts (21:4, 7; 27:3).
Cyprus was the original home of Barnabas (4:36) and Mnason (21:16).
Antioch: capital of the Roman province of Syro-Cilicia, beautifully situated on the Orontes, 15 miles from the sea. It had a population of 800,000, and ranked next to Rome and Alexandria as the third city of the Empire. The character and culture of the city were Greek, although the people were mostly Syrian, and there was a strong Jewish minority. Antioch was notorious for its low moral standards.

20. Cyrene is referred to also in 2:10, 6:9, 13:1.
Greeks: some MSS. have 'Greeks' (i.e., Hellenes), some have 'Hellenists'. If 'Hellenists' is right it must be used in the sense of 'Greek-speakers', and not in the sense of 6:1, where it means obviously 'Greek-speaking Jews'. The evangelists in question were themselves Greek-speaking Jews, and the contrast here is clearly

between those in verse 19 who addressed themselves to (Greek-speaking) Jews and those who in Antioch preached the word to (Greek-speaking) Gentiles. This for Luke is the great break-through of the Gospel. From its Galilean beginnings it has spread under the impulse of the Spirit to overseas Jews and proselytes (2:9ff.), Samaritans (8:5ff.), legally unacceptable adherents of Judaism (8:27), half-Jews (8:40, 9:32), Gentile 'God-fearers' (Cornelius and his friends), culminating now in a mission to out-and-out 'pagans'. It should be noticed that, since Luke's interest is primarily in the movement westwards from Jerusalem to Rome, he is not concerned with any possible missionary activities to the east of Palestine or south into Egypt.

the Lord Jesus: proclamation of Jesus as the Christ (Messiah) would mean little or nothing to Gentiles. Although for God-fearers like Cornelius and his friends the word 'Christ' would have deep significance (10:36), for the benefit of pure Gentiles Jesus must be presented primarily as 'Lord'.

21. the hand of the Lord: an OT expression meaning 'the power of God' (Isa. 59:1; 66:14).

22. Barnabas: as in the case of Philip's Samaritan mission (8:14), the delegation from the Jerusalem church was sent in no unfriendly spirit. This is obvious from the choice of Barnabas, himself a Cypriot like some of the evangelists at Antioch (verse 20), and who for this reason as well as on account of his character (verse 24) would be calculated to handle the new situation there with tact and sympathy, unlike the rigorists of verse 2.

25. In view of the rapid growth of the church at Antioch (verses 21, 24), it seemed to Barnabas that the best man to direct the mission there would be Paul; this confirms the indication in 9:27 that the two men knew each other well. Paul had been sent off to **Tarsus** in Cilicia for his own safety several years previously (9:30; cf. Gal. 2:1). In this period, as he says himself, he had been engaged in missionary work in the province of Syro-Cilicia (Gal. 1:21), whence having eventually located him Barnabas brought him back to Antioch where they worked together for a year building up the church (verse 26).

26. Christians: in the NT the word occurs only here, in 26:28 and in 1 Pet. 4:16; and it is not used by Christians of themselves. In Acts Christians are described normally as 'disciples', 'believers', 'saints', 'brethren' or 'Nazarenes'. It would seem that the name **Christians** would naturally originate in a Gentile community, since the word 'Christ' would be used there as a personal name for Jesus, rather than as the Greek translation of the title 'Messiah', which in such circles would have no meaning. **Christians** would probably therefore be the popular way in Antioch of describing those who claimed to be followers of Christ, as distinct from the Jewish community.

FAMINE RELIEF 11:27–30

27. in these days: while Paul and Barnabas were building up the church at Antioch.

prophets were a recognized feature in the life of the primitive Church. They were grouped with apostles, evangelists, pastors and teachers as instrumental in furthering the spread of the Gospel and the spiritual growth of Christian communities (Eph. 4:11). According to 1 C. 14:1–5 their particular function was to strengthen, encourage, console and edify; they were also, like the *OT* prophets, 'fore-tellers' as well as 'forth-tellers', both types of pronouncement being regarded as revelations imparted to the prophet by God through the Spirit. They seem to have exercised a distinctive ministry within the Church until about the end of the second century.

28. Agabus appears here, as in 21:10, in the role of 'fore-teller'. The Western text begins verse 28: 'And there was much gladness. And when we were collected together, one of them named Agabus said . . .' This odd appearance of 'we' before the beginning of the 'we'-passages at 16:10 in the standard text probably indicates a desire to identify Luke with Antioch, of which traditionally he was a native.

a great famine over all the world: while there is no evidence of a general famine over the Roman Empire **in the days of** the Emperor **Claudius** (A.D. 41–54), according to Suetonius there was frequent dearth during his reign. The phrase **over all the world,** however, may mean 'over all the land' (of Palestine). Josephus records a famine in Judaea about A.D. 46, when Queen Helena of Adiabene in Mesopotamia, who had become a Jewish convert and was on a visit to Jerusalem, bought corn and figs overseas, and had them brought to Jerusalem for distribution to the inhabitants. Such largess would presumably not be extended to the Nazarenes.

29. relief: the mother church in Jerusalem was notoriously poor, partly perhaps because of the pooling of resources in the early days, and partly because of the loss of well-to-do Hellenists by persecution. The better-off Gentile Christians at Antioch, setting a pattern later to be developed by Paul among other young Gentile churches (1 C. 16:1), express their concern and sense of solidarity by sending help to their famine-stricken **brethren.**

30. elders: the despatch of the contribution from Antioch to 'the elders' does not mean that the Apostles were no longer in Jerusalem; following the Jewish practice, elders would be heads of families, perhaps in this case presiding over the house-churches, and whose business it would be to administer relief as distinct from the apostolic ministry of preaching and teaching (cf. 6:2ff., and see on 14:23).

Barnabas and Saul: the dating of events in the early part of Acts can only be approximate. If we accept Josephus' date for the famine in Judaea as *c.* A.D. 46, and reckon the visit of Paul and Barnabas to Jerusalem with the gift from Antioch as having taken place in that year, it fits in well with what Paul himself says in Gal. 2:1–10. There he describes his second visit to Jerusalem as occurring fourteen years after his conversion, which may be dated on other grounds in A.D. 32, approximately three years after the Crucifixion of Jesus. Paul's concern at this point in his letter to the Galatians is to maintain that his fundamental proposition that Gentiles should be admitted into the Church without submitting to circumcision was approved at a private meeting he had on this visit with James, the head of the mother church, and two of the Twelve, Peter and John. It would be natural for this topic to be discussed, since Barnabas was now for the first time reporting back to Jerusalem on the Gentile mission at Antioch. It was further recognized by the leaders of the Church that Paul and Barnabas should make the mission to the Gentiles their special province, while the Apostles should operate mainly in Palestine. Paul speaks of having gone to Jerusalem on this occasion 'by revelation' (Gal. 2:2), which may be a reference to the prophecy of Agabus, and concludes his account of the visit by saying that the Apostles' request to him to 'remember the poor' was the very thing he had been anxious to do (Gal. 2:10).

Luke does not mention the circumcision issue at this point since he deals with it in detail in chapter 15 in connection with the official decision on the matter by the leaders of the Church at the Council of Jerusalem three years later in A.D. 49. In the meantime, Paul and Barnabas have completed their first missionary tour among the Gentiles (A.D. 46–8) (chapters 13–14), as agreed

on this famine relief visit, and the Jewish Christian rigorists have
been stirring up trouble on the circumcision issue both in Antioch
and in the Galatian churches which Paul and Barnabas founded
on this first missionary journey. Paul writes his letter to these
Galatians with this question in the forefront of his mind, either
after his return to Antioch or on his way to the Council of Jerusalem (14:26–15:2)—i.e. in A.D. 48 or 49.

PERSECUTION OF THE CHURCH BY HEROD AGRIPPA 12:1–25

Chronologically the events described next must have taken place
before the famine relief visit of Paul and Barnabas to Jerusalem
in A.D. 46 (11:30). Not only was Peter in Jerusalem then—
whereas in this chapter he leaves the city and disappears for his
own safety—but also, and more conclusively, Herod's death took
place in A.D. 44. Of course, it is possible that the two incidents
included here by Luke—the imprisonment of Peter and the death
of Herod—were not connected; Peter may have been arrested at
any time during Herod's reign—i.e. between A.D. 41 and 44—in
which case his departure 'to another place' (verse 17) may have
been temporary, and the death of the king may have made it
possible for him to be back in Jerusalem by A.D. 46 when Paul
and Barnabas arrived.

Dramatically, however, it is entirely appropriate that Luke
should order his material in this manner. He is stressing two
points: firstly, that by the enforced departure of Peter from
Jerusalem the stage is cleared for the emergence of Paul as the
leading figure in the expansion of the Church into the pagan world;
and, secondly, that in the violent action of Herod the attack on
the Church by the whole Jewish people reaches its climax. Christ
and his people have been finally rejected by the Jews; it is time
now to turn to the Gentiles. Luke suggests that he is less concerned
with accurate dating at this point—or perhaps he was himself
uncertain—by prefacing his account of Herod's persecution with
the vague expression 'about that time'.

1. Herod the king: this was Herod Agrippa I, grandson of
Herod the Great, to be distinguished from his uncle the Herod of
the Gospels—Herod Antipas, tetrarch of Galilee (Lk. 3:1). He
was born in 11 B.C., brought up in Rome on intimate terms with
the imperial family, and owed his Roman name to the friendship
of his father Aristobulus, son of Herod the Great, with the states-
man Agrippa who had died the year before Herod Agrippa was

born. Successive Roman emperors bestowed Palestinian territory upon him. From Caligula he received the tetrarchies of his uncles Philip and Antipas, and from Claudius Judaea and Samaria. By A.D. 41 he ruled with the title of king over almost as much of Palestine as had his grandfather Herod the Great. In his short reign of three years (A.D. 41–4) he sought to counter the distaste on the part of the Jewish religious leaders for his Roman background and Edomite ancestry by his sedulous observance of Jewish customs and support of the Jewish faith; it was, no doubt, as part of this policy that he sought to win general approval by this attack on the Nazarenes.

2. James the brother of John: James the son of Zebedee, who had been one of the earliest disciples of Jesus (Mk 1:19–20), now becomes the first of the Twelve to be martyred. It was doubtless because of the association of the two brothers in the prophetic words of Jesus in Mk 10:38–40 that it has sometimes been held that John too was martyred, either at this point, or at least before the fall of Jerusalem; there is, however, a much stronger tradition that he survived to a ripe old age at Ephesus.

3. to arrest Peter also: it is not clear why James should have been the first Apostle to be beheaded; perhaps he was the only one of the Twelve, apart from Peter, who was in Jerusalem at the time. Obviously the arrest of Peter, leader of the Twelve, pending public sentence and execution was in pursuance of Herod's policy of currying favour with the Sadducees and Pharisees, whose hostility to the Nazarenes since the persecution of Stephen's sympathizers extended to all but extreme right-wing Jewish Christians.

the days of Unleavened Bread: technically the week following 14th Nisan, the day on which the Passover was observed. As in Lk. 22:1 Luke here regards the two terms as synonymous, in the sense of the whole season of the festival (cf. verse 4), during which it would be unseemly to stage a public execution.

4. four squads: each squad or quaternion, had four soldiers who guarded the prisoner in turn during the four three-hour watches of the day and of the night.

5. in prison: probably in the Tower of Antonia, headquarters of the Roman garrison in Jerusalem.

6. soldiers . . . and sentries: this seems to imply that Peter had a soldier of the quaternion on either side of him, and that the other two were on guard outside the door of his cell.

7. an angel of the Lord appeared: Luke clearly regards Peter's escape as a miracle, a divine intervention by a supernatural visitant (cf. Lk. 2:9); some would regard it as no less of a 'miracle' if it was engineered by sympathizers among the guard. At all events, an unexpected and dramatic escape from prison would seem to be indicated. The graphic description, including the addition in the Western text of verse 10 ('they went down the seven steps') suggests Peter's own recital of the event to the astonished circle in Mary's house (verse 12), including John Mark, from whom Luke may have heard the story.

12. the house of Mary: traditionally the house with the upper room where the Last Supper was held, which for this reason had become the first meeting place of the Jerusalem Christians (1:13–14).

the mother of John ... Mark: the reference in Mk 14:51 to the 'young man' who fled from the Garden of Gethsemane is usually taken to be an autobiographical detail, and fits in with the tradition that it was from Mark's mother's house that Jesus and his disciples made their way to Gethsemane after the Last Supper. If John Mark was the young man in question, he may also have been the guide to the rendezvous referred to in Mk 14:13. His Jewish name John is gradually dropped in Acts, and his Gentile name Mark, by which he was more commonly known in the Church, is used to identify him. He features in Acts as one of the early missionaries to the Gentiles, in company with Paul and Barnabas, who was his cousin. In the NT outside Acts, he is referred to by Paul as a 'fellow-worker' (Phm. 24) and a 'comfort' (Col. 4:10–11), apparently during Paul's last imprisonment in Rome (cf. 2 Tim. 4:11). His association with Peter in Rome was even more significant, and is attested both by the NT (cf. 1 Pet. 5:13, where the suggestion seems to be that it had been through Peter's influence that Mark became a Christian) and by very early tradition. Mark is characterized by Papias as the 'interpreter of Peter' who, on the basis of that connexion, incorporated Peter's preaching in the Gospel which he compiled soon after Peter's martyrdom in A.D. 64. Luke having used Mark's Gospel in writing his own version—no doubt because of the authority of Peter which lies behind it—gives Mark more prominence in Acts than his minor missionary role would seem to warrant, both on this account and also probably because he was indebted to Mark for much of his information about the early days of the Jerusalem church.

13. the door of the gateway: the door opening from the courtyard on to the street.

Rhoda: or Rose.

15. his angel: as distinct from the **angel of the Lord** in verse 7, this means Peter's guardian angel, or spirit counterpart—or, as we should say, his 'ghost'. In late Jewish thought such an 'angel' resembled a person, and could be mistaken for him.

17. motioning to them with his hand: again the vividness of the narrative suggests an eye-witness account: the excitement of the maid too overcome to open the door, the incredulity of the household who thought the girl was 'seeing things', Peter's exasperation, and the shrill clamour of welcome which threatens to rouse the neighbours.

James and ... the brethren: the fact that James is referred to without further identification indicates, not so much an awareness on the part of Luke's readers as to which particular James was meant, as the skill of the narrator: neither Peter nor his audience would be in any doubt that this was James the Lord's brother (Gal. 1:19) who, during the absence of the Twelve on their pastoral enterprises and subsequent to Peter's final departure from Jerusalem, assumed the leadership of the mother church. For prudential reasons Peter on his escape had not gone to his house. At this early date, while the Apostles still frequented Jerusalem, the singling out of James suggests that none of them was in the city at the time. James had probably not yet gained the ascendancy which he appears to have progressively acquired, as evidenced when Paul and Barnabas visit the city in A.D. 46 (Gal. 2:1-10), at the Council of Jerusalem in A.D. 49 (15:13) and on Paul's last visit in A.D. 56 (21:18). The 'brethren' at this time would not be so much the governing body of the Jerusalem church, the 'elders' of 21:18 associated with James, but the Christian community generally, apart from those who were meeting in the house of Mary.

James (Mk 6:3) was either a full brother of Jesus, or a step-brother if Joseph had had a previous marriage, or perhaps a cousin. Understandably sceptical of Jesus' messianic role during his Galilean ministry (Mk 3:21, 31), he appears to have been converted by an encounter with the risen Christ (1 C. 15:7). Doubtless it was because of his relationship to Jesus that he became the head of the Jerusalem church. Paul seems to have regarded him as an Apostle (Gal. 1:19), and he emerges from the

record in Acts as the foremost supporter of the conservative Jewish
Christian position (15:13ff., 21:18ff.). He was called 'James the
Just' on account of his moral rectitude, and his devotion to Jewish
law and institutions made him more acceptable to the Jewish
religious authorities than the Twelve. He may be the author of the
Letter of James. He is said to have been martyred about A.D. 62.
another place: various suggestions have been made as to where
Peter went when he left Jerusalem at this time. Some scholars
believe that Peter's imprisonment preceded his missionary tour of
Palestine (9:32ff.); in this case 'another place' would mean Lydda.
The tradition that he went to Rome at this time, where he re-
mained to become bishop, cannot be accepted, since he is in
Jerusalem during the famine relief visit of Paul and Barnabas in
A.D. 46 (Gal. 2:1ff.), and again at the Council of Jerusalem in
A.D. 49 (15:2ff.). Perhaps he simply went into hiding; but pos-
sibly 'another place' may have been Antioch, where later Paul
took him to task for his ambivalent attitude to Gentile Christians
(Gal. 2:11ff.).

19. According to Roman law, a guard allowing a prisoner to
escape was subject to the same penalty as awaited the prisoner.
In this case it is more likely that Herod suspected connivance on
the part of the sentries.
Caesarea was in fact in Judaea—indeed, its administrative
capital. As a predominantly Gentile city it was, however, not
regarded by strict Jews as being properly Jewish territory.

20. Herod was angry: it is not known what occasioned the
king's anger. The account of Herod's death, which generally
agrees with that given by Josephus, would seem to have been included by Luke to round off the first section of his history of the
early Church with this evidence of God's judgment on the head of
the Jewish people which had now totally rejected Christ and his
disciples. It is, at the same time, a dire warning of the fate that
awaits persecutors of the Church.
Tyre and Sidon were the chief cities on the coast of Phoenicia,
NW. of Galilee, centres of commerce and of a far-flung shipping
trade since *OT* times and were dependent for their food supplies
on the hinterland of Galilee. Whatever had been the cause of their
dispute with Herod (probably of a commercial nature), it was in
their interests to restore good relations with the ruler of the territory which sustained their economy. To this end they had **persuaded** (i.e. bribed) **Blastus** to act as mediator to secure the

king's favour. He is described as Herod's **chamberlain,** in charge of the royal household; but he is otherwise unknown.

21-2. on an appointed day: according to Josephus (*Antiquities* XIX. viii. 2), it was at a festival in honour of the Emperor Claudius that Herod, arrayed in a silver robe, entered the theatre at Caesarea as the sun rose; the reflection of its rays on the monarch's vestments so dazzled the spectators that they hailed him as a god. Josephus does not mention the presence of the delegates from Tyre and Sidon, but such an occasion could well have been thought appropriate for Herod to make a public declaration that their plea had been granted.

23. eaten by worms and died: again Josephus gives circumstantial details which amplify Luke's narrative. He records that Herod neither rejected the divine title which the crowd bestowed on him nor rebuked them for their flattery, but that shortly afterwards he saw an owl sitting above him and, being highly superstitious and recalling an earlier prophecy that this would presage his death, he was overcome by violent internal pains of which he died in his palace five days later. Both Josephus and Luke attribute his death to his impiety in accepting **the glory** that belongs only to God. In biblical terms the **angel of the Lord** is the agent of the divine judgment (cf. 2 Kg. 19:35). The physical cause of Herod's death may have been a cyst produced by tapeworm.

24. As in 6:7 and 9:31, Luke comments on the irresistible advance of the faith, despite domestic troubles (6:1ff.), the machinations of the Jews (8:1ff.), and now the violence of a tyrant who has met his proper fate.

25. from Jerusalem: although 'to Jerusalem' is a better attested reading than 'from Jerusalem', *RSV* must be right in preferring the latter. In 11:30 Paul and Barnabas left Antioch for Jerusalem with the famine relief fund. Luke has followed this with the interlude of Peter's imprisonment and Herod's death, introduced rather for dramatic effect than because it followed in chronological order: he indicates that these events took place some time before the famine relief visit by referring to it now as an accomplished fact. The explanation of the better attested reading 'to Jerusalem' may be that a very early copyist inadvertently wrote this instead of 'to Antioch', which common sense would indicate to be what Luke meant. Paul and Barnabas are now back in Antioch, accompanied from Jerusalem by John Mark. From there they are to set out on the first of Paul's great missionary enterprises into the Gentile world.

THE PROGRESS OF THE GOSPEL FROM ANTIOCH TO ROME 13:1-28:31

FIRST MISSIONARY JOURNEY 13:1-14:28

IN CYPRUS 13:1-12

This would appear to be the half-way mark in Acts. Luke has described the advance of Christianity from Jerusalem through Palestine to Antioch, which has become the effective centre of the Church's activities. It is from Antioch that Paul now sets out on the first of his three momentous missionary tours which takes him by way of Cyprus into the heart of Asia Minor, where in the province of Galatia he founds the young churches to which, as is now generally accepted, he later writes his Letter to the Galatians. In his earlier years as a Christian Paul had embarked on missionary enterprises in 'the regions of Syria and Cilicia' (Gal. 1:21), but we are justified in calling this his 'first official missionary journey', since he now sets out as the accredited agent of the church at Antioch to proclaim the Gospel among the Gentiles.

1. prophets and teachers: it is unlikely that Luke means us to distinguish the 'prophets' from the 'teachers' among the five names given. The leadership of the church at Antioch is of this mixed character, as opposed to the church at Jerusalem, where the twelve Apostles had been predominant. Prophecy and teaching rank next in importance to the apostolic office in the order of precedence Paul gives in 1 C. 12:28 (cf. Eph. 4:11). Barnabas properly heads the list as the apostolic delegate (11:22) and Paul, as yet a comparative newcomer to Antioch, is placed last. The other three are otherwise unknown. **Symeon who was called Niger**—i.e. 'the Black'—may have been an African. Some have identified him with Simon of Cyrene (Lk. 23:26). **Lucius of Cyrene** was perhaps one of the Cyrenians mentioned in 11:20. There is no reason to connect him with the Lucius of Rom. 16:21 and, although by the fourth century the temptation to identify him with Luke proved irresistible, it is unlikely that the author of Acts threw off his mantle of anonymity at this point only. **Manaen** is described as having been the foster-brother or intimate friend of **Herod the tetrarch** (Herod Antipas), meaning that he had been brought up as a boy with the young Herod at court. It has been pointed out that Luke is particularly interested in or well acquainted with the affairs of the Herodian household, and Manaen may have been the source of his information.

2. worshipping . . . and fasting: this would seem to suggest that at a service of divine worship one of the prophets was moved by the Spirit to propose the mission of Paul and Barnabas. Fasting as a common Jewish practice had been assumed by Jesus to be part of the Christian life (Mt. 6:16).

3. laid their hands on them: in response to what was evidently the will of God, the two most outstanding figures in the church at Antioch are sent off with the blessing of the rest of the leaders. In commissioning Barnabas and Saul by the imposition of hands, the other office-bearers invest them with authority to act on behalf of the Christian community at Antioch, and symbolically identify the whole congregation with their enterprise.

4. sent out by the Holy Spirit: again Luke emphasizes that no development in the expansion of the Church happened by chance, least of all this major undertaking.

Seleucia was the port of Antioch, sixteen miles distant from it.

Cyprus was an obvious starting-point for the mission, since Barnabas was a native of that country.

5. Salamis, chief town of Cyprus, was on the east side of the island opposite Syria, and about 130 miles from Seleucia. Its site was a few miles from the present-day Famagusta.

synagogues of the Jews: there was a large Jewish element (hence the plural, synagogues) in Salamis which was a busy commercial centre. Augustus had given a half-share in the rich copper mines of the island to Herod the Great. In accordance with Paul's belief that the Gospel must be first preached to God's chosen people, the Jews, synagogues provided his natural platform in a new area. There was the added advantage, however, that they were also a point of contact with 'God-fearing Greeks' (see on 10:2) from whom there was an easy and latterly normal transition to a full Gentile mission.

John to assist them: i.e. John Mark, cousin of Barnabas (cf.

12:25). He is attached to the two senior missionaries, Paul and Barnabas, in the same capacity in which Timothy was to be associated with Paul and Silvanus on the second missionary journey (16:1ff.). His duties may have been merely to make travel arrangements, or he may also have taken some part in the teaching work of the mission.

6. Paphos: ninety miles W. of Salamis, was at that time the seat of government.

magician: there is no reason to suppose that Luke invented this incident in which Paul discomfits a magician, as Peter had already done in the case of Simon Magus (8:9ff.), to show that Paul's apostolic authority was equal to Peter's (but see on 14:8). The two occasions are quite different and magicians or astrologers were rife in the superstitious Roman world. This man, Bar-Jesus, is described by Luke as a **false prophet,** in that he wrongfully claimed to be a channel of divine communication. It was not unusual for such a character to be attached to the household of a Roman dignitary.

7. proconsul: Cyprus was a senatorial province of the Empire, and as such was administered by an official of this rank, as Luke correctly records.

Sergius Paulus: a man of this name is known to have been a *curator* of the Tiber in the reign of Claudius; he may subsequently have been made proconsul of Cyprus. He is described as **a man of intelligence** (i.e. of intellectual curiosity), who would be interested to hear the 'philosophy' of the two itinerant teachers.

8. Elymas: it is not clear what Luke means by the words in brackets. Elymas is not a translation of Bar-Jesus, though it could be that the man was known by both names. Josephus (*Ant.* xx. vii. 2) mentions a Cypriot magician called Atomos; he may have been confused with Elymas, since the Western text gives the magician's name as Hetoimas.

9. Saul . . . called Paul: like many other Jews, Paul had two names, one Jewish and one Graeco-Roman (cf. John—Mark, Symeon—Niger). His Roman name comes into use here, no doubt partly because another Paulus has just been mentioned, but principally because he is moving now into Gentile territory where he is commonly known by his Gentile name.

10. son of the devil: an allusion to the magician's name, Bar-Jesus, which means 'son of salvation'. Paul, indignant at the attempt of the magician to discredit the message of the missionaries in the eyes of the governor (verse 8) denounces him in words which echo the *OT.*

11. you shall be blind: Luke's narrative shows Paul using his apostolic authority to punish an enemy of the faith with temporary blindness; it may be a conscious repetition of his own conversion experience in reverse, in order that out of physical blindness inward light might come. Some would no doubt prefer to think that the story has grown in the telling, and that strong words of Paul referring to the magician's spiritual blindness have given rise to a legend. Luke implies, however, that it took more than words to bring about a change of heart in the governor.

12. the proconsul believed: i.e. became converted to Christianity. It is not recorded that the governor was baptized, which would have been the inevitable sequel to profession of faith. While a superstitious Roman might well have been persuaded by such a miracle—if miracle there was—the conversion of so notable a personage as the governor of Cyprus might be expected to have been made more of in later Christian tradition. Although it is perhaps too facile to say that the Apostles mistook the proconsul's courtesy for conversion, the encounter can still be counted a victory for them if they succeeded in impressing the governor with the power of their message and shook his confidence in his pet soothsayer.

AT PISIDIAN ANTIOCH **13:13-52**

13. Paul and his company: from now on Paul is the acknowledged leader of the missionary team. So far as we know, the 'company' consisted of Barnabas and Mark, but there may have been other Christians in the party making their way for various reasons to Asia Minor.

Perga in the south of Asia Minor was not itself on the coast, but lay 12 miles inland from the seaport of Attalia, from which the Apostles sailed on their return journey (14:25). In this instance also, they possibly disembarked at Attalia and made their way by road to Perga, although it had an inland harbour on the river Cestrus which may have been the ship's destination. Luke is generally particular on these matters.

Pamphylia was the district in the south of Asia Minor between Lycia to the west and Cilicia to the east. North of it lay Pisidia.

John left them: Mark's defection from the missionary team, which later led to a notable quarrel between Paul and Barnabas

(15:36ff.) has caused much speculation. Was there a clash of personalities between Paul and Mark? Did Mark resent his cousin's being relegated to second place in the team, even though Barnabas characteristically and loyally accepted it? Was he intimidated by the possible hazards of a venture into the heart of unknown territory? Did he disapprove of Paul's radical views on the admission of Gentiles into the Church? Or was he merely homesick for Jerusalem? Luke does not tell us.

14. Antioch of Pisidia: Pisidia was the southern part of the Roman province of Galatia. Antioch, though actually in Phrygia, was the chief city of the region, and a Roman colony. It lay near the border of Pisidia and was later incorporated in it. To reach it from Perga, the two missionaries had to cross the Taurus mountains, and it has been suggested that this difficult and in places dangerous journey was undertaken because the swamps of Perga had brought on one of Paul's recurring attacks of malaria— if indeed this is what the 'thorn in the flesh' was (2. C. 12:7); in writing later to the churches he founded in Galatia on this first missionary journey, he speaks of his original mission there as being the result of illness (Gal. 4:13). The highland air of Antioch, 3,600 feet above sea level, may have assisted his recovery. It has been objected, however, that since a sick man would be unlikely to face the rigours of a mountain pass, no doubt 'in danger from rivers, danger from robbers' (2 C. 11:26), Paul's real intention was perhaps to reach the great road to Ephesus which passed through Antioch, with Rome as his eventual goal. Illness at Antioch may have prolonged his stay there, and made him change his plans. On the other hand, his encounter with Sergius Paulus may have fired him with the desire to evangelize a Roman colony; he seems to have devoted much of his attention to this particular field of activity: as well as Antioch, Lystra, Philippi and Corinth were all Roman colonies (see on 16:12). Whatever brought Paul to Antioch, he made his first recorded proclamation of the Gospel to the Jewish community in the synagogue in the course of a sabbath service, as was his normal practice.

15. after the reading: the sabbath worship of the synagogue at this time consisted of a recital of the Jewish creed, or sh*e*ma ('Hear, O Israel: the Lord our God is one Lord'), followed by prescribed prayers. Then came the reading of the Law, based on a lectionary, with appropriate passages from the Prophets. The address which followed could be given by any competent person invited to speak, which he did seated (cf. Lk. 4:16ff.). On this occasion Paul 'stood up' (verse 16), and presumably moved from his place in the congregation to take his seat on the platform. **rulers of the synagogue:** the leading layman, normally an elder, was called 'the ruler of the synagogue', and was responsible for the arrangement of the services as well as for the use and maintenance of the building. He appointed members of the congregation to read the prayers and the lessons, and called on suitable persons to preach. Crispus (18:8) and Sosthenes (18:17) held such office. At Antioch there was apparently more than one ruler (cf. Mk 5:22). Paul's presence would already be known to the Jewish community, since he presumably found lodgings in the Jewish quarter; his dress probably also marked him out as a rabbi.

16–41. Paul addresses himself to the mixed congregation of Jews and Gentile adherents ('God-fearers'; see on 10:2). His sermon, which has affinities with those of Peter at Pentecost and Stephen before the Sanhedrin, is nevertheless distinctively Pauline. While Luke is responsible for this summarized form, we may take it that he gives here the gist of a typical Pauline address in hellenistic Jewish synagogues. The recital of early Hebrew history (verses 17–22), which may have been mainly for the benefit of the Gentiles in the congregation, leads up to the proclamation of Jesus as the promised Son of David (verse 23) (cf. Rom. 1:3).

19. seven nations: cf. Dt. 7:1.

four hundred and fifty years, apparently reckoning from patriarchal times to the occupation of Canaan.

20. Samuel was regarded as last of the judges and first of the prophets after Moses.

21. of the tribe of Benjamin: from which Paul himself claimed descent (Phil. 3:5).

forty years: the length of Saul's reign is not stated in the *OT*. However, this figure is also given by Josephus.

22. The quotation combines Ps. 89:20; 1 Sam. 13:14; Isa. 44:28; and the same combination of the first two texts is also found in 1 Clement (written about A.D. 95). It may have appeared thus in a collection of *OT* proof-texts (see on 3:22–3) used by both Luke and Clement of Rome.

23. as he promised: see on 2:30.

24–5. It may be that followers of John the Baptist, believing him to have been the Messiah, and constituting a sect which had spread outwards from Palestine, presented more of a problem to Christian missionaries about this time than the *NT* evidence would suggest; a hint of this is given in 19:3-5. If such were the case, it would account for Paul's strong emphasis here on John's role as merely the herald of the Messiah.

26. salvation through Christ is open both to Jews and Gentile adherents of the Jewish faith (cf. verse 16).

27-8. As in Peter's sermon (3:12ff.), Paul attributes the Crucifixion to Jewish blindness with the reluctant connivance of Pilate.

29. laid him in a tomb: Joseph of Arimathaea and Nicodemus (Lk. 23:50ff.; Jn 19:38ff.), both members of the Sanhedrin, are presumably regarded as representing the Jews in general in this compressed summary.

31. now his witnesses: it is no argument against the basically Pauline character of this sermon that he does not include himself among the witnesses to the Resurrection as he does in 1 C. 9:1, 15:3-9. Here he is describing the events of Passion Week and the immediate sequel.

33. by raising Jesus: the argument would seem to be that as God had 'raised up David', and 'promised' a 'Saviour' of David's posterity (verses 22-3) he has now 'fulfilled' this promise by 'raising' (i.e. sending) Jesus as the Messiah, the 'Son' of Ps. 2:7 (see on 4:25). The specific reference is to Jesus' Baptism regarded as his anointing as Messiah (4:27, 10:38) (cf. Lk. 3:22, where the Western text reads: 'Today I have begotten thee', instead of: 'With thee I am well pleased.').

second psalm: The Western text reads: 'first psalm'. Apparently the first two psalms were sometimes regarded as one.

34. raised him from the dead: Paul now refers directly to the Resurrection of Jesus as opposed to God's action in 'raising', or sending, Jesus in the previous verse. He regards the Resurrection as the fulfilment of **the holy and sure blessings** promised to David, the LXX version of the more familiar (*AV*) 'sure mercies of David' of Isa. 55:3.

35-7. See on 2:25-32, where Peter makes the same point.

38. forgiveness of sins is a common element in the *Kerygma*, as in 2:38, 10:43.

39. freed from . . . the law: the main lines of Paul's address have followed the normal pattern of the early apostolic preaching, as evidenced by Peter's sermons hitherto. Here, however, Paul asserts the characteristic doctrine of justification by faith, as expounded at length in Romans and Galatians. The Law could

not set men free from the sin that separates them from God and
bring them into a right relationship with himself. Only Christ
could do this. By faith in him men are **freed** (lit. 'justified', i.e.
made at one with God).

40–1. Paul concludes with a warning from Hab. 1:5, applying
the words to the coming judgment upon those who reject the
Gospel (cf. 2:40, 3:23). Parallel with the positive theme of the
preparation for the coming of the Christ through Abraham, Moses,
Samuel, David and John the Baptist, he has interwoven an ad-
monitory reminder of those who have failed to recognize the
divine plan and purpose—the Canaanites, Saul, the Jerusalem
Jews and Pilate. Now he presents the Dispersion Jews with a
similar challenge to accept or refuse the Gospel message.

43. devout converts: normally the word translated 'devout'
refers to God-fearers (see on 10:2) as distinct from 'converts', i.e.
proselytes (see on 2:10). There may be an omission of the word
'and', in which case Luke intends to cover the whole range of
Jews, God-fearers and proselytes. On the other hand, as the text
stands, he is referring simply to Jews and those who had become
Jews by full acceptance of the requirements of the Law. The
general impression conveyed is one of the keen interest aroused by
Paul's sermon, manifesting itself in further talk and discussion
elsewhere after the service.

44. almost the whole city: a pardonable exaggeration, but
presumably too large a crowd for the synagogue.

45. jealousy: on the part of the synagogue authorities, because
the new faith preached by Paul was clearly more attractive than
Judaism to the Gentile population of the city. This might also
involve the loss of God-fearers including their financial support
of the synagogue.

reviled him: lit. 'blaspheming'. Hence the meaning could be
'blaspheming against Jesus', i.e. denying his messianic status because of the Crucifixion (cf. Gal. 3:13).

46. we turn to the Gentiles: in accordance with his avowed
purpose and obligation, as expressed in Rom. 1:16, to preach the
Gospel first to the people of God's choice, the Jews, Paul pursued
this policy doggedly to the end of his missionary career. Now for
the first time Dispersion Jews follow the example of their Jerusalem counterparts in rejecting Christ, and for the first time
Paul publicly announces his intention of turning his back on them
and concentrating on a purely Gentile mission. The Dispersion

Jews can no longer claim ignorance as their excuse. Paul is to
repeat this dramatic declaration of such a change of policy on
further occasions (18:5-6; 28:25-8). There had of course previously been missionary work among mixed Jewish Gentile communities, as at Syrian Antioch; but this is the first deliberate step
towards the creation of a purely Gentile congregation.

unworthy of eternal life: i.e. unworthy to participate in the
blessings of the messianic age which was, according to the Scriptures, the future inheritance of the people of God, and which had
now become a present possibility through Christ.

47. The words of Isa. 49:6, originally addressed to the Servant
of Yahweh and then applied to Jesus (Lk. 2:32), are now adopted
by Christian missionaries as describing their own role.

48. ordained to eternal life: it has been suggested that the
word translated 'ordained' means 'disposed'—i.e. that those who
were ready to accept the Gospel message became believers. There
does seem to be more to it than that, however. The idea of a
heavenly book of life, in which the names of the faithful are
inscribed, is common to OT and NT (Exod. 32:32, etc; Lk. 10:20;
Rev. 13:8, etc.); it is a pictorial way of expressing the conviction
of the sovereignty of God—i.e. that salvation is in God's gift, and
does not depend on man's efforts. But it is not in any sense
narrowly predestinarian, as if some are scheduled for salvation
and others for damnation; the Bible constantly stresses the element
of free choice: we may accept or reject the Word of God. In this
case the Jews of Antioch as a whole reject the offer of eternal life,
while some—but by no means all—of the Gentiles accept it.
Those who do accept the Gospel fulfil the purpose of God that all
men shall be saved, and by their response they show that they are
worthy to be numbered with the saints in heaven.

49. This implies the propagation of the Gospel by the new
Gentile converts.

50. devout women: synagogue worship attracted many Gentile women as adherents of Judaism; in Asia Minor wealthy
matrons exercised much more influence than was the case in most
other parts of the Empire. Now under pressure from the Jews
—always, as Luke points out, the root of Paul's troubles—they
induce the **leading men of the city**—i.e. the magistrates, who
were possibly their husbands—to expel the missionaries.

51. shook off the dust: as a gesture of abandonment (cf. Lk.
9:5, 10:11).

Iconium: mod. Konia, about 100 miles SE. of Antioch, and within the province of Galatia. It was the chief town of the region known as Lycaonia, which included also Lystra and Derbe referred to in the next chapter. If illness overtook Paul at Antioch, he may have felt inclined to move *eastward*—and homeward—rather than to press on *westward* to Ephesus (see on verse 14).

52. the disciples: the new Gentile converts, presumably meeting in a house-church.

AT ICONIUM 14:1–7

1. together: the Greek could mean either 'together' (i.e. Paul and Barnabas), or 'in the same way' (as at Antioch). Once again the initial approach in a new town is to the Jews.

Greeks: Gentiles and, since they were present at a synagogue service, therefore God-fearers.

2–3. poisoned their minds: this implies a sustained campaign on the part of orthodox Jews, hostile to the Apostles' message, to discredit their teaching and to stir up trouble. Despite this, the missionaries persisted in proclaiming the faith.

signs and wonders: acts of healing, like those of Jesus himself and of the Apostles in Jerusalem (2:22, 43).

for a long time: a second century legendary work: *The Acts of Paul and Thecla*, enlarges on Paul's visit to Iconium about which we are told so little in Acts. However fanciful most of the details may be, the description of Paul is sufficiently unflattering to be possibly a genuine reminiscence: 'A man of small stature and scanty hair, with eyebrows meeting; a rather large nose and large eyes, bandy-legged and strongly built; of gracious presence, for sometimes he looked like a man and sometimes he had the face of an angel' (ii. 3).

4. divided: as a result of the campaign referred to in verse 2.

apostles: Luke has so far reserved this title for the Twelve. Here and in verse 14 he extends it to include Paul and Barnabas. It is not likely that he does so because he regards their commission by the leaders of the church at Syrian Antioch (13:3) as giving them apostolic status; on that occasion the participants in the ceremony were all of equal rank. Luke must be using the word in its literal meaning of 'one who is sent out': Paul and Barnabas were messengers or representatives of the church at Antioch. Paul uses the word in this wider sense in Rom. 16:7; 2 C. 8:23; Phil. 2:25.

5. molest .. stone: this appears to be a threat of mob violence with the connivance of the Jewish synagogue authorities and the Gentile magistrates; to avoid it the missionaries left the town in haste.

6. Lystra (mod. Zoldera) was about 25 miles SW. of Iconium, and a Roman colony.

Derbe may have been about 30 miles SE. of Lystra, though there is some doubt about its exact location.

cities of Lycaonia: although Iconium was officially also a Lycaonian city, its inhabitants were mostly Phrygians. Hence Luke correctly reflects the local situation by grouping Lystra and Derbe separately.

the surrounding country appears to have been mainly villages.

AT LYSTRA AND DERBE **14:8–20**

8. a cripple: this incident, selected by Luke for detailed description from among the 'signs and wonders' of the Galatian mission (verse 3), parallels the similar cure by Peter in chapter 3, and doubtless was chosen for this reason. In opposition to those who would challenge Paul's claim to apostolic authority based on his direct commission from the risen Christ, Luke is concerned to show that his hero shares with the chief Apostle the healing power vested in his disciples by the Lord himself (Jn 14:12) and exemplified in Jesus' own ministry (Lk. 7:22). It is possible that there was a trace of the same purpose in Luke's mind as he related Paul's rout of the magician Elymas (13:6ff.) and recalled Peter's successful confrontation of Simon Magus (8:9ff.).

11. in Lycaonian: Lystra, like other towns in Asia Minor, would have three languages in normal use: (i) Latin, as the official language of the Roman administration—in this case more widely used, since Lystra was a Roman colony; (ii) Greek, as the *lingua franca* of the Empire, understood and to some extent spoken by all; and (iii) the native vernacular, in the present case Lycaonian. This would be the ordinary means of communication between the townspeople, not intelligible to the Apostles, who, however, could make themselves understood in Greek.

The gods have come down: this fascinating glimpse of the superstitious pagan background of the Empire suggests the magnitude of the problem facing early Christian missionaries, and highlights the success of Paul and his associates in winning such massive response to their message throughout the Gentile mission. Luke has already drawn attention to the credulity of even a

Roman proconsul in Cyprus (13:6ff.), and later he records an incident in Malta (28:6) which elicits the same reaction on the part of more simple-minded pagans as is described here. The thought of gods coming to earth in human form was presumably already familiar in this region through the myth of Zeus and Hermes (or, in Latin, Jupiter and Mercury) visiting an aged and devout Phrygian couple, Baucis and Philemon. Ovid recounts the story in his *Metamorphoses*.

12. Zeus . . . Hermes: Barnabas, no doubt because he was older than Paul and had a more impressive appearance (see on verse 3), is taken for the father of the gods; Paul, the spokesman, is identified with Hermes, the messenger of the gods and the god of oratory. Later inscriptions found near Lystra indicate the association of these two particular gods; they were doubtless originally local gods who had been merged with the more widely known deities of the Greek pantheon, as was common practice throughout the Empire.

13. garlands: woollen bands or wreaths used to adorn sacrificial animals.

gates: most probably the city gates.

14. tore their garments: as a sign of horror when they realized by the actions of the priest what the unintelligible shouting of the Lycaonians had meant (cf. Jdt. 14:16–19).

rushed out: perhaps from the house where they were lodging.

15–17. Paul's speech here, apart from his address to the Athenian philosophers (17:22ff.), is the only example in Acts of his technique in dealing with a purely pagan audience; it is a striking example of his ability to reinterpret the Gospel in terms intelligible to his hearers. It differs widely from his approach to Jews and adherents of Judaism, as illustrated by his sermon in the synagogue at Antioch (13:16ff.), where some knowledge of the scriptures could be assumed on the part of his listeners. Here, as at Athens, he proceeds on the basis of natural revelation—the providential order of the universe—which ought to lead men's thoughts from the cult of idols to the worship of a living God, Creator of all that exists; he expounds this line of argument more fully in Rom. 1:19ff.; 2:14f., and he writes of its successful outcome at Thessalonica in 1 Th. 1:9.

Paul insists that he and Barnabas are no divine beings in disguise, but mere mortals who are nevertheless bearers of **good news** of the truth about God. He seeks to build on the pagan acknowledgment of the mystery of the created world, and to show that their explanation of this in terms of a variety of mythical gods and goddesses, each controlling one or other aspect of life and each represented by meaningless images, is woefully inadequate. There is but one God, **living** and active, whose works are clearly to be seen around them (verse 15).

Until now God has allowed the Gentiles to express their religious response in their own way (verse 16); yet he was preparing their minds for the full knowledge of his nature and purpose by the manifest evidences of his bounty in the fruitfulness of the earth and the sense of well-being that such gifts bring to men (verse 17).

19-20. Jews came: the suggestion seems to be that there were few if any Jews in Lystra, since there was no synagogue; but trouble-makers came from the synagogues of Antioch and Iconium, and stirred up local feeling against the missionaries, possibly attributing the cure of the cripple to demonic powers. Paul as the spokesman was **stoned** by the mob, and his battered body was **dragged** out of the town. With the help of those who had been converted to Christianity, he recovered sufficiently to set out next day with Barnabas for Derbe. When Paul, writing later to Corinth, says: '. . . once was I stoned' (2 C. 11:25), it is probably this occasion to which he is referring.

RETURN TO ANTIOCH **14:21-8**

21. The mission to Derbe is wholly successful, and this is the only one of the Galatian communities where no trouble is encountered. If 2 Tim. 3:11 is a genuine Pauline fragment, the Apostle recalls there his persecutions at Antioch, Iconium and Lystra. Despite this, he and Barnabas retrace their steps through these very places. It may be that the reason was that the more obvious route overland through the Taurus mountains to Tarsus and thence to Syrian Antioch was blocked in winter. More probably, in view of what follows, they turned back on their tracks in order to consolidate the new Gentile churches and provide them with some form of organization. Luke's indications of the time taken on this first missionary journey are fairly vague, but a rough estimate of two years would not be inconsistent with his narrative—say in A.D. 46-8. But, even if some time elapsed before Paul and Barnabas revisited Lystra, Iconium and Pisidian Antioch on the return journey—enough, for example, to allow for a change of magistrates at Iconium and Antioch, or even if they concentrated on establishing house-churches and abstained from public preaching—it is still a superbly courageous venture to set foot in these places again so soon.

22. kingdom of God: the young Gentile communities would, in view of what had happened, need all the **strengthening** and **exhorting** that the Apostles could give them to remain firm in the **faith**—i.e. Christianity—and the reminder that, like the Lord himself (Lk. 24:26), his disciples must expect **tribulations** as a prelude to the glory of the **kingdom of God**—in their case, life with Christ in the age to come (cf. Rom. 8:17–21).

23. appointed elders: it would be unwise to read into this basic administrative necessity later and more developed ideas of church order. Every community needs some kind of organization, and the most obvious expedient that lay to Paul's hand for these largely Gentile congregations would be to follow the pattern of the synagogue, since Jews and Gentiles alike were now incorporated into the 'Israel of God'. The elders (or presbyters), therefore, would be chosen from the older members of the community, and charged with the oversight of worship, discipline, administration and instruction—more or less along the lines of the 'rulers of the synagogue'. The church in Jerusalem had already established this office (11:30) as, indeed, had the Essenes of Qumran in different circumstances; both Christian and Essene practice ultimately derived from *OT* tradition. That the organization was fluid at this stage and that Paul was primarily concerned with the practical functions of congregational leadership are indicated by the variety of titles he uses for elders: 'guardians' (20:28), 'bishops' (Phil. 1:1)—in both cases the Greek is *episkopoi* ('overseers')—'those who . . . are over you' (I Th. 5:12).

By the time the Pastoral Epistles were written (c. A.D. 90–100), church organization had become more standardized, in that oversight of local congregations was vested in 'presbyter-bishops'. By the second century the three-fold order of ministry—bishops, priests (presbyters) and deacons—had become accepted practice.
prayer and fasting: as in the commissioning of Paul and Barnabas themselves (13:3).

24–5. Pisidia, Pamphylia, Perga, Attalia: see on 13:13–14. This is apparently the first missionary work in Perga.

26. Antioch: Syrian Antioch.
work: cf. 13:2.

27. opened a door of faith to the Gentiles: such an oppor-

tunity had been offered to Gentiles before, as in the case of
Cornelius and in Syrian Antioch itself; but Luke underlines the
spectacular advance of Christianity which had been achieved on
this first deliberate and authorized campaign into the Gentile
world. As we have seen, it is not clear why this particular area of
Asia Minor was chosen; but the campaign was significant, not
only in that for the first time churches which were either exclusively or predominantly composed of non-Jews were founded, but
also that it was to the young churches established on this journey
that Paul wrote his great manifesto on Faith and Freedom, the
letter to the Galatians.

The internal evidence of that letter, which was probably written
at Syrian Antioch after his return from this tour or on the way to
Jerusalem to take part in the meeting described in chapter 15,
is in striking accordance with Luke's narrative in Ac. 13–14. Paul
is writing to Gentiles who are under pressure from Jews. Barnabas,
who was Paul's companion only on this first journey, is obviously
well known to the readers (Gal. 2:1, 13). Paul recalls that he
visited them in the first instance because of illness (see on 13:14);
that he was received 'as an angel of God' (Gal. 4:14)—which
suggests their identification of him with Hermes (14:12)—and
that he bears on his body 'the marks of Jesus' (Gal. 6:17), which
may well be the result of his stoning at Lystra (14:19); even the
fickleness of the Galatians (Gal. 1:6) is reflected in the *volte face*
of the Lystrans on that occasion (14:18–19). Whatever was the
source of Luke's information—the vividness of the episode at
Lystra may have come from Timothy, who was a native (16:1)—
his account of the Galatian mission ties up remarkably well with
Paul's own recollections in his letter.

28. no little time: it may have been as much as a year, say
A.D.48–9.

THE COUNCIL OF JERUSALEM **15:1–35**

Perhaps it is at this point that we should turn to Gal. 2:11ff. for
Paul's account of a sharp rebuke which he delivered to Peter
in face of the congregation at Antioch. Whether this took place
before Paul set out on his first missionary journey or after his
return, it serves as an introduction to the momentous conference
at Jerusalem Luke describes in this chapter, and brings out the
issues involved; humanly speaking, these could have split the
Church in two and ultimately destroyed it.

Since its earliest days in Jerusalem, the Church had not only pushed its frontiers far beyond Palestine into the Graeco-Roman world, but, particularly as a result of Paul's missionary efforts, its membership now included probably at least as many Gentiles as Jews, if not more. Christians at this stage could include anyone from, at one end of the scale, a devout Jerusalem Jew, whose life was still focused on the Temple, and who had superimposed on his meticulous observance of the Law of Moses the belief that Jesus was the promised Messiah, to, at the other, a native of Galatia whose religious upbringing had been in a pagan temple, who knew little of Judaism or its tradition, but who had accepted Jesus Christ as Saviour and Lord and had been baptized into the fellowship of the Church.

For Peter as for Paul, this was all that a Gentile needed to do to become a Christian. Many less enlightened Jewish Christians, however, mindful of the thousand years of tradition behind them, and deeply conscious of sacred history and the heritage of God's ancient people Israel, viewed with misgiving the opening of the doors of the New Israel to Gentiles, to whom all this meant little, who had never known the salutary safeguards and restraints of the Law, and who might be inclined to treat too lightly their incorporation into the historic covenant bond between God and his chosen people. Without the strong sense of the historical continuity of New Israel with Old Israel provided by obedience to the Law, might not Gentile Christianity become a rootless faith with a Christ who was hard to distinguish from the saviours and lords of the Greek mystery-religions? Some went even further. There were those on the extreme right-wing of Jewish Christianity who reckoned that circumcision should be obligatory for all Gentiles who became Christians, as it already was for proselytes to Judaism (see on 2:10). This meant that, to become a Christian, a Gentile must first become a Jew.

For those Jewish Christians who took this rigorist view, it followed that association with uncircumcised Gentile Christians was as abhorrent as it would have been had Christian belief not been involved at all. It was the age-old horror of the strict Jew, based on the Law of Moses, of contamination with those who were technically not within the covenant relationship—outwardly signalized by circumcision—and who ate food not permitted by the Law from utensils which had not been ceremonially cleansed. Thus the issue was more than that of admission to membership of the Church. It involved also the question whether Jewish Christians ought to mix socially with uncircumcised Gentile Christians, to eat the characteristic Christian *agapē* at the same table, and to share in the same eucharistic celebration.

Peter had been dramatically shown by God, in the case of Cornelius and his friends, that the traditional Jewish distinction between 'clean' and 'unclean' had no longer relevance in the admission of Gentiles to the Church. Gentiles could become Christians by faith and baptism alone; circumcision and full acceptance of the Mosaic law were not required of them. For this reason Jewish Christians and Gentile Christians could mix freely together, and in this Peter had himself set an example (10:48), for which he had to justify himself later in Jerusalem. At that time the principle of equal rights for Jews and Gentiles within the Church had been accepted by the mother church, but no doubt even then there were mutterings from the ultra-conservative members (11:1–18; see on 11:18).

It was in accordance with this principle, as Paul recounts in Gal. 2:11–14, that Peter on a visit to Antioch had been happy to associate with Gentile Christians, including sharing the common meal, until some of the Jerusalem rigorists arrived, at which point Peter and the other Jewish Christians, including even Barnabas, segregated themselves from the Gentile Christians, perhaps eating in another room or in another house-church. For Paul this was no mere temporary concession for the sake of expediency, but a betrayal of the Gospel. It was for this reason that he took Peter publicly to task; he could not have done so if he had not known that Peter in his heart believed that he was right. If the Jewish-Christian extremists had succeeded in imposing their views on the Church, insisting on circumcision and observance of the Mosaic Law for all Christians, it would have led to two churches, Jewish Christian and Gentile Christian, since most Gentiles would certainly have refused circumcision even if they were willing to accept some of the restrictive practices of Jewish Law; more probably, it would have meant the end of Gentile Christianity, and the Church would have existed for a time as a Jewish sect, small in numbers and with dubious prospects. Either possibility was for Paul unthinkable.

The situation Luke now describes in this chapter is the appearance at Antioch of some of these fanatically extreme Jewish Christians from Jerusalem—they may even have been those referred to in Gal. 2:11ff.—claiming that circumcision was essential for salvation. Luke, writing several decades after the event, can view the issues with the calm detachment of the historian; by that time the crisis was past, and Luke had not been involved. For Paul it was a matter of the life or death of the Church, and in view of all the evidence it would seem best on balance to date his impassioned defence of Christian freedom in his letter to the Galatians at this point in time. The mischief that Luke now describes as being done by these Jewish-Christian extremists at Antioch was apparently being paralleled by similar propaganda on the part of other Christian Judaizers among the young churches Paul had so recently founded in Galatia. Having heard of this, he wrote in white heat, either from Antioch or on his way to Jerusalem, a letter which magnificently expresses the crucial nature of the issue for the future of the Church, and provides an eloquent gloss on Luke's more restrained account of the problem and its solution.

1. some men: if these are those referred to in Gal. 2:12, they had come to Antioch with some kind of commission from the Jerusalem church, but according to verse 24 they had no authority to insist that salvation depended on circumcision as the Law required, i.e. **according to the custom of Moses.**
Judaea: on the one hand, there was the conservative Jewish-Christian church in Jerusalem with its daughter churches in Judaea, and, on the other, the more liberal Gentile Christian church at Antioch with its daughter churches in Syria and Asia Minor.

2. Since the matter was vital, and agreement could not be reached at Antioch, 'conservatives' and 'liberals' must meet to thrash the matter out in Jerusalem, which was still acknowledged by all as the mother church, with James the Lord's brother as its permanent head and, behind him, the authority of the Apostles. The delegation from Antioch consisted of a party which included Paul and Barnabas. It is not stated how many of the **apostles** were involved in this Council of Jerusalem; those who were present had presumably returned after the persecution mentioned in chapter 12. The **elders** are the administrative body supporting James, last referred to in 11:30.

3. the brethren were those Jewish Christians in **Phoenicia** whose conversion is referred to in 11:19 (cf. 21:3-4), and also the Samaritans evangelized by Philip (8:5ff.). To both groups the story of the Galatian campaign would be welcome news.

5. Pharisees: these are presumably some of the right-wing Jewish Christians zealous for the Law (21:20). But it is not clear from the text whether they went as far as the bigots of verse 1 in maintaining that circumcision was essential for salvation; they may simply have insisted that Gentiles should be circumcised and observe the terms of the Mosaic law in order to be admitted to full fellowship with Jewish Christians. The fact that there were enough converted Pharisees to have an influential voice in the affairs of the Church indicates that the Jewish-Christian party had a powerful case for dictating terms to the pro-Gentile faction. At this stage it could have been argued that the mission to the Jews was as promising as the mission to the Gentiles. Jewish susceptibilities could therefore not be disregarded.

6. The Council of Jerusalem, generally dated in A.D. 49, seems to have been a public assembly (cf. verse 12), with the Apostles and elders 'on the platform', as it were.

this matter: the whole question of the conditions of membership of the Church in respect of Gentiles, and the terms on which Jewish and Gentile Christians could associate.

7. much debate: at Antioch tempers had been frayed ('no small dissension and debate' (verse 2)), and no doubt the atmosphere at Jerusalem was more restrained; but the case must have been hotly argued on both sides.

in the early days: Peter recalls the *cause célèbre* of Cornelius which about ten years previously had been the subject of a similar enquiry (11:1ff.). He identifies himself with Paul as being equally an apostle to the Gentiles, although his main work had been among the Jews (cf. Gal. 2:1–10).

8. as he did to us: cf. 10:47, 11:17. Other phrases in Peter's speech occur also in the Cornelius story.

10. God had shown his acceptance of Cornelius and his friends by the gift of the Holy Spirit based on their faith alone. To demand now that more than that should be required of Gentiles would be to question the rightness of God's action, i.e. **make trial of God.**

yoke: Peter echoes the thought of Jesus as he condemned the burdensome legalism that the Pharisees laid on men's shoulders (Mt. 23:4). They had made a 'yoke' of the Law which should have been a delight, as it was to the psalmist (Ps. 1:2).

11. Peter is very much on the side of Paul and the 'liberals', and in this verse and the preceding one his sentiments are wholly Pauline.

12. Barnabas and Paul: Barnabas, as a notable member of the Jerusalem church, is mentioned before Paul, as in verse 25. Both missionaries now recount, in support of Peter's argument, the more recent successes of the mission to the Gentiles of Galatia. **signs and wonders** would presumably not be restricted to acts of healing, but would include evidences of the power of God such as Peter had referred to.

13. James: see on 12:17. Here, despite Peter's presence, James seems to act as president of the Council, and it is his summing-up and subsequent decision which are accepted by the assembly. It is easy to understand how James had acquired this status over the years through the prolonged absences of the Twelve on evangelistic missions; Luke, like Paul (Gal. 1:19), probably counted James as an Apostle (verse 6). Although not one of the Twelve, he had acquired, by reason of his kinship with Jesus and his encounter with the risen Christ which probably led to his conversion (1 C. 15:7), what amounted to apostolic qualifications. His views would command more attention among the conservatives than those of Paul, Barnabas or even Peter. His judicious conclusion, which proves acceptable to both sides, is an admirable compromise.

14. Symeon: James uses the Jewish form of Simon in referring to Peter. This is in keeping with the markedly Jewish character of his speech.

visited: Luke uses this word to denote the intervention of God in human affairs (Lk. 1:68, 78; 7:16).

a people: normally the word is used of Israel alone as the people of God. Here James includes Gentiles as well as Jews among God's people, the New Israel, the Church.

15. the prophets: the book of the Twelve Prophets, including Amos, which James now quotes.

16–18. The quotation is mostly from the LXX of Amos 9:11–12, which differs from the Hebrew in a way favourable to James's argument. The prophecy originally referred to the restoration of Israel, and the recovery of its lost territories. Verse 17 in Hebrew reads: 'that they (Israel) may possess the remnant of Edom and all the nations who are called by my name'. In the Greek translation it has become as here: **that the rest of men may seek the Lord, and all the Gentiles who are called by my name.** Thus James can use the LXX version to support what he has already said in verse 14—namely, that the people of God

now consists of Gentiles as well as Jews. The Church has inherited the role of old Israel, and the promises made to Israel are
now being fulfilled in the life and experience of the Church.

Perhaps it would be unlikely that James, as head of the conservative Aramaic-speaking Jewish Christians, would address the
Council in Greek or quote from the LXX, especially when the
point he was making depended on a variation in the text from the
Hebrew. But, like all Galileans, he would be bilingual, and it
could have been an act of courtesy to the non-Aramaic speaking
delegates from Antioch. Nor do we know that there may not have
been many Greek-speaking Jerusalem Jewish Christians in the
assembly. Possibly, however, the quotation, which is not wholly
from Amos but includes echoes of Jer. 12:15 and Isa. 45:21, may
have been taken by Luke from a collection of OT proof-texts.

19. should not trouble: by insisting on their circumcision.

20. In return for the Jewish concession which waived circumcision in the case of Gentile converts (which was Paul's main concern), the Gentile Christians should be asked to respect Jewish-
Christian convictions on four matters which made full fellowship
difficult, especially at the *agapē*-eucharist.

pollutions of idols: in Gentile cities most of the meat for sale
in shops or markets consisted of the carcases of animals which had
been used for sacrificial purposes in one or other of the pagan
temples (cf. verse 29); in the process they had been dedicated or
offered to some god, represented by his statue. From the Jewish
point of view, the eating of such meat condoned polytheism and
was an act of sacrilege. There was the added complication that
social occasions among Gentiles involving banquets or even family
gatherings were often held on temple premises where sacrificial
meat that was abhorrent to Jews was consumed.

unchastity: there was undoubtedly sexual licence in pagan
society such as the Jews with their strict code would not tolerate;
sacramental fornication was practised as a religious act, and many
temples were little more than brothels. It was difficult for Christians
who had been brought up as pagans to break away from this sex-
ridden atmosphere as Paul found in the church at Corinth
(1 C. 6:13ff.). James can hardly, however, be referring to sexual
promiscuity, since this was forbidden among all Christians—
Gentile or Jewish—as much as it was among Jews; it is more likely
that he is concerned that Gentile Christians should observe
the OT marriage-laws of Lev. 18. Another suggestion is that

originally the Greek word may have been *choireia* ('pork'), and not *porneia* ('unchastity').

what is strangled: it was a breach of Mosaic law to eat flesh from which the blood had not been drained (Lev. 17:10ff.). Poultry, for example, must therefore be decapitated, and not have their necks drawn.

blood: this prohibition, which underlies the ban on strangulation, is based on the Noachic covenant (Gen. 9:4), which was assumed to involve all mankind, since Noah was technically a Gentile. The Hebrews regarded the blood of a man or an animal as containing his, or its, life; even animal blood was therefore in some sense sacred and mysterious and must not be eaten (Dt. 12:16, 23–25).

The Western text transforms these ritual matters into moral obligations. Whoever was responsible for this version understood the demands of the Council upon Gentile Christians to have been abstention from idolatry, fornication and murder ('blood'). Since strangulation of animals is obviously inappropriate in this context, he has substituted a negative form of the Golden Rule: 'and whatever they do not wish to happen to themselves, not to do to others'. All this indicates a complete misunderstanding of the issues at stake, and cannot be the authentic version; it did not need a solemn conclave of the Apostles and elders of Jerusalem to insist that Gentile Christians should abstain from, e.g., murder.

As they stand, the terms imposed by James as representative of the Jewish Christians were not unreasonable and could be accepted by Paul and the other delegates from Antioch as providing a working compromise. The main obstacle, circumcision, had been removed and the four-pointed concession to Jewish-Christian scruples laid no heavy burdens upon the Gentile churches. Most of the things they were asked to avoid were common practice in pagan communities, and in themselves innocuous; but if it meant the establishment of full Christian fellowship between the two sides of the Church, it was worth some inconvenience. Paul himself interpreted the spirit of the terms of the Council admirably in Rom. 14:1–15:6 and 1 C. 8.

21. Moses . . . is read every sabbath: James supports his verdict by pointing to the Jewish communities which for centuries had maintained their faith and identity, based on the Law, in foreign places far from Jerusalem. In the synagogues of the Empire many Gentile adherents had become familiar with the

Mosaic code and held it in high esteem. Jewish tradition which
meant so much to Jewish Christians should therefore be respected by their Gentile-Christian brethren.

22. it seemed good: the assembly voted, apparently unani-
mously, for James's motion from the chair, incorporating it in
a letter to Antioch (verse 23) which they entrusted to two leading
representatives of the mother church.

Judas called Barsabbas may have been a brother of Joseph
Barsabbas (1:23). He probably represented the 'Hebrew' section
of the Jerusalem church (cf. 6:1).

Silas: better known by his Latin name, Silvanus. He was to
feature largely in Paul's second missionary journey (cf. verse 40;
2 C. 1:19; 1 Th. 1:1; 2 Th. 1:1), and was the scribe of 1 Peter
(1 Pet. 5:12). Both Judas and Silas were prophets (verse 32).
Silas was also, like Paul, a Roman citizen (16:37), and was
probably chosen to represent the Hellenists in the Jerusalem
church.

23. Antioch and Syria and Cilicia: Syria and Cilicia formed
the joint province of which Antioch was the capital. The letter is
addressed to the church at Antioch and its daughter churches in
the province, since it was Antioch that had asked for a ruling on
the matter (verse 2); Paul himself later delivered copies of the
Jerusalem decree to the Galatian churches (16:4).

24. The letter repudiates the extremists of verse 1, who are
possibly also those of Gal. 2:12, as having exceeded their brief.

26. risked their lives: better, 'devoted' their lives(cf. Gal.
2:20). This warm commendation of Barnabas and Paul is in
itself a rebuke to the Judaizers.

28. Holy Spirit and . . . us: or, 'we have reached these
decisions under the guidance of the Spirit'. The terms stated in
the letter conform exactly to the proposals of James accepted by
the Council, except that the phrase 'pollutions of idols' (verse 20)
is made more explicit in verse 29.

30. they: Paul, Barnabas, Judas, Silas and the delegates from
Antioch referred to in verse 2.

31. Naturally the church at Antioch received with relief and
thankfulness the decree of the Council, which was, in effect, a
victory for the liberal point of view. It both repudiated the
Jewish Christian extremists, and made it plain that Gentile converts were not to be relegated to the status of second-class
Christians. The terms of the letter were no doubt reinforced by

fraternal encouragement from the two official representatives of the mother church (verse 32).

33. they were sent off: Judas and Silas returned to Jerusalem. The Western text, in order to overcome the difficulty of verse 40—in which Silas is on hand at Antioch to set out with Paul on his second missionary tour—adds after verse 33: 'but it seemed good to Silas to remain there'. This forms verse 34 in the *AV*, but is rightly omitted in *RSV*, since it contradicts verse 33. The explanation of verse 40 is that presumably Paul had in the meantime sent to Jerusalem for Silas to join him, as Barnabas seems to have done in the case of Mark (verse 39).

SECOND MISSIONARY JOURNEY 15:36–18:22

GALATIA REVISITED 15:36–16:5

36. Paul's second missionary journey, which may be dated in 50–2, began with the primary objective of revisiting the churches in Galatia founded on the first tour, no doubt as a follow-up to his letter to them, and now with the decree of the Council to reinforce it. However, it would seem he had more ambitious plans in mind (16:6ff.).

37-8. Barnabas, as Paul's associate in the Galatian mission, was his obvious choice for a return expedition; but Barnabas' insistence that Mark should accompany them met with strong resistance from Paul, who clearly regarded Mark as unreliable because of his defection on the previous tour (see on 13:13).

39. a sharp contention: Luke, who has never drawn a veil over the human weaknesses marring the record of the early Church, which throw its achievements into greater relief, does no less in the case of his hero now. Perhaps Barnabas regarded Paul's attitude as a slight on his family, since Mark was his cousin (Col. 4:10); but Paul was equally obstinate. The quarrel was heated, and ended in separation: Barnabas returned to Cyprus, his native country (4:36) with Mark, who had accompanied Paul and Barnabas on their earlier campaign there (13:4–12). The separation was not final, since Paul later refers to Barnabas as his partner in missionary work in Corinth (1 C. 9:6), and Mark also was later associated with Paul, who speaks of him in warm terms (Col. 4:10; Phm. 24; 2 Tim. 4:11). It has been pointed out that the quarrel had at least one good result—namely, that there were two missionary enterprises instead of one. Both Barnabas and

Mark disappear after this from Luke's record, as also does Peter after the Council of Jerusalem.

40. Silas: see on verse 22. As substitute for Barnabas, he had perhaps an advantage over him in respect of the Gentile churches which were to be visited, in that he was the accredited representative of the mother church to Antioch as guarantor of the Council decree. He had the added asset of being a Roman citizen; this was to prove useful (16:37).

41. Syria and Cilicia: the united province (see on verse 23) had been the field of Paul's early missionary activities in the years between his conversion and his summons to Antioch (Gal. 1:21); no doubt the churches mentioned here owed their foundation to him: they are included with Antioch as recipients of the decree, of which copies presumably were sent to them from Antioch independently of Paul's visit. His interest in these communities may have been less personal than in the Galatian churches, but they lay on his route which went overland through Tarsus and through the gap in the Taurus mountains known as 'the Cilician Gates'; in this way, he reached the Galatian churches in the reverse order of his initial visit (see on 14:21).

16.1. Derbe, Lystra: see on 14:6.
there: Lystra.
Timothy is described as a **disciple** which suggests that he may have been converted during Paul's previous campaign in Lystra (cf. 1 C. 4:17) and verse 2 might imply that he was already an evangelist. According to 2 Tim. 1:5, his mother Eunice and his grandmother Lois were also converts, possibly becoming Christians at the same time as Timothy. Despite their Greek names, Eunice and Lois were Jewesses, but Eunice had married a Greek. Although mixed marriages of this kind were against Jewish law—presumably there was more laxity on this point in Lystra than in Jerusalem—the son of such a union was legally Jewish, and Timothy had been brought up in the Jewish faith (2 Tim. 3:15). He was, however, suspect in the eyes of the local Jews, since his late father had been a Gentile and he had not been circumcised.

2. Iconium: see on 13:51.
3. to accompany him: presumably as a substitute for Mark and in the same capacity (see on 13:5). He becomes Paul's constant companion from now on, and Paul associates Timothy's name with his own in the opening words of 2 C., Phil., Col., 1 and

2 Th., Phm. 1 and 2 Tim. are addressed to Timothy personally.
circumcised him: This has been thought by many to be so
contrary to Paul's attitude on circumcision, as expressed in the
letter to the Galatians—especially in the case of Titus (Gal. 2:3)—
and so unnecessary after the recent decision of the Council of
Jerusalem, that it has been dismissed as impossible. Luke, however, who was closely associated with Timothy on this second
missionary journey (see on verse 10), is unlikely to have got his
facts wrong. Moreover, the cases of Titus and Timothy were not
parallel, since Titus was a pure Gentile, and not half-Gentile. Nor
can Paul be accused of a breach of principle, since, although he
hotly contended for the right of Gentiles to become members of
the Church without circumcision, he never at any point suggested that Jews were free from their obligations to the Law.
Paul's difficulty was that an uncircumcised Timothy as an assis-
tant in the missionary team would have added fuel to the fire of
Jewish opponents of Christianity who would argue that Paul as
a Jew was playing fast and loose with sacred Jewish practice. His
action in circumcising Timothy, therefore, was to regularize his
position and make him a full Jewish Christian in the same sense
as Paul himself and Silas. It was completely in accordance with
the spirit of the Jerusalem decree and with Paul's own avowed
missionary policy (1 C. 9:19-23).

4. the cities: where Paul had campaigned on the first missionary journey—Derbe, Lystra, Iconium and Pisidian Antioch.
the decisions of the Council were important for these young
Galatian churches, both because they were in effect daughter
churches of Antioch and because of the trouble stirred up in them
by the Judaizers referred to in Paul's letter to them (see p.
170). The decree fully confirmed what Paul had said in his
letter, that salvation depended on the grace of God and not on
circumcision.

5. Luke winds up this section on the Council of Jerusalem and
its sequel with an editorial summary of the progress of the Galatian
churches, before turning to the new ground broken on this second
journey—which was to take the faith into what we now know as
Europe.

AT PHILIPPI 16:6-40

6-8. Paul's route between the last of the Galatian churches,
Pisidian Antioch, and Troas is hurried over by Luke in a way that

suggests that no missionary work of note was done between the
two towns. It is as if Luke is eager to get the party to Troas; this
is understandable, since it was there that the door was opened to
the evangelization of Greece, and thus Christianity entered upon
a further stage of its progress towards the heart of the Empire.
Since Rome is the goal for Luke as it was for Paul, Troas on the
shores of the Aegean sea is a signpost that for Luke at least points
directly towards it. There is the further consideration in these
verses that it is not always clear whether Luke is using geographical
terms in a popular as opposed to a political sense—e.g. as 'Ireland'
might be used today to include the province of Ulster. The general
direction of the missionary party, however, would seem to have
been northwards from Pisidian Antioch to some point roughly due
E. of Troas, and then westwards until they reached that town.
Luke's main emphasis would seem to be that this was where they
least wanted to go, and where the unmistakable hand of God led
them.

the region of Phrygia and Galatia: what Luke means by this
would appear to be best explained by the words that follow.
Paul's original intention was probably to go west from Pisidian
Antioch, along the great highway to Ephesus in the Roman
province of Asia at the western end of Asia Minor. Prevented
from doing so, he went northwards through the Phrygian part
of the province of Galatia (see on 18:23).

forbidden by the Holy Spirit: these words, like those in the
following verse, **the Spirit of Jesus did not allow them**, indicate
that the missionary team were deterred from following the routes
they wished to take by what they regarded as divine action. Paul
may have had visions or dreams (cf. verse 9, 23:11), or inward
prompting. Silas, a prophet (15:32), may have been moved to
utter words of warning, or they may have had to change their
plans by force of circumstance (e.g. Jewish opposition), which
they afterwards recognized as the overruling intervention of
Providence.

7. Mysia was the NW. part of the province of Asia. 'Opposite
Mysia' would mean perhaps somewhere about Dorylaeum,
roughly north of Pisidian Antioch. From there they planned to go
further north, into the province of **Bithynia,** bordering on the
Black Sea, where there were several large and important towns;
but once again they were thwarted.

8. passing by Mysia: they had to go through Mysia, in wild and lonely country, in order to get to Troas. 'Passing by' possibly means that they did not linger longer than they had to.

Troas: a seaport on the coast of the Aegean Sea, frequented by shipping between Asia Minor and Macedonia. It was a Roman colony, near the site of ancient Troy. Did Paul think at this point that he had come to a dead-end, and that he was being guided to go back to Antioch?

9. a vision appeared: this dramatic dream proved the turning point, or rather the real beginning, of the second missionary journey, compensating for all the previous frustration, and indicating the divine purpose that lay behind it.

a man of Macedonia: modern Greece consisted then of two Roman provinces, Achaia in the south and Macedonia in the north. The heyday of Macedonia under Philip of Macedon and his son Alexander the Great was long past, but it must have appeared to the missionaries as a challenging and exciting new field. Paul could have recognized the man in his dream as a Macedonian from what he said; but it has been conjectured that the man might have been Luke himself, who indicates his presence at this point by changing the narrative from 'they' to 'we' in the following verse. If this were so, it would suggest that Luke, a Macedonian or of Macedonian ancestry, had encountered Paul at Troas, perhaps as a medical attendant, and pressed him to preach the Gospel to the Macedonians. In this case, his appearance in Paul's dream would make him seem to be a God-sent messenger, and would clinch the matter. This is, of course, no more than an attractive speculation.

10. we . . . us: this is the first of the 'we'-passages in Acts. The most obvious explanation is that the author now joins the missionary team; Luke accompanies Paul, Silas and Timothy to Philippi, and the narrative becomes noticeably more vivid and detailed. The possibility that Luke had been a member of the missionary team before they reached Troas cannot be ruled out; but the sudden appearance of the pronoun 'we' would seem to be significant.

11. direct voyage: with a favourable wind, the journey from Troas to Neapolis on this occasion took two days; on a later occasion the reverse journey took five days (20:6).

Samothrace: a mountainous island (5,000 ft), halfway between the two ports, where presumably they anchored for the night.

Neapolis: mod. Cavalla. This was the port of Philippi, which

lay about ten miles farther on along the Via Egnatia, the great
road which ran across Macedonia from the Aegean to the Adriatic, connecting with Asia Minor in the east and with Rome in the
west.

12. Philippi had been the scene of the notable battle almost
a century before, which ended in victory for Mark Antony and
suicide for Brutus. Thessalonica (17:1) was the capital of Macedonia, which was divided into four districts or sub-provinces.
Philippi was a **leading city** in its own **district,** but Amphipolis
(17:1), about thirty miles away, was in fact the chief town. If
Luke was a native of Philippi, or if he had been in medical
practice there, local pride may have induced him to call Philippi
the leading city (see on verse 9). A simpler explanation would be
to attribute his pride in the place, if such it was, to his sojourn
there as resident missionary (see on verse 17).

a Roman colony: although other Roman colonies feature in Acts
(e.g., Pisidian Antioch, Lystra, Troas and Corinth), it is only
Philippi that Luke specifically describes as such. Apart from the
deployment of army units throughout the Empire, the Romans
strengthened their hold on the provinces by the creation of
'colonies'. These were towns, strategically selected, whose inhabitants were given the rights of Roman citizenship, lived under
Roman law and were governed by a Roman type of constitution;
they were often used as settlements for retired soldiers of the
Roman army, and thus were tantamount to garrison towns.
Although these colonies presented the normal architectural
features of Greek civilization—temples, porticoes, theatre, and
the like—they were veritable 'little Italies' transplanted overseas,
with the Latin ethos and language much in evidence.

13. the riverside: the river is the Gangites.

place of prayer: foreign religions had to conduct their worship
outside the city (gate); in this case the river was 1½ miles to the
west of the town. Paul, as was his normal practice, would have
begun his mission in the synagogue; but in Philippi there were
apparently fewer than the ten male Jews who would technically
have constituted a synagogue where services could be held. There
was, however, 'a place of prayer', presumably an open-air meeting-place where the few Jews and Jewish adherents in the city—
mostly women—were accustomed to gather on the Sabbath.

we supposed: the words suggest that at this stage Luke had no
local knowledge of Philippi. Moreover, he gives no indication of

having any friends there, and like the other missionaries he stays at Lydia's house.

we sat down: not necessarily for formal teaching (see on 13:15), but for ordinary conversation.

14. Lydia may have been her real name, but possibly it means a woman from Lydia in Asia Minor, where **the city of Thyatira** was famous for the manufacture and export of purple dyed cloth. Lydia was the local retailer in Philippi. As a **worshipper of God** (i.e. an adherent of the Jewish faith), no doubt dating from her earlier days in Thyatira where there was a Jewish colony, she was a ready listener to Paul's message and was converted.

15. baptized with her household: baptism followed immediately on profession of faith, as in the case of the Ethiopian (8:36), and Lydia's household, as in the case of Cornelius, was included (see on 11:14). This would imply that she was a well-to-do spinster or, more likely, a widow, and thus able to offer hospitality to the four missionaries.

16. a slave girl: like Rhoda in 12:13.

spirit of divination: lit. 'a spirit, a python'. Once more Luke gives us an insight into the superstitious background of the Graeco-Roman world with which the Christian mission had to contend (cf. 8:9, 13:6). The girl was supposed to be inspired by the god Apollo, who was thought to be embodied in a snake (python) at Delphi. Anyone so possessed was reckoned to be able to foretell the future, like the original priestess of Apollo herself. Plutarch tells us that the word 'pythons' was used to mean 'ventriloquists'. In Philippi a mentally unbalanced girl was being profitably exploited by her owners to tell fortunes; this she probably did by ventriloquial utterances while in a trance, which would convince gullible clients that she was being used by the snake-god to convey messages.

17. she followed Paul: the girl attaches herself to the missionaries, pursuing them through the streets 'for many days' (verse 18) with excited parrot cries. The words she utters are reminiscent of those of the demoniac in Lk. 8:28, and the implication in both incidents is that the evil spirit recognized the presence and power of God.

and us: this is the last point in the narrative of events in Philippi at which Luke identifies himself specifically with the missionary team. Paul and Silas are the chief actors in what follows. The next 'we'-passage begins at 20:5–6, again at Philippi, which suggests that Luke stayed behind at Philippi to build up the church there, and some years later rejoined Paul and his associates on the final journey to Jerusalem which ended in Paul's arrest.

the Most High God: although this was a term widely used of the supreme deity in pagan religions (as indeed the word **salvation** was also common) it would seem that here, as in Lk. 8:28, it is meant to be taken as a Gentile title for the God of Israel. The missionaries are thus identified as Jewish rather than as Christian propagandists (cf. verse 20).

18. annoyed: Paul's motive in exorcizing the evil spirit is attributed more to irritation than compassion. The effect is, however, to restore the girl to sanity.

19. her owners have been thought to be a corporation of priests, a business syndicate, or simply her master and mistress. But violent manhandling is suggested by the word **dragged.**

hope of gain was gone: the girl's ventriloquial power had left her, and the prospect of losing a profitable source of income, as in the case of the silversmiths of Ephesus (19:24-7), was camouflaged by a display of religious principles and patriotism on the part of her aggrieved owners.

Paul and Silas are singled out for attack, perhaps not only because they were the leaders of the party, but because they were obviously Jews, whereas Timothy was half-Greek and Luke wholly 'Greek'.

market place: this was the *forum* or *agora*, now excavated at Philippi, where the courthouse and prison were situated.

20. magistrates: these are the same as the **rulers** of the previous verse. Here the word used (*stratēgoi*) is the Greek equivalent of the Latin *praetores*, the courtesy title given to the two chief officials (*duoviri*) in a Roman colony.

these men are Jews: the plaintiffs, whose real grievance is of course financial, rely on anti-semitic prejudice to sway the court in their favour. In the previous year (49) the Emperor Claudius had issued an edict expelling the Jews from Rome (see on 18:2). Jews may have been in bad odour throughout the Empire as a result of this, particularly in Roman colonies.

disturbing our city: the practice of the Jewish religion was tolerated according to Roman law, but active proselytizing of Roman citizens by Jews was not allowed. The actual charge would seem to be that the missionaries were guilty of a breach of the peace.

21. advocate customs: proselytizing on behalf of Judaism, which the magistrates would not distinguish from Christianity, could be interpreted as an insult to the Emperor. The divine honour accorded to the Caesars in Emperor-worship was anathema to Jews and Christians alike. The Philippians' pride in their Roman citizenship would combine with their dislike of Jews to sway the magistrates against Paul and Silas.

22. beat them with rods: this would be done by the attendants of the praetors—the lictors, the 'police' of verse 35—who carried the rods bound together with axes as a badge of office. Paul refers to having been beaten three times with rods in 2 C. 11:25.

23. jailer: probably a centurion, governor of the prison.

24. inner prison: possibly the dungeon, with the door secured by a bar. The **stocks** would be fastened to the wall. Paul alludes to his ill-treatment at Philippi in Phil. 1:30 and 1 Th. 2:2.

25ff. Allowing for a certain amount of pious exaggeration to heighten the effect of what must have seemed a direct intervention of God, there is nothing inherently impossible in this story. It can hardly have been a **great earthquake,** but earth tremors were common enough in these parts and one of these might quite easily dislodge bars from doors and bolts from walls without doing further damage. We must not look for circumstantial details in Luke's story, such as would be required as evidence in a court of law; for example, it has been asked: 'How did Paul in the darkness of the dungeon know that the jailer had drawn his sword?' There are reasonable explanations for this; for example, Paul may have seen the jailer silhouetted against the open door. But on this point, as on other questions that have been raised about the story, we simply do not have enough information to be certain.

25. praying and singing hymns: this is recorded as an example of the triumph of faith over affliction rather than as a petition for deliverance which is miraculously answered.

27. about to kill himself: he would be held responsible if the prisoners had escaped (see on 12:19).

28. we are all here: were the other prisoners as terrified as the jailer at what they believed to be the magical power of two Jewish sorcerers which could bring about an earthquake? This might account for their failure to try to escape.

29. fear: superstitious alarm.

30. The Western text inserts after **out:** 'when he had secured the others'.

what must I do to be saved?: if these were the jailer's exact
words they probably meant: 'How can I be saved from the
consequences of having ill-treated two obviously powerful magicians?' Paul uses the question as an opening for his Gospel
message (verse 31).

32. they spoke the word: the jailer and his family were
speedily enlightened as to the true calling of the 'magicians',
and respond in compassionate care for the missionaries' bruised
bodies.

33. he was baptized: since Luke presumably was told of all
this by Paul, we may be sure that baptism would not take place
until Paul had been satisfied that what had begun as superstitious fear ended as genuine Christian faith. Not only is it unlikely that baptism (in water from a well in the courtyard?)
would be a perfunctory formality, but we may assume that the
jailer's family were not included simply because they formed part
of his household (cf. verse 15 and see on 11:14). This practice of
reckoning a man's family and household staff as a unit for purposes of church membership may indeed, on some other occasions,
have brought a number of baptized persons into the Church
whose conversion was no more than skin-deep.

34. up into his house: this may have been above the cells.
food: the meal may have merged into a eucharistic celebration.

35. police: see on verse 22.
let those men go: this change of attitude on the part of the
magistrates has been attributed to fear of two Jewish sorcerers who
could cause earth tremors. It is at least as likely that the magistrates had ordered the beating of the missionaries mainly to
quieten the mob, and now felt that they had had adequate
punishment. They order them to leave the city.

37. uncondemned: without a proper hearing.
Roman citizens: if the beating took place amid uproar, Paul's
protestations of his own and Silas's Roman citizenship may have
gone unheard; on the other hand, he may have considered the
beating as enabling them both to share in the sufferings of Christ
(2 C. 1:5). On a later occasion, when it was the deadly scourging
that was involved, Paul invoked his Roman citizenship before the
flogging was administered (22:25); then it was essential that he
should be fit to testify to his faith. It was against Roman law to
inflict degrading punishments such as beating upon Roman
citizens, so that Paul was justified in accusing the magistrates of

committing an illegal act which might have had serious consequences for them. No doubt he also derived satisfaction from turning the tables on these Philippian officials who prided themselves on preserving the Roman character of their city; but, more important, his action may have ensured protection for the Christians who remained in Philippi.

39. came and apologized: having expressed shame, the magistrates now request the missionaries to leave the town; despite their status as Roman citizens, Paul and Silas had so roused the animosity of the mob that the praetors could not guarantee their safety.

40. Lydia and ... the brethren: this suggests that a Christian group had been established, possibly meeting in Lydia's house. Paul's arrest had been the climax of a campaign which had lasted for some time (verses 12, 18). This small group grew, perhaps under Luke's direction (see on verse 17), to become one of the most notable of the young churches; in his letter to the Philippians some years later, Paul can write to a well-established and well-organized Christian community (Phil. 1:1) from which, alone among the churches, he had accepted financial help more than once (Phil. 4:10ff.; 2 C. 11:8–9). It is pleasant to think that Lydia's initial hospitality proved to be characteristic of this warm-hearted community. Paul had nothing but praise for their loyalty to himself (Phil. 1:3–5), and his letter to them abounds in expressions of joy and affection; by that time his unhappy experiences on this first visit are past history, and he can pour out his thanksgiving to God for the outstanding life and witness of a church built, as Luke has told us, on the foundation of a successful business woman, a jailer—and, perhaps, a grateful slave-girl.

AT THESSALONICA **17:1–9**

1. The missionary party continued along the Via Egnatia from Philippi, passing through **Amphipolis** and **Apollonia,** until they reached **Thessalonica.** The distance between each of these towns is approximately thirty miles, which could suggest a three-days' journey on horseback. The fact that mention is made of a **synagogue** at Thessalonica may imply that there were no Jewish communities at the other two places where contacts could be established. Thessalonica (mod. Saloniki) was the capital of the province of Macedonia, and a free city of the Empire with a large population.

2. Paul began his mission to Thessalonica in the synagogue **as was his custom** (cf. 13:5, 14; 14:1).

for three weeks must refer to his preliminary campaign among the Jews only. His letters to the Thessalonians indicate that he stayed long enough to receive financial help from the Philippian church on at least two occasions (Phil. 4:16), although he was also supporting himself by working at his own trade—which itself suggests a longer stay than three weeks (1 Th. 2:9; 2 Th. 3:7-12). Moreover, the evidence of the letters indicates that the bulk of the membership of the church founded at Thessalonica on this occasion consisted of converts from paganism (1 Th. 1:9). Luke's narrative appears to cover the period of the Jewish mission only, which was presumably followed by a longer mission to the Gentiles. Luke uses his limited space to emphasize once more the rejection of the Gospel by the Jews.

3. to suffer and to rise: the theme of Paul's message to the Jews, probably based on proof-texts, was that their **scriptures** clearly foretold that, when Messiah came, he must suffer, die and rise again (cf. Lk. 24:13ff.). This was the substance of the preaching of Paul as well as of Peter when addressing Jewish audiences (see on 3:18). Since Jesus had in fact fulfilled these prophecies, Paul claims, he must be the Messiah.

4. devout Greeks: see on 10:2.

leading women: wives of the leading men.

5. jealous: This was a predictable reaction at the loss of prospective converts to Judaism.

Jason was probably a Jew known by the Gentile form of his Jewish name, Joshua. He was at least sympathetic to the missionaries, if not one of the converts of verse 4; he had apparently provided them with lodging, and could have been Paul's temporary employer.

to the people: Luke correctly describes the democratic constitution of Thessalonica which as a free city had its own parliament, or assembly of the people (*dēmos*), before which the mob tried to hale Paul and his associates. Failing to find them they laid hands on Jason and some of the believers.

6. city authorities: these were politarchs (the word used by Luke here); inscriptions indicate that Thessalonica had five or six of these magistrates. This technical term is almost exclusive to Macedonia. The charge preferred against Jason was that of harbouring notorious trouble-makers, whose activities were treasonable in that they proclaimed Jesus as a rival king to Caesar; this was doubtless deliberate perversion of missionary teaching about the kingdom of God.

8. disturbed: perhaps the politarchs connected the missionaries with the recent troubles in Rome, described by Suetonius as having been instigated by Chrestus, which led to the Emperor Claudius' edict expelling the Jews from the city (see on 18:2).

9. security: probably a legal undertaking not to harbour Paul any longer, and to prevent his return. Such a ban might well be the reason for Paul's reference in 1 Th. 2:17–18 to his desire to revisit the church at Thessalonica as being thwarted by 'Satan'. His words there confirm that he was forced to leave the city sooner than he intended.

AT BEROEA 17:10–15

10–13. Having left Thessalonica under cover of darkness, Paul and Silas (and Timothy (?)—cf. verse 14) made their way to Beroea (mod. Verria), about fifty miles SW. of Thessalonica, off the Egnatian Way. In the synagogue there they met with a better response from a less bigoted group of Jews (**more noble**) than at Thessalonica, who were more prepared to examine the Scriptures with an open mind. However, Paul's work at Beroea also met with interference from fanatical Jews from Thessalonica, and came to an abrupt end. Nevertheless, a church was founded; and we are told later that Sopater, one of its members, accompanied the Apostle on his last journey to Jerusalem (20:4).

14–15. It is not clear whether Paul was taken to Athens, his next centre of activity, by land or by sea. Silas and Timothy, who had been left behind at Beroea, presumably to consolidate the mission, were summoned to join him at Athens; it has been suggested that the reason for this change of tactics, as well as for Paul's apparent need of company all the way to Athens, may have been that he was suffering from one of his recurrent attacks of illness. According to 1 Th. 3:1–6, it would seem that Silas and Timothy did join Paul at Athens; and that from there Timothy was sent back to Thessalonica, and Silas, perhaps, to Beroea or Philippi, leaving Paul to go on to Corinth alone, where his two henchmen later rejoined him (18:5), and from where he wrote the two letters to Thessalonica.

AT ATHENS **17:16-34**

16. In Paul's day **Athens** had lost much of its former glory: politically it had no significance, and commercially it was outshone by Corinth. In a sense, it lived on its reputation, but it was still a lively cultural centre, and its university was world-renowned. Paul's arrival in Athens would seem to have been accidental, and he does not appear to have intended to conduct a mission there. However, he sent for Silas and Timothy and, while awaiting their arrival, he reacted strongly against the pagan cults, as evidenced in the multiplicity of temples, shrines and statues erected in honour of a wide variety of gods and goddesses. Like Savonarola in Florence, he was less moved by the beauty of the architecture than by the moral and religious plight of the inhabitants.

17. market place: having made his usual approach through the Jewish synagogue with its complement of Gentile adherents, Paul was unable to refrain from arguing with anyone who would listen in the *agora*, which was not only the market place but the centre of civic life, surrounded by public buildings, shops and colonnades, where citizens gossiped and where public speakers of all sorts sought to attract an audience. It was traditionally the resort of the Athenian philosophers who expounded their views, instructed their disciples and engaged in debate with all and sundry.

18. Epicurean and Stoic philosophers belonged to the two most influential schools of thought at that time. The Epicureans, founded by Epicurus (*c.* 300 B.C.), taught among other things that happiness was the greatest virtue, and was to be attained by living a life free from excesses of any kind, by getting rid of fear, and by loving one's fellow men. The Stoics owed their origin to Zeno (*c.* 300 B.C.), and taught that there was a great Purpose shaping nature and mankind to good ends. In so far as a man allied himself to this Purpose, he was fulfilling his destiny. What happened to him—good fortune or adversity—was of little moment; all that mattered was the pursuit of goodness for its own sake. There was much else in both systems to which any Christian missionary must take exception, but there were points of contact between Christianity and Greek philosophy at its best of which a skilful Christian propagandist like Paul was not slow to take advantage in commending the faith in the speech that follows.

babbler: this was Athenian slang (*spermologos*, lit. 'seed-picker') for a man who has picked up scraps of learning here and there, like a sparrow picking up crumbs in a city street.

Jesus and the resurrection: the reference to 'foreign divinities' suggests that some of Paul's audience thought that Jesus and Anastasis (the Greek word for 'resurrection') were two new deities, a god and a goddess, whom Paul was seeking to add to the Athenian pantheon.

19. Areopagus: or, 'Hill of Ares' (*AV* 'Mars' Hill'). This was behind the *agora* and W. of the Acropolis, and anciently had been the meeting-place of the Council of the Areopagus, the supreme judicial and legislative body in Athens. Although stripped of much of its civil power in Paul's day this court was still the supreme authority in matters of religion and education, with control over public lecturers. It met, not on the Areopagus itself, but in the recently excavated Stoa Basileios, a columned building in the *agora*. It is more likely that Paul was invited to state his views before an informal meeting of this court, or one of its committees, rather than at a judicial hearing—there is no suggestion that he was in any sense on trial; some scholars prefer to think rather of an open-air meeting on the ancient site on the hill.

21. This description of the Athenians is borne out by classical writers. Demosthenes had criticized them for constantly running around looking for news instead of guarding their liberties.

22. very religious: the Greek word is ambiguous, and can mean either 'devout' or 'superstitious'. Paul obviously believed that Athens was a hotbed of superstition; but his whole speech is conciliatory, and it would have been bad tactics to antagonize his hearers at the outset. No doubt the Athenians accepted it as a compliment.

23. To an unknown god: hitherto it has not been confirmed by archaeological or literary evidence that an altar existed in Athens bearing precisely these words; however, it is known that there were altars dedicated to 'unknown gods' and 'unnamed gods', designed to protect the citizens from the wrath of unspecified deities, and there is no reason why Paul should not have seen an altar inscribed as stated here; on the other hand, he may have changed the plural form to the singular to suit the monotheistic purpose of his speech. His point, as in Rom. 2:14–16, is that God has revealed some knowledge of himself and his will to all men, but that this has been clarified and illuminated by his special revelation through the Scriptures and now finally in the

Gospel. It is basically the same approach as in the only other address to a purely Gentile audience we have so far encountered— Paul's speech at Lystra (see on 14:15–17).

24. God who made the world: cf. 14:15.
shrines made by man: cf. 7:48, where the same argument is applied to the Temple at Jerusalem.

25. served by human hands: just as God cannot be confined within any man-made temple, so he is also not dependent on man's service. This would be a point of contact with the Epicureans, who stressed God's self-sufficiency, just as Paul's next words describing God as the author of **life and breath and everything** would meet with approval from the Stoics.

26. from one: i.e. one man, Adam. Paul's emphasis on the unity of mankind was also a tenet of the Stoics.
periods . . . boundaries: historical epochs and territorial areas.

27. God's purpose is that men should respond to him and seek to know him through obedience and service. Through their sin and folly, they often fail to find him (cf. Wis. 13:1–9, especially verse 6).
not far: cf. Dt. 4:7; Ps. 145:18.

28. It has been argued that the thought of verses 27–8 is sheer Stoic pantheism. This is not so, although some of Paul's audience may have interpreted his words in that way. The Stoics believed that the divine Reason is immanent in man, i.e. 'God is in us'; what Paul is saying here is that 'we are in God', which is in line with his general teaching that the Christian lives 'in Christ'. When he writes of Christ 'living in us' (Gal. 2:20), he is not reflecting the Stoic doctrine of the immanence of God. God is indeed 'in us', as the Stoics said, but he is not identical with us or with the natural world, which was their claim. He is independent of man and nature and is the source of all life. Paul's quotation, **For we are indeed his offspring,** if properly understood, establishes the right relationship between the Creator and the created world and refutes any suggestion of pantheism. This is from the Stoic poet Aratus; but it is not certain whether the earlier words, **In him we live and move and have our being,** are in fact a quotation. If they are, they may come from Epimenides the Cretan, who is also credited with the quotation in Tit. 1:12. The plural **poets** may refer to the fact that the Stoic poet Cleanthes has a verse similar to that of Aratus.

29. the Deity: lit. 'the divine (nature)'. However much Paul in his argument has sought to meet the philosophers on their own ground by using language and ideas that were common to both paganism and Christianity, he proceeds now to emphasize the difference. His indictment of idolatry, in line with such *OT* passages as Ps. 115:4–8 and Isa. 40:18–20, follows from the Judaeo-Christian (as opposed to the pagan) interpretation of **being . . . God's offspring:** being made in the image of God, man cannot worship a God made in the likeness of any created thing. Most of Paul's educated audience would, of course, have agreed with this point, since they did not share the popular sentiments of pagan religion.

30. The times of ignorance God overlooked: Paul can speak of 'the wrath of God' being visited upon those who fail to recognize his revelation of himself in the natural world, and who consequently resort to idolatry (Rom. 1:18–23). He can also, however, stress God's 'forbearance' of 'former sins' (Rom. 3:25). This is what he does here, as in the speech at Lystra (14:16) and as Peter had done in his conciliatory words to the Jews in 3:17. Now, however, since God has fully revealed himself in Christ, the time has come for Gentiles as well as Jews (3:19) to **repent,** i.e. turn to him, and acknowledge their past blindness.

31. The specifically Christian content of Paul's speech comes in a rush at the end: the Day of Judgment, Christ as Judge, and the Resurrection as the guarantee that this is what will be.

a day: The Day of Judgment is no more and no less imminent here than throughout Paul's letters, and indeed the rest of the *NT*. The complex texture of Jewish eschatological thinking, which was adapted to Christian circumstances by the early missionaries, including Paul, makes it impossible for us to say whether they thought of 'the Day' chronologically or theologically—that is, whether 'imminence' meant 'immediacy'. Their basic conviction was that we stand under the Judgment of God, and that the time for decision for or against the Gospel is Now. Perhaps inevitably this led them, like the *OT* prophets and the Psalmists, to speak in terms of the speedy advent of God's Judgment, or in Christian terms of the Second Coming of Christ.

he will judge the world in righteousness: a quotation from Ps. 96:13.

a man: clearly the Son of Man of Dan. 7:13 (cf. Ac. 7:56). Since this Jewish term would mean nothing to his Gentile audience, Paul substitutes 'man'.

32. resurrection of the dead: lit. 'a resurrection of dead men'. To the Greeks the immortality of the soul was a familiar idea. The thought of a dead man coming alive again was to them nonsensical; thus **some mocked.** The more polite members of Paul's audience deferred the matter for further consideration.

33. from among them: Paul left the meeting.

34. Whether we think his mission to Athens was a failure or not depends on how large Paul's audience at Athens on this occasion may have been. **some . . . believed** and **others with them** suggests that more than a few were converted; on the other hand, there is no mention elsewhere in the *NT* of a church at Athens, and we are told that when Paul went on to Corinth he reached it in 'fear and trembling' (1 C. 2:3)—and also in 'weakness', which may suggest physical illness as well as despondency (see on verses 14–15). It is also noticeable that in Corinth he forswore all efforts to convince his hearers with philosophical arguments, and reverted to his evangelical message of 'Jesus Christ and him crucified' (1 C. 1:20-5; 2:1-6). Nothing is known of **Damaris**, apart from this reference, which has led to the suggestion that she may have been either the wife of Dionysius or a courtesan.

Dionysius the Areopagite: a member of the Areopagus. There have gathered legends around him, such as that he was the first bishop of Athens, the author of a fifth-century work on mystical theology, and the original St Denys, patron saint of France. None the less, he was a distinguished convert. Paul credits the household of Stephanas at Corinth with providing the first converts to Christianity in Achaia, the Roman province in which Athens like Corinth was situated. He may be using the name Achaia in a narrower sense, meaning Corinth and district (cf. 'Achaia' (18:27) = 'Corinth' (19:1)); or Stephanas may have been converted in Athens (1 C. 16:15).

AT CORINTH **18:1-17**

1. We are not told how long Paul's visit to Athens had lasted. Luke obviously attaches much importance to it as a significant stage in the progress of the Gospel from Jerusalem to Rome, when Paul confronted the intellectual élite of the ancient world. From the point of view of the growth of the Church, however, to say nothing of the contents of the *NT*, his next port of call was to produce more far-reaching results.

To move from Athens to **Corinth** was to exchange the atmosphere of a provincial university city for that of a thriving commercial metropolis, not unlike Syrian Antioch from which Paul had set out. Characteristically, he appears to be more at home in such surroundings. Situated only fifty miles from Athens, Corinth, by virtue of its strategic position on an isthmus between the Adriatic and Aegean Seas, with a port on each, was in Paul's day the cosmopolitan capital and seat of government of the province of Achaia. It was a Roman colony, harboured a vast variety of religious cults, and had a proverbial reputation for debauchery. 'To live like a Corinthian' was synonymous with profligacy, and the temple of Aphrodite, which boasted a thousand religious prostitutes, was an attraction for pilgrims from all over the world. It is thus no accident that sexual problems loomed large in the young Corinthian church (1 C. 5, etc.).

2. Pontus: the province in Asia Minor adjoining Bithynia on the south side of the Black Sea.

Priscilla: or Prisca (Rom. 16:3; 1 C. 16:19; 2 Tim. 4:19). She is usually named before her husband, by both Luke and Paul; this may mean that she was of more distinguished ancestry, or that she was more active in the work of the Church. She has been credited with the authorship of the Epistle to the Hebrews, although this suggestion has been countered with the dry comment that 'there is no evidence that Aquila was plagued with a learned wife'. The couple had come to Corinth from Rome; they then moved with Paul to Ephesus (verses 18, 26) where their home became a meeting place for a Christian group (1 C. 16:19) as was the case when they subsequently returned to Rome (Rom. 16:3–5—unless Rom. 16 is a note attached to the copy of that letter which was sent to Ephesus).

Their enforced original departure from Rome is generally connected with the edict of the Emperor Claudius, dating probably from A.D. 49, which is referred to thus by Suetonius: 'He expelled the Jews from Rome for causing continual disturbance at the instigation of Chrestus'; Roman vagueness in matters of foreign religions points to the probable identification of 'Chrestus' with 'Christ'. Most likely the trouble was the result of Christian propaganda among the Jews settled in Rome. The edict was not fully enforced, perhaps because of the size of the Jewish community. At all events it is clear that Christianity had been established in Rome before the arrival of Paul (cf. 28:15), no doubt by the anonymous travellers and traders who were responsible for so much of the spread of the Gospel in the early days of the Church. It is not clear whether Aquila and Priscilla were already Christians when they reached Corinth; the fact that their conversion is not mentioned suggests that they were.

3. tent-makers: or, more generally, 'leather-workers'. Cilicium, a felted cloth made from goats' hair and used for making tents, cloaks, rugs and curtains, was the leading export of Cilicia, Paul's native province. As a prospective rabbi, Paul had had to learn a **trade** to support himself, since teachers of the Law were supposed to give their services free. Aquila and Priscilla would have a shop on the ground floor of their house with living quarters above, where Paul now joined them. Apart from occasional gifts (Phil. 4:15ff), Paul's practice was to be self-supporting by working at his trade and not to be dependent on the charity of church members (1 Th. 2:9; 1 C. 4:12; 9:1ff.).

4. synagogue: a fragment of a lintel found at Corinth dating from about this time bears the remains of an inscription reading: 'Synagogue of the Hebrews'. Paul began his mission at Corinth with discussions in the synagogue **every sabbath,** presumably working during the rest of the week, convincing some Jews and also some **Greeks**—i.e. Gentile adherents.

5. Silas and Timothy: see on 17:14-15.
was occupied with preaching: rather, 'proceeded to devote himself entirely to preaching'. If we have correctly interpreted the meaning of Paul's words in 1 C. 2:3 (see on 17:34), his depression on arriving in Corinth may well have had as a contributory factor his uncertainty about the success of his whole Macedonian campaign. His message and his methods might, for all he knew, have been as unsuccessful with the Macedonians as had been his encounter with the philosophers at Athens. Themes and tactics which had awakened a favourable response in Syria and Asia Minor would not necessarily have the same appeal in the West. However, as we learn from 1 Th. 3:5ff., the arrival of Timothy from Thessalonica (and Silas from Beroea or Philippi) with excellent news of the progress of the Gospel and the growth of the churches in Macedonia not only prompted Paul to write his first letter to the Thessalonians, but stimulated him into prosecuting the mission to Corinth with new vigour, as Luke here records. The words might suggest that Paul was able to devote himself to full-time missionary work, if Silas and Timothy had brought

financial help from the Macedonian Christians (2 C. 11:8f.; Phil. 4:15).

that the Christ was Jesus: since Paul was speaking to Jews who were already familiar with the idea of a Messiah, his task was to persuade them that Jesus was indeed he whose coming the Scriptures foretold.

6. shook out his garments: as a gesture of repudiation, as in 13:51 (cf. Neh. 5:13).

your blood be upon your heads: cf. 2 Sam. 1:16; Mt. 27:25. Responsibility for the rejection of their own Messiah is placed squarely on the shoulders of the Jews; Paul has done his best. 'Blood' is here used in the sense of 'destruction'.

7. there: the synagogue. As a token of his change of policy, Paul moved his headquarters from the home of the Jewish Christians, Aquila and Priscilla, to that of a Gentile adherent of the synagogue, who lived next door to it. This was not an act of provocation on the part of Paul, but a suitable venue for easy contact with the Gentiles who frequented the synagogue as 'God-fearers'. Presumably there was a room in Paul's new centre big enough to accommodate meetings for worship and instruction; possibly Paul himself continued to lodge with Aquila and Priscilla.

Titius (or Titus) **Justus:** Paul's new host may have been a Roman citizen—perhaps a colonist. It has been suggested that his full name was Gaius Titus Justus, and that he is referred to in 1 C. 1:14; Rom. 16:23.

8. Crispus is mentioned, together with Gaius (see on verse 7), as having been baptized by Paul in 1 C. 1:14.

ruler of the synagogue: see on 13:15.

all his household: see on 11:14.

9. vision: this phenomenon plays a significant part in Luke's narrative as a channel of divine revelation (9:10, 12; 10:3; 16:9; 22:17ff.; 23:11; 27:23). Paul himself speaks of his visions in 2 C. 12:1–5. In this instance, the vision encourages the Apostle to spend a longer period than usual—at least eighteen months (verse 11)—in Corinth, which in view of the subsequent importance of the Corinthian church (cf. 'many people' in verse 10) was fully justified.

12. Gallio: Lucius Junius Gallio was the brother of Seneca, the philosopher and uncle of the poet Lucan. From an inscription found at Delphi, it is known that he was proconsul of Achaia in

A.D. 52; probably he had taken up office in the summer of A.D. 51. Paul's trial before him, which is now related, can therefore be roughly, but not accurately, dated within this period. We do not know exactly at which point in Gallio's proconsulship Paul appeared before him, or whether Luke reckons the 'year and six months' (verse 11) of Paul's stay in Corinth as covering the whole period of his missionary work, including the 'many days longer' of verse 18, or whether Paul was brought to trial after he had been eighteen months in the city. In any case, there is no substantial margin of error, and we may say that the Apostle probably arrived in Corinth about the middle of A.D. 50 and left in the spring of 52.

proconsul: it is a mark of Luke's historical accuracy that he knows that Achaia was at this time a 'senatorial' province of the Empire, and therefore governed by a proconsul—as opposed to an 'imperial' province, which was governed by a legate. This is particularly noteworthy, since proconsuls had been reintroduced in Achaia only from A.D. 44 onwards, after a lapse since A.D. 15. In the intervening period Achaia was governed by propraetors.

the Jews . . . united attack: perhaps the implication may be that the arrival of a new governor encouraged the Jews to hope that they might press their case more successfully.

13. contrary to the law: it could be that the Corinthian Jews, like the plaintiffs at Philippi (16:21) and Thessalonica (17:6ff.), sought to win their case by suggesting that Paul had committed an offence against Roman law. It is more likely, however, that they argued that his teaching was not in accordance with Jewish law.

14-16. Gallio firmly distinguishes between matters of concern to the imperial government and religious squabbles among subject peoples. Criminal offences were one thing; Jewish theological disputations were another. As a good Roman administrator he dismissed the case; to him Paul was a Jewish sectary whose views were as irrelevant to Roman law and order as Jewish orthodoxy.

17. Sosthenes: probably the leader of the prosecution against Paul, he would be either the successor of Crispus (verse 8) or one of his colleagues. If he is to be identified with the Sosthenes later associated with Paul when he writes to the Corinthian church (1 C. 1:1), he must subsequently have become a Christian. His beating on this occasion **in front of the tribunal,** possibly a dais

in the *agora*, would presumably be a drubbing administered by
the Gentile audience at the public trial, venting their anti-
Jewish prejudices and encouraged by Gallio's rebuff. Gallio himself is commended by Luke for his 'correct' attitude in refusing to
intervene in a petty religious dispute. The Western text reads:
'Gallio pretended not to see.'

RETURN TO ANTIOCH **18:18–22**

18. many days: in view of the official attitude, Paul had no
reason to leave Corinth in a hurry. When he did eventually depart
(**took leave of the brethren**), Luke does no more than suggest
that the fruits of his work at Corinth were considerable. We learn
from the Corinthian correspondence that, although the Jewish
aspects of Paul's mission have occupied most of Luke's attention,
the church at Corinth was composed largely of converts from
paganism. Moreover, Paul's work would seem not to have been
confined to the city itself, or at least the influence of the mission
extended eventually throughout the whole province of Achaia
(1 C. 16:15; 2 C. 1:1). There was apparently also a Christian
group at the port of Cenchreae (Rom. 16:1). The many problems
within the congregation—immorality, schism, litigiousness and
class distinction being among them—occasioned at least four letters
from the Apostle and more than one visit. But though no church
caused him more anxiety, none in the end gave him more cause
for thankfulness.
sailed for Syria: began the return journey to Antioch (verse 22).
Cenchreae was the eastern port of Corinth on the Aegean side
of the isthmus (see on verse 1).
had a vow: this type of temporary Nazirite vow, probably in this
case connected with Paul's impending visit to Jerusalem (verse
22), was based on Num. 6:1ff., esp. verses 5, 18. It was clearly
Paul, and not Aquila, who had made the vow, although grammatically it could be either: Luke would have no interest in
recording such an action on the part of Aquila, whereas in Paul's
case it would serve in Luke's mind to emphasize to Paul's Jewish-
Christian brethren in Jerusalem his faithfulness to Jewish tradition. According to Josephus (*Wars of the Jews*, II. xv. 1), it was
customary after illness or some other misfortune to make a vow to
abstain from wine and from cutting the hair for thirty days before
offering it in sacrifice—i.e. as an offering to God of part of oneself.
This would suggest that at Cenchreae Paul **cut his hair** to mark

the completion of his vow. It is more likely, however, that he began his vow at Cenchreae, in thanksgiving for the success of the mission and his escape from his Jewish attackers (cf. verse 10), declaring that he would not cut his hair again for thirty days, and intending to offer it in the prescribed way at Passover in the Temple at Jerusalem. This would explain his unwillingness to linger at Ephesus (verse 20).

19-21. Ephesus, to which Paul was shortly to return to stay for three years, was the capital of the province of Asia, and its largest city. Here the ship probably waited for a few days, long enough to unload and reload. It gave Paul an opportunity to establish his first contact with Ephesus through the synagogue, and to make a promise to return. Aquila and Priscilla, who had accompanied him so far, remained there (see on verse 2), while Paul set sail for Caesarea, giving as his reason for haste, according to the Western text, 'I must at all costs keep the coming feast at Jerusalem'. If, as is likely, the feast was Passover, he was planning to reach Jerusalem by April, A.D. 52. This was a bad time of the year for a sea voyage, and it has been suggested that one of the three shipwrecks which Paul refers to in 2 C. 11:25 may have occurred between Ephesus and Caesarea.

22. he went up and greeted the church: having landed at Caesarea Paul went up (to Jerusalem), to discharge his vow and visit the mother church, perhaps to ventilate his plan for a collection from the younger Gentile churches (1 C. 16:1), which was the object of his fifth and last visit to Jerusalem, which is described more fully than this one in chapter 21. Since Jerusalem is not specifically mentioned, the **church** could be that at Caesarea. To 'go up' is, however, almost a technical term for visiting Jerusalem, and he would not 'go down' from Caesarea to Antioch. Having therefore paid his fourth visit to Jerusalem, he **went down** to his headquarters at **Antioch,** thus completing his second missionary journey.

Luke's narrative at this point (verses 22-3) is unusually compressed. Perhaps he did not have much information about this period, or perhaps what he did have he did not think worth recording. The text does not indicate a clear break between what are generally known as the Second and Third Missionary Journeys; indeed, the whole section beginning at 18:18 and ending at 19:41 might rather be called 'the church at Ephesus', and this may be how Luke planned his material, with only the barest travel details. However, if for nothing more than convenience, which in no way contradicts Luke's record, it is most satisfactory to regard Paul's arrival at Antioch in verse 22 as providing a breathing space before embarking on his third missionary tour, most of which was indeed concentrated on Ephesus, but which included also evangelistic activity in Galatia and Phrygia (verse 23) as well as in Macedonia and Achaia (20:1–3).

THIRD MISSIONARY JOURNEY 18:23–21:17

FROM ANTIOCH TO EPHESUS 18:23–19:1a

23. some time: an unspecified period, perhaps implying some months.

Galatia and Phrygia: Paul has set out alone, so far as we can judge, since Silas and Timothy have not been mentioned since Corinth, and no new companions appear to have replaced them. Perhaps the reason was that he seems to have broken no new ground on this journey before reaching Ephesus, but rather contented himself with calling on the churches he had founded earlier in Galatia on his first missionary tour. His route would follow that of his second missionary tour overland from Antioch through the Cilician Gates to Derbe, Lystra, Iconium and Pisidian Antioch; no doubt his pastoral visitation would include also the churches of Syria and Cilicia mentioned in 15:41. The phrase here, 'through the region of Galatia and Phrygia', is therefore roughly equivalent to that of 16:6, and refers to that part of the province of Galatia in the area of Pisidian Antioch (see on 13:14). Paul appears to have been heading more or less directly for Ephesus, choosing, however, to take a more northerly road ('the upper country' of 19:1), rather than the main road along the Lycus valley, which would have taken him through Colossae and Laodicea which later he says he had not visited (Col. 2:1).

24. The next few verses provide an interlude, bringing us up-to-date with events in Ephesus between Paul's brief visit in 18:19–21 and his arrival in 19:1 for a much longer stay. Luke is also providing an introduction to Paul's encounter with some disciples of John the Baptist described in 19:1–7.

Apollos, we are told, was a Jew, and a native of Alexandria, which had a very large and constitutionally independent Jewish community. Philo, the notable bridge-builder between Judaism and Greek philosophy, was the most influential of these hellenistic

Jews; but Alexandria was also noteworthy as the place of origin
of the LXX. Apollos is referred to as being **eloquent** or 'cultured'
and **well versed in the scriptures**—i.e. the *OT*. The combination in the unknown author of the Letter to the Hebrews of
these two characteristics, together with a type of exegesis familiar
in Alexandrian teachers, has led many commentators from Luther
onwards to attribute that writing to Apollos.

25. According to Luke, when Apollos reached Ephesus he was
already sympathetic to Christianity.

He had been instructed in the way of the Lord: the Western
text adds 'in his own country'. This implies that Christianity was
known in Alexandria by about A.D. 50, which is not surprising.
Apollos already knew what Christians believed, and something
about the Christian way of life; he also had an accurate knowledge of the works and words of Jesus (**he spoke and taught
accurately the things concerning Jesus**). He was **fervent in
spirit,** an inspired preacher, full of enthusiasm. But the only
baptism of which he knew was the **baptism of John** the Baptist.
This suggests that for Apollos baptism was merely an outward
symbol of inward repentance and cleansing, but that he was un-
aware of, or so far unwilling to accept, baptism 'into the name of
Jesus' (with its normally attendant experience of the possession
of the Holy Spirit), which involved acknowledging Jesus as the
Messiah.

26. This imperfect presentation of the Gospel was being **boldly**
proclaimed by Apollos in the **synagogue** at Ephesus. Whereupon
he was taken to task by **Priscilla and Aquila,** and shown the
defectiveness of his message. We are left to assume that he was
then baptized, and we are told that, when he reached Corinth,
his message was an unequivocal proclamation to the Jews that 'the
Christ was Jesus' (verse 28).

Luke's brief and rather vague account does not enable us to say
with certainty very much about Apollos' background. Had he
learned about Christianity from someone of the type of the twelve
'disciples' referred to in 19:1-7—who would almost certainly
seem to have been members of a John the Baptist sect? That Luke
saw a connection between Apollos and these twelve disciples is
beyond doubt, but whether Apollos had belonged to the same
category as they before he came to Ephesus it is impossible to say.

27. the brethren: this implies the existence of a Christian
group at Ephesus, which can hardly be attributed wholly to

Paul's lightning visit in 18:19–21. Perhaps Apollos, enlightened by Aquila and Priscilla—or Priscilla and Aquila!—had built on his foundations. With a letter of commendation from the Ephesian Christians in his hands, Apollos sailed to **Achaia** ('Corinth', 19:1). There, as we learn from Paul's correspondence with Corinth, he became a powerful figure in the Christian community—to such an extent, indeed, that a faction in the Corinthian church declared itself to belong to Apollos' 'party', as opposed to those professing allegiance to Peter or Paul (1 C. 1:12). There is no evidence, however, that Paul considered Apollos to be in any sense his rival (1 C. 3:6), but rather acknowledged him as an apostle of Christ like himself (1 C. 4:9).

AT EPHESUS **19:1b–20:1a**

19:1b. Paul arrived in Ephesus when Apollos had gone to Corinth, having reached it **through the upper country** after leaving the Galatian churches (see on 18:23).

disciples: normally in Acts, this would be the equivalent of Christian believers; on the other hand, Luke in his Gospel uses the word **disciples** also with reference to followers of John the Baptist (Lk. 5:33, 7:18, 19). In view of the preceding passage about Apollos, it is at least possible that the men here regarded themselves as followers of John the Baptist and of Apollos. They were presumably Gentiles, and may have come under the influence of Apollos before he was 'more accurately' instructed by Priscilla and Aquila; it is not clear whether they were in any way attached to the Christian community in Ephesus or not. Indeed, the whole account of Paul's encounter with these people is rather obscure. Is Luke simply giving us one of his pen-picture illustrations of yet another problem that faced Paul and other early Christian missionaries—namely, the existence of groups of so-called Christians who had been inadequately taught and had to be fully enlightened? Or were these 'disciples' members of a Baptist sect who were absorbed into the Church? There is evidence that a John the Baptist sect existed as late as the second, or possibly even the third, century, originally in friendly relationship with the Christian communities, but later, because of its claim that John and not Jesus had been the Messiah, in a state of rivalry; but it seems to have declined in numbers, and eventually it disappeared. The Fourth Gospel, with its insistence on the inferiority of John the Baptist to Jesus, may point to the presence

later in the century of a Baptist sect in Ephesus, where that
Gospel traditionally was said to have originated (see also on
13:24-5).

2. We know too little of the background of these 'disciples' to
say precisely what this verse means. If they had been well taught,
and assuming the synoptic record of John the Baptist's teaching
to be accurate, they must have known that John claimed to be the
herald of the Coming One who would baptize them with the
Holy Spirit (Mt. 3:11; Mk 1:8; Lk. 3:16-17); therefore they
would not be able to maintain that they had **never even heard**
of the Holy Spirit. What they may have done was to plead
ignorance that the messianic age of which John had spoken had
in fact begun, and they may not have known about Pentecost and
its sequel.

3. Like Apollos (18:25), they had been baptized as a symbol
of repentance only.

4. This verse must summarize a more extended course of
instruction provided by Paul, in which he expounded the Scriptures and showed the preparatory nature of John's ministry.
Messiah had now come, and Jesus was he.

5. baptized in the name of the Lord Jesus: this second
baptism, the only case of re-baptism in the *NT*, involved con-
fessing Jesus as Messiah and Lord, and signified incorporation
into the fellowship of his people.

6. Paul . . . laid his hands upon them: this laying-on of
hands following baptism seems to be a parallel with the same procedure in the case of the Samaritans, and is followed by a similar
special manifestation of ecstatic utterance (see on 8:14-17). It
may mark the importance Luke attached to Ephesus as the future
great centre of the Gentile mission in Asia Minor; it is less likely
that he is anxious to show that what Peter and John could do,
Paul could do also!

7. about twelve of them in all: since Luke normally
qualifies numbers by prefacing them with 'about', it has been
suggested that the 'twelve' here may point to the existence of a
'college' of twelve, set up by Paul for the organization and government of the church at Ephesus.

8. the synagogue, which he had previously visited briefly
(18:19).

kingdom of God: see on 1:3.

9. the Way: see on 9:2.

the hall of Tyrannus: having proclaimed the Gospel to the Jews first without much success, Paul concentrates on a mission to the Gentiles, as he had done on previous occasions. The lecture-**hall of Tyrannus** served the same purpose as the house of Titius Justus at Corinth (see on 18:7). The Western text adds at the end of the verse: 'from the fifth to the tenth hour'—i.e. 11 a.m.–4 p.m., the normal siesta time; thus the picture we get is of Paul working at his trade daily from daybreak to 11 a.m. (20:34; 1 C. 4:12), and then engaging in teaching and discussion for the next five hours with any who were prepared to listen, when Tyrannus had finished his lectures and the room was available.

10. for two years: presumably somewhat over two years, which, together with the 'three months' of verse 8 and the 'for a while' of verse 22, would correspond to the 'three years' Paul mentions in 20:31, presumably in round figures. If he reached Ephesus at the beginning of A.D. 53 (see on 18:21, 23) this would bring his Ephesian mission to an end in the autumn of A.D. 55.

all the residents of Asia: this does not necessarily mean that Paul himself was personally responsible for all the evangelistic work in the province which seems to have taken place at this time (1 C. 16:19). The churches in the Lycus valley—at Colossae, Laodicea and Hierapolis—would appear to have been either founded or supervised by Epaphras, one of Paul's missioners (Col. 1:7; 2:1; 4:13); indeed, the Seven Churches of Asia referred to in the book of Revelation (Rev. 1:9–3:22) were possibly all founded during these years. We may think of the 'hall of Tyrannus' as the centre of Paul's activity, attracting many Gentile enquirers from the province generally, who in due course became themselves, like Epaphras, faithful ministers of Christ on Paul's behalf (Col. 1:7).

11. extraordinary miracles: Paul himself claims to have had the gift of healing (Rom. 15:18–19; 2 C. 12:12), perhaps literally laying his hands on the sick.

12. handkerchiefs or aprons: 'sweat-rags' and leather aprons used by Paul in his trade as a tent-maker. It is in keeping with the atmosphere of magic which pervades this passage (verses 11–20) and the reputation of Ephesus as a centre of the black arts that Christians, in that place and at that time, were apparently no less credulous than pagans. We are not entitled to say that, if those who were sick in mind or body believed that Paul, like Peter (see on 5:15–16), was a channel of the healing power of Christ, contact with items of his clothing may not have brought about effective cures, as in the case of Jesus himself and the woman with the haemorrhage (Lk. 8:44). Luke had heard that this had happened, and obviously believed it to be true.

13. itinerant Jewish exorcists: exorcism—expelling evil spirits by adjurations, prayers and ceremonies—was common in the ancient world; holy names—whether pagan, Jewish or Christian—were used indiscriminately by the less reputable among its practitioners. The great Paris magical papyrus, dating from the third century, invokes the names of Abraham, Isaac, Jacob, Jesus and the god Sabarbarbathioth. It was a practice obviously open to abuse, encouraging charlatans to exploit the gullibility of the people; on the other hand, exorcism in the name of God or of Jesus was recognized in the Church by the creation of an order of exorcists, which functioned for centuries until the office became restricted to priests. Jewish exorcists are mentioned in the Gospels (Mt. 12:27; Lk. 11:19) and, outside Palestine, Jewish magicians were notorious. Those referred to here would seem to have been quacks who used the name of Jesus as a magic incantation; this practice was later condemned by the rabbis.

14. Sceva: whoever he was, he was not a Jewish high priest who had held office in Jerusalem, since their names are all known; nor is it likely that he even belonged to a high-priestly family. It is possible that he may have been a self-styled 'high priest' of one of the innumerable pagan cults, who found that it paid him to pass himself off as a Jew. Or the **seven sons** may have invented their distinguished parent, and could therefore claim to know the unutterable name of the God of the Hebrews.

15-16. The demon being exorcized is represented as recognizing the names of Jesus and Paul, but questioning the right of the non-Christian exorcists to use them. Instead of the madman becoming subdued, the indignant demon possessing him makes him even more violent, so that he sets about the exorcists. The point of this highly unedifying story is presumably to contrast Paul's success with the failure of his imitators, and to show that the name of Jesus cannot be used in such cases with impunity by those who do not believe in him; Jesus himself took a different view (Mk 9:38–40; Lk. 9:49–50).

17. Whether the incident has any factual basis or not, no doubt Luke is right in saying that such a tale would have this effect on the superstitious inhabitants of Ephesus.

18. divulging their practices: revealing their spells. There is no necessary connection between verses 18–19 and what precedes them; rather, what is now described is regarded as the effect of Paul's missionary activities, namely that many practitioners of the black arts had renounced their sorcery and now disclosed their secrets.

19. books: scrolls containing magic spells and incantations were known as 'Ephesian letters', and fetched high prices. This particular bonfire, if the **pieces of silver** were drachmas, was worth approximately £2,500.

20. This sober statement, reflecting the solid gains of Paul's Ephesian ministry, is in striking contrast to the rest of this section (verses 11–20), which seems to be based largely on gossip. How much of it Luke himself believed we cannot say; but he does use it to convey most vividly the hold that magical practices had over this city, the magnitude of Paul's task, and the measure of his achievement.

21. It was while he was near the end of his stay in Ephesus that plans began to take shape in Paul's mind, as always under the guidance of the Holy Spirit, to visit Jerusalem by way of Macedonia and Achaia, and then to proceed to Rome. Luke no doubt implies that it was for this reason, and not because of the riot which is next described, that Paul left Ephesus. He does not mention here, although he knew of it (24:17), the purpose of Paul's visit to Jerusalem, which was to take a collection from the younger churches for the relief of the mother church (see on 20:4). Paul's motive was twofold: to increase the sense of solidarity within the Church; and to demonstrate the unity of the Jewish and Gentile elements which composed it. As we can see from his letters to the Corinthians and to the Romans, this collection was a matter of the highest importance for Paul. Luke, writing a few decades later, sees it in perspective as less significant than what happened to Paul when he reached Jerusalem. Thereafter Paul did indeed visit Rome, but in circumstances far different from what he expected. He confirms his intention of visiting Rome, and then of going on to Spain, in his letter to the Romans written soon after this from Corinth (Rom. 15:24–7).

22. Timothy now reappears in the story, having been last heard of when he arrived in Corinth from Macedonia (18:5); he may indeed have accompanied Paul to Ephesus like Priscilla and Aquila when Paul left Corinth (18:18), or have joined Paul at

Ephesus later. Now he is sent to Macedonia, doubtless to arrange
for the collection (cf. 1 C. 16:1–5), together with **Erastus,** who,
if he is the same as the man mentioned in Rom. 16:23, was the
city treasurer of Corinth (cf. 2 Tim. 4:20); but this is unlikely.

23. Luke now describes an anti-Christian riot at Ephesus, in
which, as at Philippi, vested interests were disguised as local
patriotism—in this case also under the cloak of religious zeal.

24. Artemis: the Ephesian goddess of this name was vastly
different from the chaste huntress Artemis, or Diana, of Greek
and Roman mythology. She was a form of the great mother-
goddess of Asia Minor, symbolic of fertility; and she was represented in statuary as many-breasted, though her 'breasts' are
thought by some to have been originally clusters of dates or
swarms of bees! Her cult attracted pilgrims from far and near,
and the **craftsmen** of Ephesus, such as **Demetrius,** did a
profitable trade in the manufacture and sale of votive images of
the goddess. Demetrius, described here as a **silversmith,** may
also have been a vestryman of the temple, since the word 'shrine-
maker' was a technical term for such officials.

silver shrines: miniature temples with a statue of Artemis.
None have been found, presumably having been melted down for
other purposes; but samples of terra-cotta and marble shrines
have been unearthed, some as far away as Pompeii.

27. temple: the temple of Artemis at Ephesus was one of the
Seven Wonders of the World. Situated about a mile outside the
city, built of marble blocks reputed to have been held together by
gold instead of mortar, it is said to have been capable of holding
50,000 people. Demetrius harangues his fellow-craftsmen to the
effect that, not only is their trade at risk through Paul's campaign
against idolatry, but that their glorious goddess and her world-
wide cult are in peril.

29. the theatre, whose ruins have been excavated, was also
vast, and is reckoned to have held up to 25,000 spectators. This
was a natural meeting-place for the assembly of citizens in such a
crisis.

Gaius and Aristarchus, Macedonians: Gaius is mentioned
again in 20:4 (and in 1 C. 1:14; Rom. 16:23. See also on 18:7).
There he is described as a native of Derbe, i.e. a Galatian; here
he is called a Macedonian. It is possible that 'Derbe' in 20:4
should read 'Doberus' (as in the Western text), which is a town in
Macedonia. Aristarchus is also referred to in 20:4 and in 27:2

(also in Col. 4:10 and Phm. 24) as a native of Thessalonica. Perhaps they were Luke's authorities for the details of this dramatic
event.

30. crowd: although this was technically the *dēmos*, or popular
assembly (see on 17:5), in its present excited state it was more like
a wild mob. Perhaps this is what Paul had in mind when he
wrote of 'fighting with beasts at Ephesus' (1 C. 15:32).

31. Asiarchs: men of substance and influence in the cities of
the province of Asia who were or had been presidents of the
provincial council, which dealt principally with organizing the
games and with ceremonial matters connected with Emperor-
worship. During his term of office, the Asiarch was styled 'high-
priest' of the imperial cult. Some of those in Ephesus were
apparently better disposed to Paul than the rabble.

32. assembly: Luke uses the technical term (*ekklesia*) for
meetings of the *dēmos* to transact legislative business, here perhaps
with his tongue in his cheek.

33. Alexander: it is not clear what part Alexander was playing; he was apparently a Jew. Does **prompted** mean 'instructed'
or, as the Western text has it, should it be 'pulled down'? And was
this Paul's 'Alexander the coppersmith' who 'did him great harm'
(2 Tim. 4:14; cf.1 Tim. 1:20)? At all events, he seems to have
been a spokesman of the Jews, perhaps delegated to dissociate
them publicly from the Christians. The pagan crowd looked on
Jews and Christians as 'six of one and half a dozen of the other'.

35. the town clerk: executive officer and chairman of the
dēmos, and a most important personage.
temple keeper: a title of honour bestowed by Rome upon certain cities possessing temples of the imperial cult. In the second
century Ephesus was recognized as 'twice temple-keeper', i.e.
warden of the emperor's cult and of that of Artemis.
sacred stone that fell from the sky: probably a meteorite.
This would be the town clerk's answer to Paul's attack on 'gods
made with hands' (verse 26). It was presumably a roughly
shaped stone recognizable as an image of Artemis.

37. sacrilegious: lit. 'robbers of temples'. Paul himself refers
to this as a particularly abominable crime, even in those who
abhor idolatry (Rom. 2:22).

38. the courts are open: if the craftsmen have a grievance
they should take action through the law courts.
there are proconsuls: i.e. there are such people as proconsuls.

Ephesus, as the capital city of the province of Asia, was the seat of government, and Luke correctly notes that the title of the governor was in this case 'proconsul'. It was he who presided at the assizes.

39. regular assembly: the *dēmos* met three times a month, according to the constitution. The present riot was an 'irregular assembly'.

40. The town clerk emphasizes that the imperial government would not look favourably on such a disorderly occurrence, which might have unfortunate consequences for the privileged position of the city.

20:1a. It would seem that Paul left Ephesus soon after the riot. Luke has singled out for mention three episodes which highlight some of the problems Paul had to cope with at this particular stage of his mission: the Baptist sect, black magic, and vested interests in idolatry. What Luke does not tell us is that, all this while, Paul was agonizing over the church at Corinth, to which he had to write at least four letters (three of them from Ephesus itself), and had to pay a hurried visit in an effort to bring order into its troubled affairs. It may well have been the fear that all his work at Corinth had been a failure that led him to write of 'the affliction we experienced in Asia', when for a time he was in a mood of the most profound despair (2 C. 1:8).

Apart from his anxiety concerning the Corinthian church, Paul seems to have had other troubles at Ephesus (1 C. 16:8–9), which he later refers to in his address to the Ephesian elders at Miletus (20:19); his letters to Corinth make many allusions to hardship and suffering (1 C. 4:9–13; 15:30; 2 C. 4:8–12; 6:4–5; 11:23–7), although it is impossible to say how much of this is specifically associated with his Ephesian ministry. Some scholars argue that he was imprisoned in Ephesus (cf. 2. C. 11:23), and that all the Captivity Epistles, or at least Philippians, date from this time.

FROM EPHESUS TO JERUSALEM **20:1b–21:17**

20:1b. (Paul) . . . departed for Macedonia: although it is extremely difficult to date Paul's movements accurately, this departure may have been in the late summer or early autumn of A.D. 55. Paul's aim was to reach Jerusalem by Pentecost (verse16), which would be in the year A.D. 56. Verses 1–5 are extremely compressed, and include three months at Corinth. Some scholars think that verse 2 includes the problematical visit to Illyricum (Rom. 15:19), which might make Paul's arrival in Jerusalem

a year later—in 57. There is a marked contrast between the sparse
information of verses 1–5 and the detailed description of the rest
of the journey to Jerusalem from verse 6 onwards, when the re-
sumption of the use of 'we' indicates that Luke was once again
present in person. We should assume from Acts that the ship from
Ephesus would follow the coastline of Asia Minor northwards
before crossing the Aegean to Macedonia. Paul himself fills in
the details in 2 Corinthians; apparently he was still so concerned
about affairs in the church at Corinth that, when he stopped at
Troas, presumably to change ships, he had no heart to embark
on a preaching mission (2 C. 2:12). He had expected to find Titus
awaiting him at Troas, having returned from his fact-finding
mission to Corinth. Restlessly Paul went on to Macedonia
(2 C. 2:13), where Titus joined him—perhaps at Philippi—with
good news that the Corinthian troubles were over (2 C. 7:5–16).
Paul's relief and joy at the happy outcome are manifest in 2 C. 1–9,
which he wrote at this point. On all this Luke has no space or
inclination to dwell.

2. these parts: the most likely meaning is that Paul was
revisiting the churches he had founded on his second tour—
Philippi, Thessalonica and Beroea (but see on verse 1b above).
His main purpose there as in **Greece** (i.e. Achaia = Corinth) was
to collect the contributions of the Gentile churches in these provinces for the relief of the poorer Jerusalem Christians (see on
19:21) (cf. 1 C. 16:1ff.; 2 C. 8:1–9:15; Rom. 15:25ff.).

3. three months: probably during the winter of A.D. 55–6
(cf. 1 C. 16:5–6). It was during this visit to Corinth that Paul
wrote the letter to the Romans (Rom. 16:1, 23). His intention had
apparently been to return to Palestine by sea as before (18:18ff.);
but news of a plot to murder him, presumably by fanatical Jews
likewise travelling to Jerusalem on a pilgrim ship, who would find
the collection money an added inducement, persuaded him to
make the journey by a more circuitous route; this would have the
added advantage of enabling him to pick up the delegates from
the Gentile churches with their contributions on the way (cf. 1 C.
16:1–4).

4. accompanied him: some of Paul's party are mentioned
elsewhere, but others only here. **Sopater,** who apparently represented the church at Beroea (17:10ff.), may be the Sosipater of
Rom. 16:21. The delegation from the church at Thessalonica consisted of **Aristarchus** and **Gaius** (see on 19:29), who had been

with Paul in Ephesus, and **Secundus,** who is otherwise unknown. Following these representatives from the churches in the province of Macedonia, **Timothy** is included, perhaps because he had been instrumental in collecting some of the contributions there (see on 19:22). Two delegates from the churches in the province of Asia are next mentioned: **Tychicus** (Col. 4:7) and **Trophimus,** who is described as an Ephesian in 21:29 (2 Tim. 4:20). No mention is made of delegates from Corinth or Philippi. Paul may have taken charge of the Corinthian contribution, and Luke himself may have done the same service for Philippi.

5. These went on: probably only the 'Asians', Tychicus and Trophimus, who may have taken ship from Ephesus to Troas, and waited there for the remainder of the party to cross the Aegean from Philippi, i.e. from its port at Neapolis (16:11).

us: this is the first appearance of the first personal pronoun in the narrative since Philippi on Paul's second missionary tour (see on 16:17). We cannot say whether Luke had been all this while in Philippi—presumably as resident missionary—or whether he may not have been in contact with Paul in the meantime. Was he perhaps present in Ephesus during the riot in the theatre? At all events, we may take it that he is with Paul from now on until they reach Jerusalem, and that he accompanies him on his final journey to Rome.

6. days of unleavened bread: the week following the Passover (see on 12:3), which Paul no doubt observed at Philippi.

five days: the voyage in the reverse direction had taken only two days (16:11). On this occasion the wind was presumably against them.

7. first day of the week: Sunday. Since the service described took place in the evening, it could have been after 6 p.m. on the Saturday, if Luke was using the analogy of the Jewish sabbath which began on Friday evening. However, Paul's departure would be on the Monday (**the morrow**), and so the service must have been held on the Sunday night.

to break bread: see on 2:42.

Paul talked with them: i.e. preached, and that at great length, **until midnight.**

8. many lights: oil lamps.

9. Eutychus, no doubt tired after the day's work and overpowered by the heat of the lamps and the stuffiness of the crowded room, nodded off during Paul's sermon and fell fast asleep. The room in which the meeting was held was on the **third story,** normally the top floor of the house, which presumably fronted on to the street. Eutychus was perched on the window ledge, and since the window would be unglazed, there was nothing to stop his falling out. When he was examined, he was to all intents dead.

10. embracing him: Paul's action, reminiscent of the stories of the restoration of the widow's son by Elijah (1 Kg. 17:17ff.) and of the Shunammite's son by Elisha (2 Kg. 4:34ff.), is no doubt regarded by Luke as the cause of the boy's recovery. Paul's own words are not inconsistent with this (cf. Mk 5:39); cases are frequently reported in the press of people being temporarily 'dead', and this may have been a similar occurrence.

11. The implication is that Paul returned to the gathering, the *agapē* eucharist then took place in the early hours of the morning, and the meeting continued **until daybreak.**

12. Meantime Eutychus was taken to his own house, presumably to complete his recovery.

13. Assos: the main party sailed from Troas round Cape Lectum to Assos. Paul stayed on a little longer at Troas, and went by road across the neck of land to Assos, a distance of about twenty miles, which would take less time than going by ship.

14. Mitylene: having taken Paul on board at Assos, the coaster called next at Mitylene, the main town on the island of Lesbos.

15. Miletus: a few days later the ship reached Miletus, having called at or anchored for the night at some point opposite the island of **Chios,** the island of **Samos,** and, according to the Western text, Trogyllium.

16. Miletus was about thirty miles S. of **Ephesus,** which the ship had bypassed. Luke gives as Paul's reason for choosing a ship which did not call at Ephesus that he was in a hurry to get to Jerusalem in time for **Pentecost** (see on 2:1); his attendance at the festival would demonstrate to the Jerusalem Christians his loyalty to Jewish tradition, and a visit to Ephesus and district (**Asia**) would inevitably have been protracted because of his many friends there. Paul's stay at Troas, which lasted a week (verse 6), was probably due to difficulty in finding a ship. There is no cause to suppose, as has been suggested, that Luke has suppressed the true reason for Paul's avoidance of Ephesus—namely, that he had been expelled by the city authorities and forbidden to return.

17. The ship presumably was scheduled to stop long enough at Miletus for a message to be sent to Ephesus and for the elders to respond to Paul's summons. This would take perhaps three days, but a visit to Ephesus itself would undoubtedly have taken much longer.

elders: see on 14:23. Here Luke presumably means the ministers of the house-churches in Ephesus and district.

18-35. Whatever may have been Luke's sources of information for the contents of Paul's previous speeches in Acts, on this occasion Luke himself was almost certainly present, since Paul's meeting with the Ephesian elders comes between two clearly defined 'we'-passages (20:5–16 and 21:1–18); it is the only example in Acts of a speech by Paul addressed to a specifically Christian audience. Luke may have made notes at the time; while he has, as in the case of the other speeches in Acts, provided a summary rather than a transcript, and is responsible for the final form of the address, the sentiments and language are strongly reminiscent of Paul's letters, and the personal references are wholly in accordance with what we gather must have been the state of the Apostle's mind at that time. Although the thought and actual phrasing can be paralleled in the Pauline Epistles, the speech cannot be regarded as in any sense a pastiche concocted from them, since there is no evidence elsewhere that the author of Acts paid any attention to them, even if he had read them (see Introduction, p. 28). The speech is in the nature of a farewell address by a pastor to chosen leaders of a church he has laboured hard to establish and build up, amid much opposition and many disappointments. Since the discovery of the plot against his life (verse 3), Paul seems to have had a presentiment that this journey to Jerusalem would be his last, and Luke succeeds in conveying the atmosphere of foreboding, both here and indeed until Paul reaches the Holy City, as he had already done in his Gospel in the narrative of Jesus' last journey to Jerusalem.

18. you yourselves know: cf. 1 Th. 2:1.

from the first day: cf. Phil. 1:5.

19. serving the Lord: cf. Rom. 12:11.

with all humility: cf. Eph. 4:2.

tears: cf. 2 C. 2:4.

trials ... plots of the Jews: Luke mentioned Jewish opposition at Ephesus (19:9), but concentrated rather on antagonism from Gentile quarters which culminated in the riot (see on 20:1a).

20. I did not shrink from declaring: cf. Rom. 1:16.

in public: in the synagogue and the lecture-hall of Tyrannus.

from house to house: in the house-churches.

21. The **Greeks** had been summoned to turn to God. The **Jews** had been called to believe that Jesus was the Messiah.

22. bound in the Spirit: inwardly compelled by the Holy Spirit.

23. Although specific intimations of impending disaster at Jerusalem are not mentioned until after this speech—such as those at Tyre (21:4) and Caesarea (21:11)—Paul had every reason to fear the worst following the discovery of the assassination plot in Corinth (verse 3). He expresses his apprehensions in his letter to Rome written at that time (Rom. 15:30–1).

24. Paul's complete surrender of himself to the service of Christ is paralleled in such passages as 2 C. 4:7ff.; Phil. 3:8. He speaks of having 'finished the race' (or **course**) in 2 Tim. 4:7, and of his **ministry** frequently (e.g., 2 C. 5:18).
the gospel of the grace of God is not, as it stands, a Pauline phrase, although all its elements are constantly found in his letters. It is, however, a perfect summary of his whole message, and is identical with 'preaching the kingdom' in the next verse.

25. all you ... will see my face no more: it is difficult to draw firm conclusions from these words, as has been done, regarding the date of Acts and the authenticity of the Pastoral Epistles. We know that Paul had recently spoken of his plan to evangelize the West after visiting Rome (Rom. 15:23–5); on the other hand, following the murder plot, he is now resigned to seeing these plans come to nothing. However, it is unlikely that in amplifying his notes of Paul's speech in this way Luke did not know of the Apostle's subsequent martyrdom at Rome, or that his premonition of never visiting Ephesus again had been right.

26–7. innocent of the blood of all of you: Paul claims that, having done his best to proclaim the Gospel in all its fullness, his conscience is clear before God (cf. Jer. 23:1–2).

28. guardians: or bishops (*episkopoi*, lit. 'overseers'). Obviously the word is synonymous with 'elders' in verse 17 (see on 14:23), and refers to the function as distinct from the office. The thought is of shepherds, or 'guardians', who have been put in charge of the **flock**, and who must **feed** it properly (cf. Ezek. 34:12–16; 1 Pet. 5:1–4).
the church . . . blood: the *RSV* has undoubtedly the correct sense here, but according to the best mss. the original reading should probably be translated: 'the church of God which he

obtained with the blood of his Own One'. In either case, the
Pauline doctrine of redemption through the death of Christ is
clearly intended.

29. wolves: heretical teachers (cf. Mt. 7:15). There is a reference
to false teachers later at Ephesus in 1 Tim. 1:3–7 and Rev. 2:2ff.
(cf. Jn 10:12).

31. three years: see on 19:10.

32. the word of his grace: the Apostle's message as in verse 24.
build you up: cf. 1 C. 3:9ff.

inheritance . . . sanctified: cf. Col. 1:12. The meaning is that
the Gospel can **build up** the Church, and guarantee its members
the **inheritance** which awaits all who belong to the new Israel.

33. apparel was regarded as part of a man's wealth. Samuel
makes a similar point in his farewell speech in 1 Sam. 12:3–5.

34. these hands ministered: cf. 1 C. 4:12; 1 Th. 2:9; 4:11;
2 Th. 3:7–12, and see on 19:9. No doubt this was said with a well-
remembered gesture.

35. help the weak: those unable to work for their living; cf.
Eph. 4:28; 1 Th. 5:14.

It is more blessed to give than to receive: this saying, here
attributed to Jesus, is not found in any of the canonical Gospels.
It may have appeared in some collection of sayings of Jesus in
circulation at this time, or it may have been preserved in oral
tradition; however, we should have expected Luke to include it
in his Gospel if he had known of it before. The saying, which is
echoed by pagan and later Christian writers, may have been
proverbial, and, as such, may have been quoted by Jesus. Alternatively Paul may have regarded these words as summing up the
spirit of Jesus' teaching.

36. knelt down: the normal practice in the early Church was
to stand for prayer (cf. Mk 11:25); kneeling implied a particularly
solemn occasion.

37. wept . . . embraced . . . kissed: The scene has an *OT*
flavour; cf. Gen. 33:4; 45:14; 46:29.

21:1. Setting sail once more, Paul and his party were taken to
Patara in Lycia on the south coast of Asia Minor, calling at the
islands of **Cos** and **Rhodes** on the way. The journey would appear
to have taken three days. The Western text adds 'and Myra' after
Patara; this is probably correct. Myra was further east along the
coast than Patara, and was the major port for larger ships crossing
to Syria and Egypt (see on 27:5).

2-3. After transferring from the coaster to a bigger vessel, they headed straight across the eastern Mediterranean towards **Phoenicia,** sighting **Cyprus** to the north, and landed at **Tyre** (see on 12:20), a distance of about 400 miles.

4. Sea journeys in the ancient world depended on finding shipping available, and accepting delays arising from loading and unloading. It is therefore not inconsistent that Paul was in haste to reach Jerusalem by Pentecost, yet had stopped for a week at Troas, and now spends a week at Tyre; he would have no choice. Moreover, he would now have time in hand because of taking the fast boat across the sea to Syria instead of hugging the coast. There is no record in Acts of the foundation of a church at Tyre; it may have owed its origin to the anonymous missionaries who evangelized Syria following their expulsion from Jerusalem after Stephen's martyrdom (11:19). Paul apparently knew of the existence of a Christian group in the city (cf. 15:3).
Through the Spirit: perhaps by ecstatic utterance, or merely expressing their judgment as responsible Christians (cf. 1 C. 7:40). Paul chose to disregard their advice **not to go to Jerusalem**; presumably he put more trust in the guidance he was himself being given by the Spirit to make Jerusalem his goal (19:21; 20:22).

5. When the ship was ready to sail, the whole Christian community escorted Paul and his party from the town to the beach, where, as Luke recalls, a touching farewell took place as at Miletus.

7. Ptolemais (mod. Acre or Akka) was about twenty miles S. of Tyre. It is not certain from the text whether the party reached it in the same ship, or in another smaller coastal vessel. The church there probably dated from the same time as that in Tyre (see on verse 4).

8. Caesarea was about forty miles S. of Ptolemais. The missionaries may have reached it by sea or by road.
Philip was last heard of in Caesarea in 8:40. He is presumably called **the evangelist** to distinguish him from Philip the Apostle, although later the two were often confused, as in the case of the two Johns (the Apostle and the elder).
one of the seven: see on 6:3.

9. daughters who prophesied: i.e. had the gift of prophecy. Since we are not told of any of their prophecies, it is possible that Luke mentions them because he was indebted to them for some of his information in the early chapters of Acts, and for some of the material peculiar to his Gospel. He had opportunity for such questioning, not only during this visit, which lasted **for some days,** but even more so during the two years when Paul was in custody in Caesarea (24:27).

10. Agabus is presumably the same **prophet** who appeared in 11:28. Although Caesarea was also in the province of **Judaea,** it was as a Gentile city, and the seat of the Roman administration, not regarded as part of the 'land of the Jews'.

11. The action of Agabus is a piece of prophetic symbolism such as is frequently found in the *OT* (cf. 1 Kg. 11:29ff.; Isa. 20:2ff.; Jer. 13:1ff.; Ezek. 4:1ff.). Such a symbolic act on the part of a prophet, now in a Christian *milieu* (**Thus says the Holy Spirit** corresponding to: 'Thus says the Lord'), was regarded as setting in motion the impending purpose of God. The prophecy was not precisely fulfilled in Jerusalem, since it was the Gentiles who delivered Paul from the hands of the Jews. In the long term, however, Paul met his death at Gentile hands, ultimately at the instigation of the Jerusalem Jews, as had been the case with Jesus.

12. Agabus had not advised Paul against continuing his journey to Jerusalem, but all who had heard his words **begged** the Apostle not to proceed.

13. Paul refuses to be deflected from the path which he believes to be the will of God (cf. Lk. 22:42) and, as his Master had done, 'set his face to go to Jerusalem' (Lk. 9:51).

15. made ready could mean 'hired horses'. This would be the most obvious way of covering the distance from Caesarea to Jerusalem, which was about sixty-five miles. Such a journey could be done in two days.

16. It would thus seem likely that **the house of Mnason of Cyprus** was half-way between the two cities. Mnason is described as **an early disciple,** which presumably means that he had been a Christian from the first days of the Church in Jerusalem; Cypriot believers have already been mentioned in 4:36 and 11:19f. Perhaps the reason why some of the members of the church at Caesarea accompanied Paul's party thus far on the way to Jerusalem was that Mnason lived in some obscure village off the beaten track. All this seems at all events more likely than that Mnason lived in Jerusalem, and that the only hospitality that could be found by the Jerusalem church for the man who had organized a substantial collection for the relief of their poor was at the home of an otherwise unknown member of the Jerusalem Christian community.

17. Luke's words here suggest that, on the contrary, when Paul's party reached Jerusalem they were well received, and no doubt appropriately housed with Hellenist members of the Jerusalem church. We are also left to understand that Paul had arrived in time for Pentecost.

PAUL'S ARREST, TRIAL AND APPEAL TO CAESAR **21:18–26:32**

PAUL IS ARRESTED IN JERUSALEM **21:18–36**

18. with us: this is the last use of the first person plural until 27:1. We may take it that we are not meant to assume that Luke disappeared at this point, to rejoin Paul in time for the voyage to Rome; rather he effaces himself from the narrative and lets Paul hold the centre of the stage during his arrest and subsequent encounters with the authorities. If Luke was not present on all these occasions, we may suppose that he was never far away. The **us** in this case means the delegates from the Gentile churches who had brought their contributions for the relief of the mother church (24:17). **James,** the Lord's brother, whom we last heard of at the Council of Jerusalem in chapter 15, is now clearly undisputed head of the mother church (see on 12:17; 15:13). There is no longer mention of any of the Apostles, and the government of the church seems to be solely in the hands of James and a body of supporting **elders** (see on 11:30).

20. they glorified God: partly on hearing Paul's detailed account of the spread of the Gospel among the Gentiles; partly, no doubt, on receipt of the generous gifts which had been brought by the representatives of the younger churches; and perhaps partly, also, out of relief on learning that the allegations (verse 21) made against Paul were untrue.

how many thousands . . . zealous for the law: the leaders of the Jerusalem church have their own problems, to which they now draw attention. Even if the figures (lit: 'how many tens of thousands') are exaggerated, and refer to Judaea as a whole rather than merely to Jerusalem itself, the spread of the Gospel among the Jews had met with considerable success; the prospects for Jewish Christianity were not to be lightly dismissed, however spectacular might have been Paul's successes in the Gentile world. Not only were these Jewish Christians (many if not most of whom probably belonged to the Pharisaic party; cf. 15:5) highly sensitive themselves to their heritage and traditions, dating back through centuries of Israel's history, but they had to live among orthodox Jews who tolerated their odd beliefs about Jesus of Nazareth only because they were otherwise scrupulously observant of the Law and of Jewish institutions.

21. Tales had been carried to Jerusalem, not only that Paul had let it be known in the course of his missionary work among the Gentiles that cherished provisions of the Law, such as circumcision, were inapplicable to Gentile Christians, but also that even Jews of the Diaspora had been encouraged by him to jettison their ancient sacred practices and, above all, to disregard the commandment that all Jewish male infants should be circumcised; that this was a mischievous calumny is attested both by Paul's own letters and Luke's narrative in Acts (see on 16:3). The leaders of the Jerusalem church therefore now propose that Paul should make public demonstration of his respect for Jewish tradition by participating in a distinctively Jewish act of piety.

23-4. under a vow: this would seem from the description that follows to have been a temporary Nazirite vow taken by four Jerusalem Christians, of the same type as the one Paul himself had observed a few years previously (see on 18:18). The regulations for the observance of the vow are found in Num. 6:1ff.; even there they are not altogether clear, so it is not surprising that Luke appears to be rather hazy about the details. The minimum duration of such a vow, according to Josephus, was one month. Paul on this occasion could not have associated himself publicly with these four men for that length of time. There is, however, provision in the regulations in Num. 6:9–12 to cover breaking of the vow through some accidental ceremonial defilement; this called for a period of purification of seven days (cf. verse 27), followed by shaving of the head and the offering of appropriate sacrifices in the Temple. The completion of the full vow called for more elaborate and more expensive sacrifices. It is more likely that what is involved here is the temporary defilement within the period of the vow, although Luke's account seems to confuse the two. At all events, the suggestion of the Church authorities is that Paul should be seen to be officially identified with the four votaries and should pay the expenses of their sacrifices. Such an act of charity by a wealthier donor on behalf of poorer members of the Jewish community was commonly recognized as a demonstration of piety; Josephus relates that Herod Agrippa I, in order to win favour with the Jews, made himself financially responsible for many Nazirites in this way (*Antiquities*, XIX. vi. 1). This incident implies that Paul had now money of his own, an impression strengthened as Luke's narrative proceeds. He had to maintain himself in prison at Caesarea; the procurator Felix expected to be bribed by him (24:26); he had to bear the heavy cost of an appeal to Caesar (25:11); and he was able to rent a house for two years in Rome (28:30). It is unlikely that all this was financed by contributions from the churches, and it has been suggested that Paul may perhaps have inherited money about this time. There are, indeed, various indications that, although Paul as a missionary chose to support himself by working at his trade, and was assisted by occasional help from congregations or individuals, he came from a well-to-do family, and had influential connections.

25. This repeats the terms of the decree of the Jerusalem Council (15:20, 29), which of course Paul already knew, since he had conveyed it to the Gentile churches (16:4). James is making the point that the decree has made plain all that Jewish Christians demand of Gentile Christians: they are not expected to conform to traditional practices which are observed by their Jewish Christian brethren. Paul, as one of these Jewish Christians, need therefore have no fear that his present action in Jerusalem will give offence in the Gentile churches, whereas it will do much to allay Jewish suspicion that he sits lightly to the customs of his own race.

26. It may be that what is meant is that Paul took a temporary vow (i.e. **purified himself**), implying that he too had been guilty of ceremonial defilement through his Gentile associations, and then officially gave notice in the Temple of his intention to make himself responsible for the sacrifices which had to be offered by the four men. Paul's readiness to comply with the suggestion of the Jerusalem church leaders is wholly explicable in the light of his anxiety to further harmonious relations between the Jewish and Gentile elements in the Church (cf. 1 C. 9:20).

27. Jews from Asia: i.e. from the Roman province of Asia, the capital of which was Ephesus. Paul had already suffered at the hands of Asian Jews (20:19), large numbers of whom would be in Jerusalem at this time for Pentecost. Now their hatred of him as the renegade Pharisee who had done so much to undermine the mission of Judaizers to the Gentiles made of no avail the modest combined effort of the Jerusalem Christians and Paul to

placate Jewish public opinion. Luke makes it plain that it was the
orthodox Jews and not the Jewish Christians who were responsible
for the riot that followed; the Jerusalem church seems to have
been powerless to intervene.

28. the law and this place: the same charge was made against
Stephen (6:13).

brought Greeks into the temple: non-Jews were allowed into
the Temple, where the Court of the Gentiles provided for their
use symbolically indicated that God was concerned for their
salvation. In Jesus' day it was more like a market-place (Lk.
19:45). Gentiles (i.e. **Greeks**) could gain access to the inner
courts of the Temple only on becoming proselytes (see on 2:10);
those who had not done so were prohibited from passing beyond
a barrier bearing an inscription in Greek and Latin intimating
that any who did so would bring their deaths on their own heads.
Paul, as a Jew, was of course entitled to pass the barrier (probably
'the dividing wall of hostility' of Eph. 2:14), and technically the
death penalty would be applicable only to any Gentile, even
including Roman citizens, who violated the injunction. The
charge against Paul was, however, serious enough, in that he was
accused of infiltrating 'unclean' persons into the sacred confines
reserved for Jews, so that the Temple became ritually **defiled.**

29. Trophimus the Ephesian: see on 20:4. Like Paul himself, he would be known to some of the Asian Jews. In the light
of Paul's recent efforts to appease the Jews, it is unthinkable that
he would have been guilty of such a heinous offence in Jewish eyes.

30. all the city was aroused: the Temple was a fetish for all
Jews, but for none more so than fanatically devout pilgrims from
the Diaspora, who had travelled far to celebrate the festival of
Pentecost in the holy city.

out of the temple: Paul was seized, presumably in the Court of
the Women or, if he was involved in transactions on behalf of the
Nazirites, in the Court of Israel (see on 3:3), and manhandled out
of the Temple proper into the Outer Court or Court of the Gentiles.

the gates were shut no doubt on the orders of the *Sagan* (see on
4:1) to prevent further disorder within the inner precincts.

31. the tribune of the cohort is later (23:26) identified as
Claudius Lysias. The Roman garrison in Jerusalem was quartered
in the fortress of Antonia, in the NW. corner of the Temple area,
and at full strength it numbered 760 foot-soldiers and 240 horse-
men. Among other duties, they were responsible for keeping the

peace within the Temple precincts, and for quelling riots in the city during the great festivals.

word came to the garrison commander, presumably from guards patrolling the roofs of the Temple colonnades on the look-out for riots, or from sentries in the fortress itself.

32. centurions: the plural suggests that at least 200 men were called into action (see on 10:1).

ran down: there were two flights of steps leading down from the fortress, or tower, of Antonia into the Outer Court.

33. bound with two chains: manacled to a soldier on either side of him (cf. 12:6).

34. barracks: the fortress, up whose steps Paul was now carried by the soldiers for his own protection.

36. Away with him!: that is, 'Kill him!' Similarly the crowd at the trial of Jesus (cf. Lk. 23:18; Jn 19:15).

PAUL ADDRESSES THE MOB **21:37–22:29**

37. Do you know Greek?: the tribune has apparently mistaken him for a notorious terrorist, and is surprised to find that his dishevelled captive speaks good Greek.

38. the Egyptian: Josephus (*Wars of the Jews*, II xiii. 5) tells of an 'Egyptian false prophet' who raised a revolt and threatened Jerusalem during the procuratorship of Felix, in about A.D. 54; the rebellion was quelled by the Roman garrison, the rebels were scattered, captured or killed, while their leader escaped. Claudius Lysias thinks he has now caught him. Josephus, whose numbers are generally inflated, gives the total of the insurrectionists (i.e. **Assassins**) as 30,000. Luke's more modest figure of **four thousand** is probably nearer the mark.

39. Paul asserts his right as a **Jew** to be in the Temple, and explains his fluency in Greek by his upbringing in **Tarsus in Cilicia,** which, as he says, was **no mean city.** This was no idle boast since, with Athens and Alexandria, Tarsus was one of the three chief centres of learning in the ancient world, as well as being the capital of Cilicia and a free city of the Empire.

40. in the Hebrew language: Paul speaks to the crowd in Aramaic (**Hebrew**), the language most acceptable to Jewish traditionalists (see on 22:2).

22:1 brethren and fathers: cf. the same words at the opening of Stephen's speech to the Sanhedrin (7:2).

defence: Paul is concerned to defend himself against the charge

that he has been disloyal to his people, the Law and the Temple
(21:28). He does so by emphasizing his Jewishness and his past
zeal for the Law. But God had shown him on the Damascus road
that Jesus of Nazareth was the long-awaited Messiah, and nothing
but a divine revelation such as he had received after his conversion
could have persuaded him to proclaim this to Gentiles rather than
to his own countrymen. Paul's speech is interrupted before he has
an opportunity to answer the specific charge of introducing
Gentiles into the Temple.

2. Hebrew language: see on 21:40. Luke may have known
enough Aramaic to get the gist of Paul's speech. Aramaic was not
merely the vernacular of Palestine, but was also the *lingua franca*
of those who did not speak Greek in the eastern parts of the Roman
Empire.

3. brought up in this city: it is not clear how old Paul was
when he left Tarsus for Jerusalem. It has been argued that the
word for **brought up** is a technical term meaning 'nurtured from
infancy', which would imply that Paul spent his childhood and
boyhood in Jerusalem, and had left Tarsus as an infant (cf. the use
in Stephen's speech of 'born . . . brought up . . . instructed' in the
case of Moses (7:20–2)); however, it is difficult to reconcile this
with his statement in 21:39, to say nothing of his excellent command of Greek, his constant use of the LXX, his frequent allusions
in his letters to features of Greek life, and his universalist outlook.
All this, of course, may have sprung from his subsequent missionary
activity in the Gentile world; on the other hand, there appears
to have been more hellenistic influence on orthodox Judaism in
Jerusalem than was at one time supposed.

at the feet of Gamaliel: cf. Lk. 10:39. Paul could not have been
a pupil of Gamaliel before his student days. Probably the punctu-
ation of the *RSV* is wrong, and the word **educated** should go
with **at the feet of Gamaliel** (cf. *NEB*: 'I was brought up in this
city, and as a pupil of Gamaliel I was thoroughly trained in every
point of our ancestral law'); cf. Phil. 3:4ff.

Gamaliel: see on 5:34. Obviously he had not communicated his
liberal attitude to his pupil.

zealous for God: cf. Gal. 1:14; Rom. 10:2. Paul had shown his
zeal by persecuting the Nazarenes.

as you all are this day: this is handsomely said.

4. I persecuted this Way: see on 9:2 and on 8:3.

to the death: at least in the case of Stephen (verse 20).

5. the high priest: i.e. at the time of his conversion: Caiaphas, High Priest in A.D. 18–36; the High Priest at the time of this speech was Ananias (see on 23:2). Presumably Paul is referring to earlier official records which would confirm his statements.

council of elders: the Sanhedrin; cf. Lk. 22:66 (see on 4:5).

brethren: in this case Jewish brethren.

to take those also who were there: see on 9:2.

6–11. This is the second account of Paul's conversion in Acts. In the first account (9:3ff.) Luke was the narrator. Here and in 26:12ff. Paul himself describes his experience. The differences in detail are negligible, and can probably be attributed to the fact that Paul may not always have told the story in exactly the same way. The main points, however, remain unchanged (see on 9:1ff. (pp. 125–9)).

6. about noon: this detail, repeated in 26:13, is not given in chapter 9.

8. Jesus of Nazareth: see on 2:22.

12. Ananias: for the benefit of his Jewish audience, Paul emphasizes the fact that Ananias was a Christian, who was none the less a devout Jew in good standing with his compatriots in Damascus. It was such a man, Paul implies, who welcomed him into the fellowship of the Nazarenes. Nothing is said here of Ananias' vision (cf. 9:10ff.), but the following verses (13–16) correspond to 9:15–17. For the apparent contradiction between the part played by Ananias (and the Damascus Christians) and Paul's words in Gal. 1:11ff., see on 9:19b (pp. 131–2).

14. The God of our fathers . . .: Ananias uses the language of a pious Jew.

the Just One: see on 3:14.

15. witness: Paul could claim to be an Apostle, in that he had now seen and heard Jesus in as real a sense as the original Apostles, who had been commanded on that account to be his 'witnesses . . . to the end of the earth' (see on 1:8).

16. calling on his name: see on 2:38.

17. when I had returned to Jerusalem: three years after Paul's conversion, according to Gal. 1:18 (see on 9:19b (pp. 131–2)).

trance: see on 18:9. Paul speaks of his visions in 2 C. 12:1ff.; this particular vision may be the one referred to in 2 C. 12:2–4. Paul draws attention to the fact that this happened when he was performing his duty in the Temple as a loyal Jew.

18. Here Paul's reason for leaving Jerusalem is given as being his response to the vision. In 9:29–30 he went off to Tarsus on the advice of the Jerusalem Christians. His departure may have been the result of both combined.

19–20. The point is that, in view of Paul's past record of persecuting the Christians and assisting in Stephen's execution, the Jews should have recognized that only some divine intervention could have brought about so dramatic a change in his behaviour. They might therefore have been expected to listen to his 'testimony'.

21. The Apostle claims that his mission to the Gentiles was undertaken at the Lord's command given in his own Temple.

22. Paul's audience had no objection to proselytizing among Gentiles; the Jews themselves practised this. What roused them to an outburst of unbridled fury at this point was that a man who claimed to be a loyal Jew asserted that he had been divinely enjoined to propagate his notoriously heretical views in the pagan world—such as that compliance with sacred Jewish law was not obligatory for all who professed to belong to the people of God, and that uncircumcised Gentiles would be regarded as equal with Jews in the sight of God.

23. waved their garments: as an expression of horror at blasphemy (see on 14:14).
threw dust into the air: see on 13:51. As has been pointed out, mud is more readily available in England.

24. scourging with whips of loaded leather thongs was the normal Roman method of extorting information from slaves and aliens. The tribune, not understanding Aramaic, was at a loss to know what had caused the uproar, and wished to find out the truth.

25. tied him up with the thongs could be translated 'stretched him out for flogging'. Roman law prohibited such treatment for Roman citizens; hence Paul's protest now. The lictors' rods at Philippi had been gentle compared with this grim prospect (see on 16:37).

28. for a large sum: normally Roman citizenship was not purchased, although large sums of money could be spent on bribing officials to include one's name on the list of candidates for enfranchisement. It is known, however, that in the reign of the Emperor Claudius (A.D. 41–54) there was a traffic in citizenship, and money payments were made to secure it. Since the name of the tribune was Claudius Lysias (23:26), it is likely that he acquired his citizenship in this way during the reign of that particular emperor; a newly-created citizen commonly adopted the name of the ruler at the time. Lysias may have been a Greek. The Western text reads: 'I know what it cost me to obtain this citizenship', which implies perhaps a sneering reference to Paul's bedraggled appearance after being mauled by the mob. The implication is: 'Anybody can apparently be a citizen nowadays.' This would justify Paul's retort: **But I was born a citizen.** It is not known how Paul's father or earlier forebears obtained their citizenship. Paul seems to have treated it largely as a convenience to be resorted to in an extremity (cf. 16:37), and shows more pride in his citizenship of Tarsus and his Jewish origins. The tribune, however, was obviously more impressed by Paul's Roman credentials.

29. had bound him: for flogging. It may seem surprising that the tribune accepted Paul's word without question. Probably in a matter of this serious nature he could not afford to take chances which might involve him in subsequent prosecution. Furthermore, the punishment for making a false claim to Roman citizenship was so severe that no one would lightly risk the consequences.

PAUL BEFORE THE SANHEDRIN **22:30–23:11**

30. The tribune was the chief executive of Roman authority in Jerusalem, and directly responsible to the procurator at Caesarea. A Jew who had, for some religious reasons beyond the understanding of a simple soldier, caused a riot in the Temple and had narrowly escaped lynching by the mob, had turned out to be no local terrorist, as the tribune had at first suspected, but an educated rabbi who claimed Roman citizenship. In the interests of Roman justice, it was therefore proper to have the case investigated by the statutory Jewish court, in the hope that the rights and wrongs of the matter might emerge, and that the prisoner should either be released if found to be innocent or, if found guilty of a capital crime, should be remitted to the procurator for proper trial and sentence. Accordingly, the tribune summoned a special meeting of the Sanhedrin (see on 4:5) on the following day, and Paul was brought down from the guardroom of the fortress to face the inquiry.

23:1. The abrupt beginning of the proceedings is no doubt due to the necessity imposed upon Luke of providing, once again, merely a summary of what was said on this occasion. He therefore dispenses with the preliminary introduction—charges, evidence and so on—and comes to the major issues and events.

Brethren: Paul addresses the Council as his equals (cf. Peter in 4:8: 'Rulers and elders'; and Stephen in 7:2: 'Brethren and fathers').

in all good conscience: Paul implies that, as a good Jew, he has done nothing to be ashamed of in becoming a Christian, and that he can answer for it before God. This infuriates the High Priest.

2. Ananias was High Priest from A.D. 48 until his deposition about ten years later. Josephus describes him as 'a bold man in his temper and very insolent. He was also of the sect of the Sadducees, who are very rigid in judging offenders above all the rest of the Jews' (*Antiquities*, xx ix. 1). He was murdered by Jewish patriots in A.D. 66 as a lackey of the Romans. His hot-tempered action now in ordering Paul to be struck on the mouth is in keeping with Josephus' account of him. Jesus had been similarly treated at his trial (Jn 18:22).

3. God shall strike you: Ananias' fate may have been in Luke's mind as he wrote this.

you whitewashed wall: Jesus had used a similar expression, 'whitewashed tombs' (Mt. 23:27), in castigating the scribes and Pharisees of his day for their hypocrisy in being outwardly respectable but inwardly corrupt. The sepulchres were, in fact, whitened to protect passers-by from defilement by touching them inadvertently. Paul's words may be an allusion to this, or they may reflect Ezek. 13:10–16, where the prophet uses the metaphor of a wall being daubed with whitewash to make it look solid, but which nevertheless crumbled and fell when the Lord sent his stormy wind to destroy it. The High Priest, who posed as an impartial judge, had broken Jewish law by ordering the prisoner to be assaulted before he had been found guilty.

4. Would you revile God's high priest?: the question following the blow is so reminiscent of Jesus' appearance before Annas (Jn 18:22), that Luke must be consciously drawing a parallel between the trial of Jesus and that of Paul. As we have already noted, Luke has seen the whole pattern of events in the last journey of Jesus to Jerusalem being repeated in the experience of his Apostle.

5. I did not know . . . he was the high priest: it has been suggested that this is an indication of Paul's bad eyesight; or that

Paul did not know that it was the High Priest who had given the order to strike him since the tribune was presiding and the High Priest was sitting among the Council, or that Paul had never personally encountered Ananias previously. Surely the explanation is that Paul's words are spoken with biting irony: such a man as Ananias made a mockery of the office of High Priest. Paul, as a devout Pharisee, refuses to recognize this corrupt Sadducee as in any sense worthy of the respect which all loyal Jews would normally give to the holder of this distinguished position, as enjoined by the Law itself in Exod, 22:28, which the Apostle now quotes. Some may feel, with St Jerome, that the contrast between the patience of Jesus at his trial and the violent outburst of the Apostle underlines the splendour of Christ's witness; but Paul was at times, as we learn from his letters, guilty of similar passionate utterances on other occasions (cf. Gal. 2:11; 5:12; Phil. 3:2), and this whole scene is so unexpected, Paul's attitude so impolitic, and his outburst so violent, that Luke could not have brought himself to record it if he had not known it to be true (cf. 15:39).

6. when Paul perceived: Paul obviously already knew the composition of the Sanhedrin. The point must be that it suddenly occured to him to change the situation to his own advantage by exploiting the ancient rivalry between the two parties.

Sadducees: see on 4:1.

Pharisees: see on 5:34.

I am a Pharisee, a son of Pharisees: there is no contradiction between these words (and similar words in 26:5) and Paul's statement in his letter to the Philippians (3:4–7), where he claims that since his conversion to Christianity his former pride in his Pharisaic upbringing has seemed pointless (cf. 2 C. 11:22). In that letter Paul was writing to Gentile Christians, and the views he expressed there on the relationship between Christianity and Judaism were the same as the views whose forceful propagation in the pagan world had led to his present predicament. It is perfectly plain, however, both from the letters and from Acts, that Paul the Christian was still Paul the Pharisee and that, like many other Christian Jews, he saw no contradiction in this (cf. 15:5). Christianity was for him the fulfilment of the Law and of prophecy, and his hope as a Jew loyal to the traditions of his people was that all Jews might come to recognize this as he himself had done. His emphasis on his Pharisaic background here in this wholly Jewish setting is no less in character than his reference to his birth in a

Greek city and his Roman citizenship in his dealings with Claudius
Lysias; it has, of course, the added point that he was identifying
himself with the Pharisaic members of the Sanhedrin, who like
most Jews, including Paul, had no love for the priestly time-serving
Sadducees.

the hope and the resurrection of the dead: i.e. the hope of
the resurrection of the dead. Paul was indeed ultimately **on trial**
because of his preaching of the risen Christ, although the specific
charges (21:28) were more inflammatory. For Paul, the Resurrection of Jesus was the guarantee of a general resurrection of the
dead (1 C. 15:12-16), which latter was a belief common to
Christians and Pharisaic Jews, as opposed to Sadducees.

7. In the theological dispute which now breaks out between
the two parties in the Sanhedrin, as Paul intended, the charges
and, indeed, the prisoner become almost a side issue.

8. Luke's explanatory note to the effect that the Sadducees,
unlike the Pharisees, did not believe in a general resurrection of
the dead is confirmed by the Gospels (Mk 12:18 and parallels)
and by Josephus (*Wars of the Jews*, II viii. 14). In their view this,
like the belief in hierarchies of good and evil spirits (**angel . . .
spirit**), was a development of post-Exilic Judaism which had no
justification in the Pentateuch. It was in keeping with the belief
of the less conservative Pharisees in an ever-developing interpretation of the Scriptures that they accepted such doctrines as part
of orthodox Jewish faith.

9. scribes of the Pharisees' party: scribes—i.e., experts in
the Scriptures—were mostly Pharisees (cf. Mk 2:16; Lk. 5:30).
Luke notices a similarly sympathetic attitude on the part of
scribes to Jesus' teaching on the subject of resurrection (Lk. 20:39;
cf. Mk 12:28).

a spirit or an angel: here regarded as synonymous. The reference would be to Paul's experience, either on the road to Damascus
(22:6-11) or in the Temple (22:17-21), both of which he had
related to the crowd on the previous day. The scribes seem to
suggest that it may have been the 'departed spirit' of Jesus which
had spoken to Paul.

10. The tribune again takes Paul into protective custody to save
him from physical violence, by sending for a detachment of
soldiers from the fortress to come down to the Council chamber in
the outer precincts of the Temple where the Sanhedrin held its
meetings.

11. Once more at a critical juncture in his life, Paul has a vision of Christ (cf. 18:9–10) confirming his purpose to reach Rome (19:21), and perhaps hinting at his subsequent appeal to Caesar as the only way now left open to him to achieve this end.

PAUL IS SENT TO CAESAREA 23:12–35

12–13. There is no good reason to suppose that Luke, in his desire to demonstrate the consistently favourable attitude of Roman officials towards Paul and Christianity, and accordingly to place all the blame for Paul's misfortunes on the shoulders of the Jews, should have invented the story of the conspiracy for this purpose. It may be that Paul, as a Roman citizen, would have been sent to the procurator at Caesarea for trial in any event, since the tribune had no power to deal with the matter himself; but this vivid narrative, giving an added reason for Paul's speedy removal from Jerusalem, is perfectly credible as it stands in the light of the fanaticism and terrorism of this period (cf. Josephus, *Antiquities*, xx viii. 5) which ended in the terrible Jewish-Roman war of A.D. 66–70. Paul's assassination had already been in the minds of such Jewish religious fanatics as those described here (20:3). The **oath** was not so suicidal as it seems, since provision was made by the rabbis for releasing participants from the consequences of failure to carry out their purpose if external circumstances had made it impossible.

14. they went to the chief priests and elders: the Sadducean faction, as being more sympathetic to their design than the Pharisaic scribes.

15. A bogus meeting of the Sanhedrin was to be called on the pretext of further investigation of Paul's case. Before the Council met, Paul was to be murdered on the way between the fortress and the Council chamber.

16. the son of Paul's sister is an intriguing new *dramatis persona*: we know little or nothing about Paul's family. This married sister apparently lived in Jerusalem. If her husband was a member of one of the high priestly families, it might explain how the youth had learned of the plot, and why he was apparently allowed access to the fortress where Paul was merely under open arrest, since he was able to receive visitors.

17. Paul, furthermore, is in sufficiently good standing with the tribune to be able to order a centurion to treat this as a matter of urgency.

21. promise: i.e. 'waiting for your consent'.

23. at the third hour of the night: about 9 p.m. The size of the escort is not excessive, in view of the troubled times and Jewish fanaticism. Despite his early rough handling of Paul, the tribune may also have come to the conclusion that his prisoner was a man of considerable importance in his own right, apart from Lysias' responsibility for his safety as a Roman citizen. It must have been known to the tribune by this time that Paul had extensive contacts in the pagan world, that he had brought a considerable sum of money for the relief of the poor of Jerusalem, that he was on good terms with the highly respected James the Just, head of the sect of the Nazarenes in Jerusalem, and that he had some support from the Pharisaic party; his murder might well have sparked off a riot. The word translated **spearmen** (*dexiolabous*) is otherwise unknown in this period; this has given rise to the suggestion that it might mean 'led horses', thus providing for a change of horses. The size of the escort thus would be smaller (see on verse 32).

24. mounts could be either horses or mules.

Felix the governor: Roman procurator of Judaea. Antonius Felix, a freedman, held this office from A.D. 52 until he was recalled to Rome, probably in A.D. 58. He was the brother of Pallas, the favourite and minister of the Emperor Claudius, and it was no doubt due to this that Felix obtained the procuratorship. According to Tacitus, his influence at court led him to think that 'he could commit all kinds of enormities with impunity' (*Annals*, xii. 54), and it was also with reference to him that Tacitus coined the epigram: 'with all manner of cruelty and lust, he exercised the functions of a prince with the disposition of a slave' (*History*, v. 9). With this view Josephus concurs (*Wars of the Jews*, II xiii. 2), and Luke also touches on his corrupt administration (24:26). His rule in Judaea was marked by fiercely repressive measures, and his eventual recall to Rome arose from charges of unnecessarily massacring his rebellious subjects.

25. Luke would not have seen a copy of the letter, which would be in Latin; but he may have heard it read at Paul's trial in Caesarea, and got the gist of it. It was customary to send such a document with a prisoner being referred to a higher court.

26. his Excellency: the same title is applied in a more general sense to Theophilus (Lk. 1:3; see on 1:1), to Felix once more by Tertullus (24:2), and to Festus by Paul (26:25).

27–30. Lysias in his letter puts the best face on his own handling of the affair. He suppresses the fact that he was about to have a Roman citizen flogged, and was only saved from the consequences of this by Paul's last-minute protest. He emphasizes that, in his view, the charges against Paul were not offences against Roman law, but were purely matters of Jewish religious concern, as had emerged at the hearing before the Sanhedrin. His attitude was similar to that of Gallio (18:15).

31. Antipatris: the exact site of this place is not certain, but it is thought to have been about forty miles from Jerusalem, possibly mod. Ras El 'Ain, roughly two thirds of the way to Caesarea. It was rebuilt by Herod the Great, and renamed in memory of his father Antipater.

32. on the morrow they returned: a journey of eighty miles in twenty-four hours obviously would have been impossible for foot-soldiers; this suggests that the 'spearmen' of verse 23 should be 'horses' (see *ad loc.*). After Antipatris the journey would be through open, mainly Gentile, country to Caesarea, which would make the larger escort unnecessary.

34. to what province: Roman legal procedure provided that a prisoner could be tried in his own native province or in the province where the alleged crime had been committed. In this case there could be no choice, since at this particular time Cilicia, in which Tarsus was situated, was part of the province of Syria, and not a province in its own right, as was the case a few years later. This is another indication of Luke's remarkable historical accuracy in such matters. Felix therefore undertakes to hear the case himself, as deputy of the legate of Syria as well as procurator of Judaea (cf. Lk. 23:6–7).

35. when your accusers arrive refers back to verse 30. **Herod's praetorium:** Herod the Great's palace at Caesarea had been taken over as the Roman government house.

PAUL AND FELIX **24:1–27**

1. after five days: see on verse 11.
Tertullus: his name suggests that the advocate engaged by the prosecution may have been either a Roman or a hellenistic Jew (see on verse 6).
2. when he was called: i.e. Paul.
much peace: although the procurator's methods of ensuring 'peace' were barbarous in the extreme, there was a measure of

truth in the otherwise empty flattery of Tertullus' opening remarks. To have preserved some kind of order in Judaea, by whatever means, for even a few years was no small achievement.
this nation: the Jews.

4. detain: or 'weary'.

5-6. The charge is framed in such a way as to suggest that this
is no mere religious dispute, but a threat to the stability of Roman
government. Paul is accused of being generally a trouble-maker
throughout the Empire, a promoter of a particular messianic
movement (which would suggest political agitation to the procurator), and a violator of the Sadducean regulations for the
sanctity of the Temple, which were guaranteed by the Romans.

5. Nazarenes: see on 2:22.

6. tried to profane the temple: a milder form of the charge
in 21:28, but still a capital offence.

we seized him, suggesting an orderly arrest instead of the maul-
ing by a mob lusting for Paul's blood, which was what actually
happened (21:30-1).

After these words the Western text adds (verses 6b-8a): 'and
we would have judged him according to our law. But the chief
captain Lysias came and with great violence took him out of our
hands, commanding his accusers to come before you.' This may
well be correct, and strengthens Tertullus' case. He blames
Lysias—falsely, of course—for interfering in the seemly handling
of the matter by the Jews themselves. This points forward to the
procurator's decision to postpone judgment until Lysias should
appear to give evidence (verse 22). If the Western text is correct,
and unless Tertullus is identifying himself professionally with his
Jewish clients, his references to 'we' and 'our law' would indicate
that he was himself a Jew and not a Roman. Furthermore, if we
accept the Western text, 'examining him' in verse 8 will refer to
Lysias and not to Paul, although the word is normally used of
examining a prisoner rather than a witness.

10b. for many years: if this trial took place in A.D. 56 (see
on 20:1b), Felix had been procurator of Judaea for only four
years. Previously, however, he had been governor of Samaria for
about the same length of time.

11. not more than twelve days: this is probably not intended to be an exact figure. It is not clear how long Paul was in
Jerusalem before he was arrested (see on 21:23-4) but, if we
assume that it was anything up to a week, and if we include the

journey to Caesarea and the 'five days' of verse 1, the 'twelve days' here will mean 'about a fortnight'. Paul emphasizes that he had gone to Jerusalem **to worship,** i.e. to attend the festival, and not to engage in 'Nazarene' propaganda.

14. the Way: see on 9:2.

a sect: the Jews regarded Christianity as a heretical variety of Judaism (cf. 28:22).

the God of our fathers: Paul insists that, as a follower of **the Way,** he worshipped the God of Abraham, Isaac and Jacob, like his accusers. Thus he implicitly claims the same privilege for Christianity as was extended by the Roman government to Judaism—that of being a *religio licita*.

believing everything . . . law . . . prophets: Paul means this in the sense that he claims Christianity to be the fulfilment of the Scriptures, not in the sense of ascribing permanent validity to the detailed requirements of the Law; this, indeed, he could not have done, in view of such statements as Gal. 3:15–25; Rom. 7; 10:4, however much he conformed with the traditional practices of his people, in Palestine at least, in the interests of the unity of a Church which included Jews and Gentiles.

15. having a hope in God: as in 23:6.

which these themselves accept: this implies that some of the 'elders' in verse 1 were Pharisees.

a resurrection of both the just and the unjust: as in 23:6. Paul bases the expectation of a general resurrection, which was common to both Pharisees and Christians, on the fact of the Resurrection of Christ. Here, as in Dan. 12:2; Jn 5:28–9; Rev. 20:11–15, the resurrection includes **both the just** (for reward) **and the unjust** (for punishment).

16. The Judgment associated with the general resurrection has its implications for day-to-day behaviour. Paul stresses his concern to have **a clear conscience toward God and toward men,** not least toward his own people who are now accusing him. However, far from wronging them, Paul, as he now goes on to say, has been engaged in raising money for the benefit of those of his countrymen in Jerusalem who have chosen to become Nazarenes.

17. after some years: Paul's last visit to Jerusalem was a fleeting one (18:22) some three years previously. Perhaps he is thinking here of his momentous visit to the city at the Council of A.D. 49.

alms and offerings: this scanty reference to the collection for the poor of the mother church organized by Paul among the young Gentile churches with such energy and personal involvement is at least an indication that Luke knew of its existence. For Paul at the time, it was a massive testimony to the solidarity of the Church and a recognition on the part of the Gentile section of the debt they owed to the Jewish origins of their faith; for Luke it was, like Paul's insistence on his apostolic status, a matter of only temporary importance in the early days which could now be seen in its proper perspective (see on 19:21).

18. purified in the temple: a reference to 21:26.
Jews from Asia: cf. 21:27. These are the people, says Paul, who ought to be in the witness-box now if there is any truth in their allegations.

21. except this one thing: Paul is making no apology. He stands by what he said before the Sanhedrin (23:6), and, indeed, he has just repeated it. His claim is that the prosecution has no case. The only charge they could possibly prefer is on a point of theology—his preaching of the Resurrection—and even on this issue some of his opponents hold views which ought to range them on his side.

22. a rather accurate knowledge of the Way: Felix, as we are told (verse 24), had a Jewish wife from whom he may already have learned something about the beliefs of the Christians.
put them off: adjourned the hearing, pending the arrival of Lysias.

23. Paul is detained in a kind of open custody, possibly in a guardroom of the praetorium rather than in the common gaol, with certain privileges including access for his friends.

24. Drusilla was the youngest daughter of Herod Agrippa I (see on 12:1) and sister of Agrippa II, who appears later in Luke's narrative (25:13). She had been enticed away from her first husband Azizus, king of Emesa, a small Syrian state, to become the procurator's third wife.

The Western text interpolates an explanatory note at this point: 'And she asked to see Paul and hear the word. So desiring to satisfy her he sent for Paul'.

25. In the light of Felix' general reputation and political record (see on 23:24), Paul's choice of topics—righteousness, self-control and the Judgment to come—was highly relevant, and the governor's alarm was no doubt genuine. His frequent interviews with Paul subsequently (verse 26) would suggest that his dismissal of Paul at this point was due to pressure of affairs, and not to a reluctance to face up to the Apostle's challenge.

26. money: although provincial governors were prohibited by law from taking bribes from prisoners, the practice was common and, in the case of Felix, quite in character. The governor's two-fold motive in seeing Paul often—theological and monetary—is not impossible. For Paul's financial circumstances at this time see on 21:23–4.

27. when two years had elapsed: this might mean that Felix's term of office came to an end two years after he had been appointed, but the more natural interpretation is that it was two years after the procurator's first encounter with Paul; as always in Acts, there is difficulty in establishing the dates with absolute certainty. The best we can hope to do in arriving at a chrono-logical account of Paul's life is to reach conclusions which are defensible and consistent; even with this proviso, scholars' con-jectures as to the date of Felix's replacement by Festus range between A.D. 55–60. If we adhere to the scheme so far followed in this commentary, Paul first appeared before Felix in A.D. 56, and remained in custody in Caesarea until 58, at which point Felix **was succeeded by Porcius Festus.** The main objection to this dating is that, according to Josephus (*Antiquities*, xx viii. 9), Felix only escaped punishment at Rome for his malpractices in Judaea, about which the Jews themselves had complained, through the intervention of his brother Pallas with the Emperor Nero, who had succeeded Claudius in A.D. 54 (see on 23:24). Tacitus, however, gives the date of Pallas' deposition from ministerial office by Nero as A.D. 55 (*Annals*, xiii. 14). Probably Tacitus gives the date correctly, and Josephus may also be right in attributing Felix' acquittal to his brother's efforts; but it may be that, even after his deposition, Pallas had some influence at court.

Porcius Festus, who succeeded Felix, but of whom little is known apart from Acts, appears to have been an exemplary governor who did his best to restore order in Judaea after Felix's unsuccessful regime. The task would seem to have proved impossible, and he died in office a few years later (Josephus: *Wars of the Jews*, II xiv. 1; *Antiquities*, xx viii. 9, ix. 1).

desiring to do the Jews a favour: or, perhaps, 'anxious to ingratiate himself with the Jews'. Felix had every reason to try to placate the Jews by any means, apparently unsuccessfully, since they were the instigators of his recall to Rome for trial.

left Paul in prison: a Western addition here reads: 'because of Drusilla'. If Drusilla had taken exception to something Paul had said about her marital adventures (verse 25), her revenge for his outspokenness may be a milder parallel to that of Herodias in the similar case of John the Baptist (Mk. 6:17ff.). It was, apparently, wholly within the power of a Roman provincial official such as Felix either to keep a prisoner indefinitely in custody or to release him at will; Roman justice outside the imperial capital was at this time very dependent on the whim of the local governor.

If these two years of enforced captivity at Caesarea were frustrating for Paul—and there is no solid evidence that any of the so-called 'Captivity Epistles' date from this imprisonment—they may well have been fruitful for Luke. Assuming that he was free to travel at his own discretion throughout the area, with the innumerable contacts it afforded, it is not unreasonable to suppose that much of the information which was later incorporated in his Gospel (or even Proto-Luke) dates from this time, and that indeed Acts itself owes much to what he was able to glean in these two years.

PAUL AND FESTUS 25:1-27

1. The new procurator, **Festus,** very properly paid an official visit at the earliest opportunity to **Jerusalem,** the religious capital of his troubled territory; there, rather than at the administrative centre at **Caesarea**, he could judge the political temperature for himself.

his province: the province of Syria, of which Judaea was a part.

2. Amongst other matters the case of Paul is raised by the Sanhedrin. This body would seem to be indicated by the phrase **the chief priests and the principal men;** cf. verse 15.

3. The ostensible request is to have Paul delivered into the hands of the Jewish religious authorities, presumably relying on the governor's inexperience in Jewish affairs and ignorance of the background of the case. From the Western tradition comes the suggestion that the true motive to have Paul assassinated **on the way** was inspired by the same group of conspirators who had been foiled before (23:12).

4-5. Festus was too shrewd to accept the Jewish plea at its face value, and instead suggested that representatives of the Sanhedrin should make the journey to the recognized seat of Roman law and government at Caesarea and state their case.

6. Luke seems to be anxious to indicate the speed and efficiency of Roman judicial procedure when a competent governor such as Festus (as opposed to Felix) was in charge.

7. Since they had little to go on except hatred of a renegade rabbi and jealousy of a successful protagonist of a rival faith to orthodox Judaism—neither of which would impress a dispassionate Roman arbitrator—there was little left to the Sanhedrin representatives but to invent **serious charges**, e.g. treasonable activities, which they could not substantiate. This seems to be borne out by Paul's reply.

8. Violation of Jewish ritual law (of which Paul was guilty in Jewish eyes, but which was not an offence against Roman law) or of the sanctity of the Temple (which was guaranteed by the imperial government, but of which Paul had not been guilty) could be easily dealt with. It would appear, however, that vague charges had now been levelled against him of undermining law and order—**against Caesar** (as at Thessalonica; cf. 17:7)—which was a grave matter for any procurator.

9. Festus had no such cogent reason as Felix for ingratiating himself with the Jews (see on 24:27) but, as the new governor of a turbulent country, it behoved him to handle carefully a case of this kind in which passions were running high. His suggestion of meeting the Jewish authorities half-way by holding the trial in Jerusalem, with himself as presiding judge, was on the surface not unreasonable; but it is not easy to see what procedure could in this case have been adopted. Paul was being charged with a combination of religious and political offences; the former were a matter for the Sanhedrin, and the latter were the concern of the Roman governor. It is unlikely that a formal session of the Sanhedrin could have been held with Festus as president. What may have been in the procurator's mind was a trial in Jerusalem before the Sanhedrin on the religious charges—contravention of Jewish law and, in particular, violation of the Temple—followed by a trial on the political charges before the procurator himself. Paul may have felt that the dice were loaded too heavily against him, or that the procurator was already unsympathetic, and would no doubt be more so after the undoubtedly hostile verdict of the Sanhedrin. He may have felt that Jerusalem was altogether too dangerous for him, or he may have been weary of the apparently interminable series of enquiries and delays. At all events, it was at this point that he made his dramatic plea to be tried by the

Emperor's court in Rome, thus removing the matter from Jewish influence entirely.

10. Paul speaks as a Roman citizen, insisting on his right to be tried by a Roman court. The procurator's court at Caesarea met this requirement since, by delegation of authority, it was in effect **Caesar's tribunal.** This would not be the case with any hearing in which the Sanhedrin was involved.

11. I do not seek to escape death: the words suggest that, whatever charges of a political nature were now being made against Paul, they were such that the death penalty could be involved. Starting a riot in the Temple was a serious enough crime, but perhaps hardly a capital offence; there must have been other allegations, possibly connected with his earlier missionary activities. **I appeal to Caesar:** according to Roman law at this time, a Roman citizen had the right to appeal to be tried by the Emperor —assuming that he could afford the expense—and whenever this occurred the local magistrate, in this case Festus, was obliged to allow it. There were no doubt many occasions in the provinces when this right was ignored; Festus seems to suggest (verse 25) that it was open to him to refuse Paul's request. He could also have set him free (26:32).

12. his council: his legal advisers.

13. Agrippa the king: this was Herod Agrippa II, son of Herod Agrippa I (see on 12:1), and great-grandson of Herod the Great; as was characteristic of the whole Herodian family, he had from the outset cultivated Roman patronage. Despite the fact that Agrippa was in Rome when his father died in A.D. 44, and in high favour with the Emperor Claudius, Claudius was dissuaded from bestowing the whole of the territories of Herod Agrippa I on his son, then a mere boy of seventeen, and Judaea reverted to government by Roman procurators; however, successive emperors, including Claudius, presented him with other regions of the Levant, most of which had been in the hands of members of the Herodian dynasty. Having been given the title of King in A.D. 53, he made Caesarea Philippi his capital. In addition, he had been made custodian of the Temple treasure at Jerusalem, and had been granted the right to appoint the High Priest. He was therefore, although obviously under the thumb of Rome, an important Palestinian princeling who could pay a State visit to welcome the new procurator of Judaea, and could meet him on equal terms. At this time he would be a man of about thirty years of age.

Bernice, his sister, after two marriages, was then a widow living at her brother's court. It was said that Agrippa had an incestuous relationship with her; later she had another short marriage, and later still was openly the mistress of Titus when he became Roman Emperor. She has been described as 'a Jewish Cleopatra on a small scale'. One year younger than Agrippa, she was ten years older than her sister Drusilla, the wife of Felix. In her favour, it should be said that she risked her life to intercede for the Jews when the brutal procurator Gessius Florus was bent on massacre in Jerusalem; Agrippa too must be given credit for having tried to avert the Jewish-Roman War (Josephus, *Wars of the Jews*, II xv. 1; xvi. 4).

14-22. It is unlikely that Luke knew exactly the contents of the conversation between Festus and Agrippa. We may regard it as an intelligent reconstruction, based on the narrative of verses 1-12, of what must have led to Paul's appearing before the king and his sister in verse 23. Festus represents himself as a fair-minded Roman judge faced with a difficult problem, and anxious only that justice should be done—which was more or less the case. He obviously makes no mention of the motive which Luke ascribes to him in verse 9!

19. their own superstition: as in 17:22, the Greek *deisidaimonia* can mean either 'religion' or 'superstition'. Since Festus is addressing Agrippa, who at least nominally professed the Jewish faith, he can hardly have meant the word to be taken in the uncomplimentary sense. It has been suggested that the procurator might have been referring to Paul, in which case '*his* own superstition' would be possible.

one Jesus . . .: Luke's words express perfectly the perplexity of the procurator over what seemed to him an incredible proposition. Less well-informed than his predecessor about the Way (24:22), at least the procurator is given credit for seeing that the Resurrection of Jesus was the real point at issue.

22. Herod Antipas had expressed a similar desire to meet Paul's Master (Lk. 9:9; 23:8), and thus, like Jesus, Paul appears before 'Gentiles and kings' (cf. 9:15). With the right of patronage in High Priestly appointments and his involvement in Temple affairs Agrippa had an added reason for wishing to hear Paul for himself.

23. Despite the ceremonial and the formal setting in the **audience hall** of the Praetorium, this was merely an informal interview.

military tribunes: there were five cohorts at Caesarea, each
commanded by a tribune. These, like **the prominent men of the
city**, were doubtless Gentiles.

24. all who are present with us: advisers and officials.
the whole Jewish people: strictly speaking, it was only the
religious leaders who had **petitioned**; but they represented the
mob in the Temple of 21:30ff. Festus makes it plain that Paul's
execution had been demanded, on whatever charges.

The Western text has a longer and livelier account at this
point: 'The whole Jewish people petitioned me, both in Jerusalem
and here, that I should hand him over to them for punishment.
But I was unable to hand him over without defence, on account
of the instructions which we have from the Emperor. So I said
that, if anyone was going to accuse him, he should follow me to
Caesarea where he was in custody. And, when they arrived, they
cried out that he should be put to death. But when I had heard
both sides, I found that he was in no respect worthy of death. But
when I said: "Are you willing to be tried before them in Jerusalem?" he appealed to Caesar . . .'

25. decided to send him: 'Send' here as in verse 21 has the
sense of 'remand'.

26. my lord: *kurios* is rather more than a title of honour: used
of the Emperor—in this case Nero—it had overtones of divinity.
In the East, particularly in Egypt, the kings had been regarded as
gods, and it became part of the cult of emperor-worship in the
West from Caligula onwards to ascribe divine status to the
monarch. The universal homage which was thus demanded was
primarily a political expedient to bind together the diverse peoples
of the Empire in a common loyalty transcending their worship of
their own particular deities.

something to write: as in the case of Lysias' letter to Felix
(23:26ff.), Festus has to send a report with the prisoner who is
being remanded to a higher court. We may sympathize with the
procurator in the difficulty in which he found himself; unfamiliar
with Jewish religious affairs he has to compose a statement for the
Emperor's information in a complex and confused case in which
the rights and wrongs are by no means clear to him. It is not surprising, therefore, that he seizes the opportunity of taking a
second opinion from his royal guest, a Jewish layman who had the
reputation of being well versed in Jewish religious matters, but
who had no ecclesiastical axe to grind. Paul is thus invited to state

his case, and uses the occasion to witness to his faith. His speech has sometimes been described as his *Apologia pro Vita Sua*.

PAUL BEFORE AGRIPPA 26:13-2

1. stretched out his hand: this would seem to have been a characteristic Pauline gesture when addressing an audience (cf. 13:16; 21:40). Here it is probably in the nature of a respectful salute.

2-3. It was customary on such an occasion to begin a speech with a few complimentary remarks to gain the goodwill of the president of the court; both Tertullus and Paul had already done so in the presence of Felix (24:2f., 10). In this case, however, Paul could express his genuine pleasure at finding himself before Agrippa, since the latter was more knowledgeable than Roman procurators in matters of Jewish religion and was also, despite his Roman allegiance, a recognized defender of Jewish interests. He would at least understand Paul's position.

4. among my own nation and at Jerusalem: this would seem to refer to Paul's upbringing in Tarsus and subsequent years in Jerusalem. 'Nation' could mean either Paul's own province of Cilicia or the Jewish community in Tarsus; in either case it suggests that Paul was more than an infant when he left Tarsus for Jerusalem (see on 22:3).

5. lived as a Pharisee: see on 23:6.

6-8. Paul has already (23:6; 24:15) spoken of the **hope** of a resurrection which was common to both Pharisaic Jews and Christians. Here he widens the context and speaks of **hope in the promise made by God,** i.e. the promise of future blessing made to the **fathers** of Israel—Abraham, Isaac and Jacob. This had developed into the more specific hope of the messianic age, in which, as at least the Pharisees believed, the faithful would be raised to a new life in a general resurrection. Paul's claim is that Jesus, as the long-awaited Messiah, has by his Resurrection given the only guarantee of any resurrection for faithful Israelites (and Gentile believers belonging to the new Israel, whom he obviously has no reason for mentioning here, cf. Rom. 9:4ff.). How can it be thought **incredible by any of you** (the Jews present on this occasion) that God should have raised Jesus from the dead, since the whole substance of the hope of the **twelve tribes,** i.e. the Jewish people (cf. Jas. 1:1), rest on the belief that the dead will live again?

9ff. Paul now goes on to show how God convinced him on the

Damascus road that Jesus of Nazareth was indeed the Messiah, through whom the fulfilment of Israel's hope had begun to be realized. But first he recounts his own unwillingness to recognize this, and identifies himself in his pre-conversion state with those who still found the Resurrection of Jesus unbelievable.

10. As in 22:4, Paul recalls his personal vendetta against the Jerusalem Christians (**saints;** see on 9:13).

when they were put to death: we have not been told by Luke of any martyrs other than Stephen and the Apostle James; but there may have been others whose names have not been recorded. **I cast my vote against them:** this need not necessarily imply that Paul was a member of the Sanhedrin, even if the Sanhedrin had the power to impose the death penalty. It may mean no more than that he approved of the persecution of the Nazarenes, as in 8:1; 22:20.

11. blaspheme: against Jesus (cf. 1 C. 12:3: 'Jesus, be cursed'). **foreign cities:** Damascus was a case in point.

12–18. This is the third account of Paul's conversion in Acts (see on 9:1–9; 22:6–11). Where there are minor discrepancies in the narrative it is idle to speculate which version represents the actual sequence of events most closely, or how much Paul himself reads back into his experience in the light of later reflection. There is general agreement in the three accounts, both among themselves and with Paul's autobiographical statement in Gal. 1.

14. when we had all fallen to the ground: this appears to contradict 9:7, where Paul's companions 'stood speechless'. They could, however, have risen before he did. **in the Hebrew language:** Aramaic, as in 21:40. This is indicated by the form of his name, '*Saoul, Saoul*', here and in 9:4; 22:7. **it hurts you to kick against the goads:** this is a new element in the story as recorded in the previous two accounts. It was a proverbial saying, common in Greek and Latin, indicating that no man can resist the will of the gods. The metaphor is that of the stubborn ox kicking back at the driver who is prodding it on in the direction he wants it to go; it expresses vividly Paul's growing doubts before his conversion as to the justice of his course of action in persecuting the Nazarenes, his increasing conviction that Stephen may have been right and he himself wrong, and his re-doubled fury against the Christians in an attempt to kill his conscience.

16–18. These verses summarize for Agrippa's benefit Paul's

conviction of his God-given destiny to carry the Gospel to the
pagan world. They combine his commission on the Damascus
road (9:6; 22:10), the charge laid upon him by the Lord through
Ananias (9:15; 22:14ff.), and the divine command given to him
in the Temple (22:17ff.). The part played by Ananias is not mentioned, since clearly this obscure 'devout man according to the
law' would be of less interest to Agrippa than to the Jerusalem
Jews. Paul's language here becomes noticeably more biblical; he
sees his call as a commission to become one of God's prophets like
Ezekiel or Jeremiah and to share the role of the Servant of
Yahweh.

16. rise and stand upon your feet: God speaks to Paul
through the risen Christ in the words of Ezek. 2:1, summoning
him to rise up and stand, like the prophet, to receive his commission which is to **serve** and **witness,** like the original Apostles
(1:8).

the things in which you have seen me: the vision on the
Damascus road.

those in which I will appear to you: the visions which Paul was
later to experience (e.g. 18:9; 22:17; 23:11).

17. Paul's visions generally came at moments of crisis, promising
deliverance. Here the words reflect the call of Jeremiah (Jer.
1:7-8). Paul's need at this point was more for deliverance from his
own countrymen than from the Gentiles.

18. to open their eyes, like the Servant of Yahweh in Isa.
42:7 (cf. Isa. 35:5).

turn from darkness to light, as in Isa. 42:16. This whole verse
is reminiscent of Col. 1:12-14.

20. all the country of Judaea: there is no difficulty here, if
Paul is simply giving a general summary of the territorial extent
of his total missionary activities up to the time of making this
speech: Damascus, Jerusalem, Judaea and the Gentile world. If,
on the other hand, he is to be understood as describing these
activities in chronological order from his conversion onwards, his
words here contradict his statement in Gal. 1:18-22 to the effect
that he had no contact with the Judaean churches apart from the
Jerusalem Christians until many years later (see on 9:19*b*-31
(pp. 131-2)). As it stands, the Greek text is grammatically
awkward; it may originally have read: 'to those at Damascus and
at Jerusalem, and throughout every country, both to Jews and
Gentiles'.

repent and turn to God: the terms are synonymous.

22. Paul insists once again that the Gospel is the fulfilment of *OT* Law and prophecy.

23. the Christ must suffer: see on 3:18 and 17:3. Although it has been maintained that the belief in a suffering messiah existed in some Jewish circles before the time of Jesus, there is no clear evidence that early Christian conviction on this point springs from any other source than the mind of Jesus himself. He saw his role as that of the Servant of Isa. 53 who by his suffering would bring men to the knowledge of God. Literally translated, this verse reads: 'whether the Messiah should suffer, whether he should be the first to rise from the dead and (whether he) should proclaim light . . . to the Gentiles'. It has been suggested that Luke is summarizing the topics Paul expounded at length to Agrippa. The early Christians may have collected under such headings Old Testament proof-texts or Testimonies, showing how the words of the Scriptures had now come true.

the first to rise from the dead: cf. 1 C. 15:20 and see on 23:6.
proclaim light: the light of salvation; see on 13:47, and cf. 2 Tim. 1:10.

24. Paul, you are mad: a splendidly realistic reaction on the part of the matter-of-fact Roman procurator who has listened patiently so far to a disquisition directed to Agrippa, who was obviously more at home in these murky theological waters. Festus is not unfriendly and recognizes Paul's dialectical skill, but his prisoner's whole argument points to the fact that he is slightly off his head!

25. Paul is polite but firm. He claims that he is perfectly sane, and **speaking** nothing but **the sober truth.**

26. done in a corner: again a Greek proverbial expression (cf. verse 14), implying that Agrippa at least must know of the events on which the Christians based their claims.

27. Paul appeals directly to the King. Anyone who believed the prophets—and Paul gives Agrippa credit for so believing—must support the Christian case, since it rested precisely on what the Scriptures promised. Of course, Agrippa, like most Jews, could accept the words of the prophets about the coming of the Messiah without believing that in Jesus of Nazareth they had now been fulfilled.

28. Agrippa makes an evasive reply and, whatever precisely his words mean, they almost certainly do not mean that Paul had nearly convinced him by his arguments. The famous *AV* translation is misleading: 'Almost thou persuadest me to be a Christian!' Agrippa is being sarcastic, not sympathetic. Perhaps, of the many attempts to render the undoubtedly difficult sentence into colloquial English, the best is: 'You make short work of turning me into a missionary!'

29. short or long: probably a play on Agrippa's words.
except for these chains: presumably Paul at this point gestures to indicate his fetters.

31–2. Again Luke probably gives the sense of the conversation between Agrippa and Festus after the dignitaries have left the audience chamber. There were many in attendance from whom the information must have leaked that both Agrippa, from an expert and impartial Jewish standpoint, and Festus, as an honourable Roman judge, agreed that there was no case against Paul, but that his appeal to Caesar must take its course. Thus in this scene, which is clearly the climax of the various confrontations between Paul, his Jewish opponents and disinterested judges, Luke has finally established that, in the eyes of all except bigoted Jews, Christianity emerges as a responsible and respectable religion, and Paul himself as guiltless of any offence against the imperial government.

VOYAGE TO ROME 27:1–28:16

CAESAREA TO MALTA 27:1–44

This fascinating description of a sea voyage and shipwreck, such as Paul had already experienced on more than one occasion (2 C. 11:25), demonstrates Luke's power as a narrator at its best, and makes us the more regret his absence on some of the other adventures which Paul briefly mentions in 2 C. 11:25–7. It is related in the first person plural which, on any reasonable view, implies that the author shared the experiences of the voyage. This is much more likely than the suggestion that Luke invented the whole story or that he cast around to find a convincing tale of a Mediterranean voyage, including a shipwreck, into which he fitted some personal references to Paul. The classic study on this last journey of the Apostle is still *The Voyage and Shipwreck of St Paul*, by James Smith of Jordanhill, near Glasgow, first published in 1848. After careful examination of the details of the narrative, Smith establishes that, on grounds of geographical accuracy, knowledge of weather conditions and navigational practice in ancient times, this is the record of a real, and not of an imaginary, voyage. We may further assume, in the light of the previous 'we' passages in Acts, that the use of the first personal pronoun in this extremely vivid piece of reporting is no journalistic trick, but that it betokens a genuine eye-witness account by our author himself.

1. we should sail: this is the first reappearance of 'we' since 21:17–18. It may mark the transition from Luke's association with Paul in the wider field of Jerusalem and Caesarea, where we may take it that they at least maintained constant contact, to the closer companionship of life on board ship.

they: the Roman authorities.

Paul and some other prisoners: the distinction is not made simply to draw attention to Paul, but because any prisoner who was a Roman citizen and on his way to trial before Caesar was in a different category from the rest, who may indeed have been criminals destined to die in the arena in Rome.

Augustan Cohort: for **centurion** and **cohort,** see on 10:1. The association of an emperor's name with a cohort as an honorary title frequently occurred in the case of auxiliary troops. There is inscriptional evidence of the existence of an Augustan Cohort in Syria in the first century A.D. Like Cornelius (10:1ff.), this centurion **Julius** plays a praiseworthy role in Luke's narrative (see also on verse 11).

2. Adramyttium in Mysia, where the ship belonged and where apparently it was returning for the winter, lay to the south of Troas and further east along the bay than Assos (cf. 20:13).

the coast of Asia: the W. coast of Asia Minor. Presumably the centurion intended to transfer his prisoners at one of the **ports** of call there to a ship bound for Rome, unless he thought of completing the journey to Italy by land along the Via Egnatia (see on 16:11).

Aristarchus: see on 19:29. Since he is mentioned in Col. 4:10 (cf. Phm. 24) as Paul's 'fellow-prisoner', we may assume that he accompanied Paul all the way to Rome—perhaps, as has been suggested, in the capacity of a personal servant.

Sidon on the Phoenician coast was about 70 miles N. of Caesarea. As it was a notable centre of commerce, the ship no doubt called there for trading purposes.

his friends: lit. 'the friends', which may suggest to us that Christians were sometimes known as 'the Friends' (cf. 3 Jn 15;

Jn 15:14). The church at Sidon, like those at Ptolemais and Tyre, probably dated back to the time of Stephen (see on 11:19; 15:3; 21:4, 7).

4. under the lee of Cyprus: keeping to E. of Cyprus, then turning westward to have the north coast of Cyprus on the port side and the mainland of Asia Minor on the starboard side. The advantage of this procedure was that the prevailing wind came from the W. or NW. at that time of the year, making the crossing of the open sea directly from Caesarea to Myra (verse 5) more difficult. By the same token on a previous journey in the opposite direction from Patara, near Myra, to the Syrian coast Paul's ship had taken the straight route across the E. Mediterranean, leaving Cyprus 'on the left' (21:1–3).

5. when we had sailed across the sea: the Western text adds: 'in fifteen days', which may well be right. Their route would be along the coasts of **Cilicia** and **Pamphylia** before reaching **Myra** on the coast of **Lycia**, where they transferred to a larger ship. This, according to the Western text, was the port where Paul had changed ships (rather than Patara) on his way to Jerusalem (see on 21:1). The normal route for sea traffic from Egypt to Italy was to head northwards to Myra, and then to sail westwards, taking advantage of such protection as the islands afforded.

6. a ship of Alexandria: since, and no doubt before, the days of Joseph, Egypt had been the granary of the East. Many of its huge grain ships such as this (cf. verse 38) were at this time engaged in the service of the Roman government. It would therefore be in order for a centurion to requisition accommodation on such a vessel for prisoners on their way to Rome.

7. Cnidus: from a glance at the map it would seem that, even against a moderate wind, the captain of a sailing-ship would have preferred to steer a course round the N. of Rhodes. That in this case the ship had to sail as far north as Cnidus, which lay on a promontory in Caria, at the SW. corner of Asia Minor, is a measure of the force of the wind, which Luke consistently emphasizes, and which might have driven the ship on to Rhodes itself. From off Cnidus the captain has to tack south, passing **Salmone,** the headland on the E. of **Crete.**

8. The ship now sails along the S. coast of Crete, presumably in calmer water. The **difficulty** Luke refers to may have been caused by the rocks off Cape Salmone.

Fair Havens is a small bay about half-way along the S. coast of

Crete, not far from the ruins of the **city of Lasea** which perhaps
they visited, since Luke specifically mentions it. The modern name
of Kalolimonias preserves the Greek for 'Fair Havens'. The bay
did not afford sufficient protection to form a good winter harbour,
and just beyond it the coast turns northwards, thus exposing
shipping to the strong NW. wind.

9. the fast had already gone by: the fast referred to is the
Day of Atonement which occurred towards the end of September
or in the beginning of October. The time indicated therefore is the
autumn of A.D. 58 (see on 24:27). Mid-September was considered
to be the end of the period for safe navigation of the Mediterranean, and after the middle of November sailings normally
ceased for the winter because the sea was too dangerous, although
occasional winter crossings were not unknown. Luke's point is
that, not only was the weather extremely bad, but that the time
for possible sailing at all was quickly running out. The date may
have been fixed in his memory if Paul had observed the fast at
Fair Havens or Lasea.

10. Paul therefore, from his own considerable experience of
Mediterranean travel, advises against continuing the voyage, perhaps at a meeting called by the centurion at which he sought
advice from more seasoned travellers than himself (verse 11).

11. Since this was a vessel in the service of the Roman government, the **centurion** was in effect the senior officer in command.
His concern was to deliver his prisoners safely in Rome. The
captain, responsible for navigation and recruitment of the crew,
was employed by the civilian **owner of the ship,** who in this case
would be under contract to the imperial government. The
prominent role played by the centurion might lend colour to the
suggestion that the Augustan Cohort (verse 1) may have been a
corps of special agents, all of the rank of centurion, who acted as
couriers between the Emperor and his armies in the provinces,
supervised the proper delivery of supplies and conducted prisoners
to Rome.

12. If this was a council of four, the centurion, the ship-owner,
the ship's master, and Paul (perhaps representing the passengers),
the **majority** would be three against one. Since Fair Havens was
unsuitable as a winter anchorage, it was not taking an unreasonable risk to attempt to reach a better harbour further along the
coast, and Paul may have concurred. From verse 21, however, it
would appear that the others may have been prepared to contem-

plate the possibility of continuing the voyage to Italy; Paul opposed this.

Phoenix: the identification of this harbour based on Luke's description is in some doubt, perhaps because the ship, with Luke on it, never went there. It may be either Lutro or Phineka, both lying about forty miles further west along the S. coast of Crete, separated by a headland, and both at that time favoured with better facilities than Fair Havens. The apparently odd discrepancy between the *RSV* text **north-east and south-east** and *RSV* marg. 'south-west and north-west' arises because the Greek words refer to winds, and the question is whether they relate to the direction in which the winds blow or to the direction from which they come.

13. Encouraged by a southerly breeze which had sprung up they ventured out of the bay of Fair Havens, hoping with this favourable wind to sail westwards to Phoenix or even to chance continuing towards Italy. They would cling to the coast of Crete as far as Cape Matala, about five miles from Fair Havens. Having rounded this point, however, a new peril faced them.

14. a tempestuous wind called the northeaster: 'northeaster' is the translation of a hybrid word 'Euraquilo', a compound of 'the east wind' and 'the north wind'. This was a sudden typhoon, blowing down from the mountains of Crete; against this a large ship with its great unwieldy mainsail was helpless.

15. They were no longer able to hug the coast, but were driven out into the open sea. The gale was so strong they they could make no headway, and had to run before it.

16. Cauda (mod. (Italian) Gozzo) is **a small island** roughly 25 miles S. of Crete. In the relative shelter afforded by this island they took steps to haul up the dinghy, which was normally tied to the stern and by now would probably be waterlogged. Luke himself, no doubt with the other passengers, seems to have taken part in this operation.

17. undergird the ship: the subsequent **measures** taken would seem to have been more technical, and thus left to the crew (cf. 'they' replacing 'we'). 'Undergirding' could mean passing ropes under water round the ship's hull to hold the timbers together, or stretching tautened ropes above deck from the bow to the stern to prevent the ship from breaking its back. This latter practice is attested elsewhere in ancient times. Another possibility is that they strengthened the ship by holding its sides together with ropes stretched internally below the deck, or else tightened the hull with cables passed lengthwise round the outside.

Syrtis: submerged sandbanks off the coast of Libya. It was quite conceivable that a helpless ship could eventually have been driven on to them.

lowered the gear: perhaps the topsails, or a sea-anchor to act as a brake. The precise nature of these technical operations is obscure, presumably because Luke was not a seaman. One can only guess that at this point the mainsail was not included in **the gear,** since this was their only hope of steering clear of the Syrtis.

18. Since matters did not improve, they sought to lighten the ship by dumping overboard most of the **cargo** of wheat.

19. The **tackle** followed—probably such sails, spars, and other equipment as could be dispensed with.

with their own hands suggests a mood of desperation.

20. Since the sky was continuously overcast, the captain had nothing to steer by. The only compass in the ancient world was the **sun** and **stars**. Thus they were drifting completely at the mercy of the gale, and knew neither where they were nor where they were heading for. If the ship had also begun to leak—which would not be surprising—it is little wonder that crew and passengers alike **abandoned hope**—all, that is, except Paul.

21. as they had been long without food: perhaps because cooking had become impossible, or because their stores had been ruined by salt water; a more likely explanation might be seasickness. It sounds, at all events, as if they were all in pretty bad shape. By contrast, Paul's mastery of the situation based on his faith is underlined.

22. Paul has changed his pessimistic view as expressed in verse 10 in the light of what he goes on to describe.

23. this very night: i.e. 'last night'. Paul's vision confirms that of 23:11.

26. This may be Luke's addition in the light of the shipwreck.

27-8. the fourteenth night: since leaving Fair Havens. According to James Smith, it would have taken a ship under such conditions just about that length of time to reach Malta.

the sea of Adria: together with the Gulf of Adria (now the Adriatic Sea), it was reckoned to stretch from Sicily to Crete, and from Venice to North Africa.

the sailors suspected . . . land: probably because they heard the noise of breakers. Soundings confirmed this.

29. four anchors from the stern: normally anchors would be dropped from the prow, but in ancient ships both ends were alike. The procedure adopted here, assuming that a north wind was blowing them towards the N. coast of Malta, would ensure that the ship's bow would be kept pointing to the shore.

prayed for day to come: in order to see if a safe landing was possible.

30–2. The storm must have died down sufficiently to enable the dinghy to be lowered. Since we do not know what went on in the sailors' minds, we cannot say whether the group who scrambled into the dinghy were bent on escape—a dubious adventure on a dark night, on an unknown shore and amid the sound of breakers —or whether they did in fact mean to fix anchors to the bow. At all events, Paul's judgment was sound enough that all hands would be needed to get crew and passengers ashore. Whether the soldiers misunderstood him or not, their action in cutting loose the dinghy meant that there was now no chance of the total ship's company rowing ashore in relays and thus reaching safety in relative comfort.

33–4. Paul urges his shipmates, now within reach of land, to strengthen themselves for the last hazard of their harrowing voyage.

having taken nothing is doubtless a dramatic way of saying 'having eaten very little'.

not a hair is to perish: a proverbial OT expression (e.g. 1 Sam. 14:45); cf. Lk. 21:18.

35. The nature of Paul's actions and in such circumstances— **he took bread ...** gave **thanks to God ...** and **broke it**— suggests so strongly a eucharistic occasion (cf. Lk. 24:30; 1 C. 11:23ff.) that it seems to impoverish the significance of the occasion to reduce it to the normal Jewish and Christian practice of saying grace before meals. Obviously it could not be a meaningful occasion for the mainly pagan crew, but if we are to be guided by the Western text which adds, after **began to eat,** the words 'distributing also to us', we may think of Paul, Luke and Aristarchus, at least, treating this as no ordinary meal, but as one with hallowed sacramental significance.

37. two hundred and seventy six: this is more probable than the variant marginal reading of 'seventy six' or 'about seventy six'. Seventy six would be a small complement of passengers, soldiers and crew for a large grain ship; much greater numbers are known to have made the voyage to Rome (cf. Josephus, *Life*, 3). Perhaps the point of mentioning a number at all is that at this point food had to be rationed.

38. throwing out the wheat, thus completing the action mentioned in verse 18. The purpose would be to attempt to run the ship aground, as far up the beach as possible.

39. a bay with a beach: this has been convincingly identified as St Paul's Bay on the N. coast of Malta, about eight miles from Valletta.

40. the rudders were large steering paddles, one on each side of the stern of the ship, which would be raised and made fast while the ship was at anchor. Now these lashings are loosened, and a small sail is hoisted on the foremast to bring the ship ashore.

41. striking a shoal: lit. 'lighting upon a place between two seas'. This could be a submerged spit of land lying between two stretches of deeper water. James Smith, however, believes that they tried to navigate the narrow creek between the small island of Salmonetta, which protects the NW. end of the bay from the sea, and the mainland. In so doing, the prow of the large ship stuck fast in the muddy bottom of the channel while the stern began to be pounded to pieces by the waves.

42-4. The ship is now aground and breaking up, a short distance from land. According to Roman law, soldiers were responsible, on forfeit of their own lives, for the lives of their prisoners (cf. 12:19; 16:27); in this case, the guards are not prepared to take the chance that any of them might escape. Mercifully the centurion—mainly, it would seem, for Paul's sake—intervenes and prevents the soldiers from killing off the prisoners. Those who can swim ashore do so; others reach safety on **planks** or other bits of wreckage. No lives are lost. The phrase **on pieces of the ship** reads literally 'on some of the (things) of the ship'. Alternatively it might mean 'on some of the (people) of the ship', i.e. on the backs of some of the crew. If Luke happened to be one of those thus rescued, it might account for the safe preservation of his notes or travel-diary; according to Suetonius, Julius Caesar on one occasion swam about 330 yards carrying his papers which survived intact. Luke's main emphasis, however, throughout this whole narrative of the voyage and shipwreck has been that despite every hazard and adversity it was the will of God that Paul should be spared to bring the Gospel to Rome, and that the Apostle himself was aware of this.

MALTA TO ROME **28:1–16**

1. we then learned: many of the seafaring members of the
ship's company would no doubt have been familiar with the
harbour of Valletta, but not with the bay in which the ship had
been wrecked.

Malta: Greek *Melitē*. At one time it was thought that the island
was Meleda, off the Dalmatian coast. This was due to a misunderstanding of 'Adria' (27:27) as meaning the present-day Adriatic
Sea. In any case a 'northeaster' from Crete (27:14) would not
have driven the ship up the Adriatic.

2. the natives (*barbaroi*) were in no sense 'barbarians', but
civilized Semites of Phoenician extraction. To the Greeks *barbaroi*
were those who spoke a language other than Greek (cf. 14:11). In
this case it was a Phoenician dialect.

rain ... cold: as one might expect in late October.

3. Paul was characteristically lending a helping hand. Poisonous
adders are no longer found in Malta, although they may have
been in Paul's day. This particular snake perhaps looked like one
of the twigs that Paul had gathered. Luke and the 'natives' clearly
thought that its bite was lethal.

4. justice may have been originally referred to under the
Maltese name for the goddess here given as *Dikē*, the name of the
Greek deity (see on 14:12). The friendly but superstitious inhabitants conclude that, one way or another, divine vengeance
will catch up with Paul; as an obvious criminal who has by a
fluke escaped drowning, he must sooner or later pay the price.

5. suffered no harm: did Luke as well as the Maltese expect
Paul to drop down dead? If so, he may have seen this incident as
a fulfilment of Jesus' words in Lk. 10:19.

6. he was a god: a realistic and humorous comment from a
medical practitioner who was well aware of the strange workings
of the human mind (cf. the Lycaonians in 14:11ff.).

7. the chief man of the island: the title of an official, and not
a general description of a person, as is evidenced by inscriptions.
This reference to the *prōtos* of Malta, like the earlier reference to
the politarchs of Thessalonica (17:6), is yet another example of
Luke's remarkable accuracy in details of this kind. The man concerned, popularly called **Publius,** may have been either a native
dignitary or the local representative of the Roman government.

8. The governor's father, suffering from what sounds like

intermittent attacks of gastric fever (lit. 'fevers'), which is still
common in Malta, is **healed** by Paul through prayer and the
laying on of hands (cf. 9:17; and also Jesus' healing of Peter's
mother-in-law (Lk. 4:38–9), followed by many others (Lk. 4:40)).

9. Further cases were 'attended to' or 'treated', as distinct
from 'healed', perhaps by Luke. The Greek words are different.

10. many gifts: it has been suggested, improbably, that this
is a technical medical term for 'large fees'.

11. after three months: the three winter months—November, December and January—were the period when sailing was
generally impossible or at least most inadvisable. The voyagers
would thus set out on the last lap of their journey to Rome about
February, A.D. 59 (see on 27:9).

which had wintered in the island, i.e., according to normal
shipping practice, and probably in Valletta.

a ship of Alexandria: possibly another wheat ship like the one
that had been wrecked.

the Twin Brothers: Castor and Pollux, the Heavenly Twins of
Greek mythology. These sons of Zeus and Leda were regarded by
sailors as their patron deities, and a glimpse of the constellation
(Gemini) was reckoned to bring good luck in stormy weather. The
ship would take its name from its **figurehead.**

12. Syracuse, the port on the east coast of Sicily, about a
day's sail from Malta. The stay of **three days** there may have
been due to lack of wind.

13. made a circuit is an obscure expression which may mean
'had to tack'.

Rhegium (mod. Reggio) is on the southern tip of Italy, almost
opposite Messina in Sicily, which is separated from the mainland
at that point by the narrow Straits of Messina.

Puteoli (mod. Pozzuoli) on the Bay of Naples was, apart from
Ostia, the main terminus for the Alexandrian grain ships. The
distance from Rhegium to Puteoli is about 210 miles, which the
ship covered in less than two days—a good indication of the speed
at which such a vessel could travel with fair winds, in contrast to
the earlier part of the journey. According to Pliny, the average
travelling time in good weather from Puteoli to Alexandria was
less than ten days.

14. brethren: the Christian group in Puteoli, no doubt
originating from the church in Rome, which, as Luke has already
at least hinted, was in existence before Paul arrived (see on 18:2).

were invited to stay with them for seven days: it has been objected that prisoners would not be treated by a Roman centurion with such consideration. But we do not know what happened to the other prisoners who accompanied Paul; what we do know is that the centurion Julius had throughout the journey from Caesarea treated Paul as a 'special case' (cf. 27:3, 43). We should not assume that any preferential treatment of the Apostle is grounded on Luke's desire to emphasize the magnanimity of Roman officialdom for the benefit of Theophilus and other Gentile readers. Paul was no ordinary prisoner, far less a common criminal who would take the first opportunity to escape; moreover, throughout the voyage the centurion had had good cause to be grateful for Paul's sound judgment and co-operation. He could thus safely leave this particular captive lightly guarded if he had himself to be off on other business for a week.

and so we came to Rome: this is merely the narrator's anticipation of the actual arrival of the party in verse 16. There were still 140 miles of road to cover.

15. Their route lay along the Via Campana to Capua and from there by the Via Appia to Rome. At the **Forum of Appius**, a town about 40 miles from the city, they are greeted by a welcoming party of Christians from Rome, who had heard of Paul's arrival and had come out to meet him. Ten miles further on at **Three Taverns** ('shops' rather than 'inns'), they are welcomed by a second deputation. It becomes almost a triumphal procession. With good reason Paul **thanked God** for his safe arrival in the capital which he had so long hoped to visit (cf. 19:21), albeit in circumstances other than he would have wished. He **took courage**, after all he had been through and now facing the unknown outcome of his appeal, from the knowledge that he was welcome and among friends.

16. when we came into Rome: this would be by the Porta Capena.

At this point the 'we'-passage ends. The Western text reads: 'The centurion handed the prisoners over to the stratopedarch, and allowed Paul . . .'. This official may have been the officer in charge of the special couriers (see on 27:11), or the prefect of the praetorian guard (or his deputy) to whom prisoners from the provinces had to be delivered.

stay by himself: Paul is permitted to live in his own quarters, 'in free custody' or 'under house arrest', with a single soldier to guard him, to whom he would be attached by the wrist with a light chain (cf. verse 20).

PAUL IN ROME 28:17–31

17. After three days: Paul loses no time after his arrival in Rome. His mission, here as elsewhere, is to preach the Gospel, and as was his wont his initial overture was to the Jews. Since he is unable to proclaim Christ in the synagogues, he invites to his house the **leaders** of the Jewish community—probably elders from the main synagogues in Rome—in order to introduce himself and to explain his position. He asserts his loyalty to his people and their traditions. Despite this, he had been accused by them in Jerusalem and handed over to the Roman authority for trial.

18–19. The Romans had found him not guilty of any capital offence, and had wished to release him. This had not been acceptable to the Jews; hence the Apostle's appeal to Caesar, which was his reason for being in Rome. He had no countercharge to bring against his people; he was simply in Rome to defend himself and plead for his life.

20. His purpose in making contact with the local Jews was to make it plain to them that the only reason why he was a prisoner was that he believed that the hopes and prayers of Israel had now been fulfilled by the coming of the Messiah, Jesus of Nazareth (see on 23:6; 26:6).

21–2. The Jewish reply is cautious. They have had no communication from the Jerusalem religious authorities about Paul, nor have they had any reports regarding him, favourable or otherwise, from any Jerusalem Jews who have come to Rome. They are, moreover, anxious to hear from Paul's own lips the beliefs of this **sect** of the Nazarenes (cf. 24:5), about which they claim to know little or nothing except that it is generally condemned. Luke is, of course, not presenting a verbatim account of the exchange between Paul and the spokesmen of the Jews in Rome; but there is no reason to suspect that his summary is inaccurate. Paul's statement in verses 17–20 is factually correct; the statement by the Jewish leaders in verses 21–2 is also perfectly credible as it stands. Once the case had been handed over to the Roman judiciary, the Jerusalem religious authorities would have been ill-advised to attempt to interfere with a Roman citizen's impending appeal to the Emperor's court, or to make any official comment on it in writing. They had already been unsuccessful in their efforts to get Paul publicly condemned or privately disposed of, and the favourable verdicts of both Festus and Agrippa must have become known to them.

It was probably an exaggeration to say that no Jerusalem Jews visiting Rome had commented adversely on Paul, but for diplomatic reasons it would be advisable for the leaders of the Jewish community in Rome to plead complete ignorance of the whole matter. Similarly, it cannot have been strictly true that they knew of the Christian 'sect' only at second-hand, and only to its discredit. There had been Jewish 'visitors from Rome' present at Pentecost (2:10); Christian propaganda among the Jews in Rome had, in all probability, led to the edict of Claudius banning Jews from the capital several years earlier (see on 18:2); Paul's letter to the Roman church implies the existence of converted Jews within its membership; parties of Christians had gone out from the city to welcome the Apostle on his arrival (verse 15). All of this can hardly have escaped the notice of the Jewish dignitaries in the city! They may have wished to appear conciliatory, since this was Rome and not Jerusalem; and their affected ignorance of Christian belief and practice, as of Paul's own activities, may have been equally politically motivated.

23. at his lodging: some kind of informal reception is indicated. **testifying to the kingdom of God:** see on 1:3. Luke summarizes the message that Paul had consistently proclaimed to Jews, the good news of salvation through Christ in fulfilment of all that was written in their own sacred Scriptures, both in the **law** and in the **prophets.**

24–5. Paul's exposition receives a mixed reception, and the meeting ends with the Jews disagreeing among themselves after Paul's final sally.

26–7. Paul quotes Isa. 6:9–10 (LXX) as evidence that the rejection of the Gospel by the Jews was also a fulfilment of prophecy. He had already used Isa. 29:10 to the same effect in Rom. 11:8; the passage may have been a popular proof-text used in this connection by the early Christians, possibly quoted from a list of such testimonies. Its use is attributed to Jesus in Mt. 13:14–15; Mk 4:12; Lk. 8:10; cf. Jn 12:40.

28. This, with its reference to Ps. 67:2, could well be described as summarizing in one verse the main theme of Acts. Paul has already warned the Jews of Asia Minor (13:46) and of Greece (18:6). Now he confirms the Jewish rejection of the Gospel, and justifies the mission to the Gentiles in Rome itself. He wrestles in Rom. 9–11 with the problem that this presents for Christian theology. Verse 29 (see *RSV* marg.) is added in the Western text, but merely repeats the first half of verse 25.

30. two whole years: A.D. 59–61.

at his own expense: see on 21:23–4. Prisoners awaiting trial were allowed to work at their trade, according to a third-century Roman jurist.

31. Luke leaves us with the picture of Paul as a favoured prisoner, receiving visitors and still exercising his ministry of **preaching** and **teaching** to all who would listen. The Captivity Epistles, assuming that they were written from his prison in Rome, indicate that he was also able to keep in touch with the young churches, and that he was surrounded by friends. The commission of the risen Christ to his first disciples to be his witnesses from Jerusalem to the end of the earth (1:8) has been fulfilled in richest measure by the greatest of all the Apostles. The Gospel has been firmly planted in the capital of the Empire, and, with the intimation that it was being proclaimed there by Paul **quite openly and unhindered**, Luke brings his masterly account of the first three decades of the history of the Church to a perfect dramatic conclusion (see Introduction, pp. 29–30).

THE JOURNEYS OF ST. PAUL

KEY
1st ————
2nd ·········
3rd ——— (alternative route ····
4th ———————
Roman Empire frontiers ———

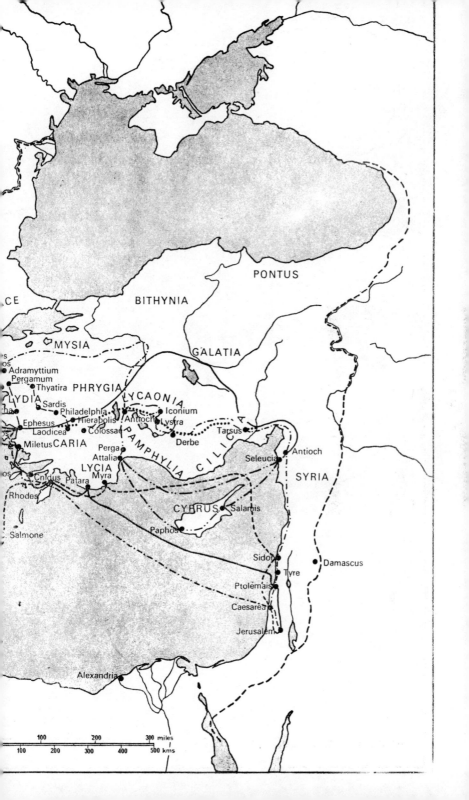

INDEX OF MODERN AUTHORS

GENERAL INDEX